The Clothed Body
in the Ancient World

The Clothed Body in the Ancient World

Edited by
Liza Cleland, Mary Harlow
and Lloyd Llewellyn-Jones

Oxbow Books
Oxford and Oakville

Published by
Oxbow Books, Oxford, UK

© Oxbow Books and the individual authors, 2005
Reprinted 2010

ISBN 978-1-84217-165-3

A CIP record for this book is available from the British Library

This book is available direct from

Oxbow Books, 10 Hythe Bridge Street, Oxford OX1 2EW
(Phone: 01865-241249; Fax: 01865-794449)

and

The David Brown Book Company
PO Box 511, Oakville, CT 06779, USA
(Phone: 860-945-9329; Fax: 860-945-9468)

or from our website

www.oxbowbooks.com

Front cover: Attic Hydria from Cyrenaica.
Back cover: Hedy Lamarr as Delilah
in Cecil B. DeMille's 1949 film Samson and Delilah.

Printed in Great Britain by
CPI Antony Rowe, Chippenham and Eastbourne

Contents

List of contributors vii
Acknowledgements x

INTRODUCTION
'I Wear this Therefore I Am': The Clothed Body in the Ancient World xi

PART I. THE CLOTHED BODY IN EGYPT AND THE AEGEAN

1. The Decorated Body in Ancient Egypt: Hairstyles, cosmetics and tattoos
   (Joann Fletcher) 3

2. The Fashioning of Delilah. Costume Design, Historicism and Fantasy
   in Cecil B. DeMille's *Samson and Delilah* (1949) *(Lloyd Llewellyn-Jones)* 14

3. Reconstructing Aegean Bronze Age Fashions *(Ariane Marcar)* 30

4. Trailing Tunics and Sheepskin Coats: Dress and status in early Greece
   (Hans van Wees) 44

PART II. THE CLOTHED BODY IN CLASSICAL GREECE

5. Constru(ct)ing Gender in the Feminine Greek *Peplos* *(Mireille Lee)* 55

6. New Clothes, a New You: Clothing and character in Aristophanes
   (James Robson) 65

7. Beauty in Rags. On *rhakos* in Aristophanic theatre
   (Silvia Milanezi) 75

8. The Semiosis of Description: Some reflections on fabric and colour in
   the Brauron Inventories *(Liza Cleland)* 87

9. Viewing and Obscuring the Female Breast: Glimpses of the ancient bra
   (Emma J. Stafford) 96

PART III. THE CLOTHED BODY IN ROME AND LATE ANTIQUITY

10. The *toga praetexta* of Roman Children and Praetextate Garments
    (Judith Sebesta) 113

11. What Made the Roman Toga *virilis*? *(Glenys Davies)* 121

12. Men are Mars, Women are Venus: Divine costumes in Imperial Rome
    (Shelley Hales) 131

13. Dress in the *Historia Augusta*: The role of dress in historical narrative
    (Mary Harlow) 143

14. Get Your Kit On! Some issues in the depiction of clothing in Byzantium
    (Liz James and Shaun Tougher) 154

15. Tunics from Kasr al-Yahud *(Orit Shamir)* 162

Bibliography 169

Contributors

Liza Cleland
MSc *Clothing Regulations of Ancient Greek Religious Cults*; PhD *Colour in Ancient Greek Clothing: A Methodological Investigation* from University of Edinburgh. Co-editor of *Colour in the Ancient Mediterranean World* (BAR, 2004) and the current volume. Forthcoming *The Clothing Inventories of Brauron: Text, Analysis and Translation*. Main research interests: methodological issues in historical colour research, and cultural epistemology – particularly of colour and clothing.

Glenys Davies
Senior lecturer in Classical Art and Archaeology in the School of History and Classics, University of Edinburgh. Her research interests include Roman funerary art, body language in Classical art, and other aspects of Classical (especially Roman) self-representation and social behaviour (including dress).

Joann Fletcher
Honorary Research Fellow in the Department of Archaeology at the University of York and Consultant Egyptologist for Harrogate Museums and Arts. She specialises in forms of body adornment in the ancient world and has studied and excavated human remains at various sites in Egypt, the Yemen and South America.

Shelley Hales
Lecturer in Art and Visual Culture in the Classics and Ancient History Department at the University of Bristol. She works on Roman domestic and personal art and its relation to issues of social identity and notions of self.

Mary Harlow
Senior lecturer in Ancient History, Institute of Archaeology and Antiquity, University of Birmingham. She is also an associate lecturer at the Open University. In 2000–2002 she received a Leverhulme Special Research Fellowship for the study of dress in late antiquity.

Liz James
Reader in Art History, Department of Art History, University of Sussex. She has published on light and colour in Byzantine art and on Byzantine empresses, and is currently working on a project on the manufacture of Byzantine mosaics.

Mireille M. Lee
Teaches Classics and Art History at Macalester College in St. Paul, Minnesota, USA, and has written on various aspects of Greek dress in art and literature.

Lloyd Llewellyn-Jones
Author of many articles on ancient dress and gender, including the 2003 monograph *Aphrodite's Tortoise: the veiled women of ancient Greece* and editor of *Women's Dress in the Ancient Greek World* (2002). He has worked as a historical costume adviser for several television and film companies, most recently for Oliver Stone's 'Alexander'. Lloyd also works on the reception of antiquity in popular culture as well as on the history of Achemenid Persia. He is currently preparing (with James Robson) a translation and commentary of Ctesias' *Persica*.

Ariane Marcar
Specialist in Aegean Bronze Age archaeology, focusing on textiles and costume (production and consumption, including issues related to ethnicity); Aegean LBA figurative fresco painting; and trade, notably between the Aegean, Egypt, Anatolia, the Levant and Southern Italy/Sicily. She is now teaching Archaeology at the Mediterranean Center for Arts and Sciences in Syracuse, Sicily. Alumna of Institute of Archaeology, London (UCL) and member of the British School at Athens.

Sylvia Milanezi
Maître de conferences in the Université François Rabelais of Tours in the Department of History, where she teaches Greek History. Research centres: Phéacie (directed by P. Schimitt) and Centre Gernet (directed by Fr. Lissarrague). A long time student of ancient theatre, her thesis is on the memory of Dionysiac contests at Athens (fifth to third century BC): a study dealing with epigraphic and literary sources.

James Robson
Lecturer in Classical Studies at the Open University. His main area of research is Aristophanes, in particular his use of humour and obscene language. Current work also includes a translation with commentary of the fragments and testimonia of Ctesias (with Lloyd Llewellyn-Jones).

Judith Lynn Sebesta
Professor of Classics at the University of South Dakota, she is also a weaver, and has published on Roman clothing and Roman women. She is Executive Secretary of the National Committee for Latin and Greek and a member of the American Philological Association, the Classical Association of the Middle West and South, and the American Classical League.

Orit Shamir
Specialises in ancient textiles, loomweights and spindle-whorls (from the Chalcolithic to the Mediaeval period) in Israel. Masters: *Textile Production in Eretz-Israel at the Iron Age in the Light of the Archaeological Finds*. PhD: (submitted June 2004): *Textiles in the Land of Israel from the Roman Period till the Early Islamic Period in the Light of the Archaeological Finds* at the Institute of Archaeology, The Hebrew University, supervised by Prof. G. Foerster and Dr. J-P. Wild. Position: Curator of Organic Materials for the Israel Antiquities Authority. Contact: orit12@israntique.org.il

Emma Stafford
Lecturer in Classics at the University of Leeds. Her research interests lie in various aspects of Greek cultural history, especially religion, myth and iconography. She is author of *Worshipping Virtues: Personification and the Divine in Ancient Greece* (Swansea 2000), *Ancient Greece: Life, Myth and Art* (London 2004), and co-editor of *Personification in the Greek World: From Antiquity to Byzantium* (Aldershot 2005).

Shaun Tougher
Lecturer in Ancient History in the Cardiff School of History and Archaeology at Cardiff University. He specialises in late Roman and Byzantine history, and has written several articles on subjects such as eunuchs, Julian the Apostate and Leo VI. He is the author of *The Reign of Leo VI (886–912)* (1997) and the editor of *Eunuchs in Antiquity and Beyond* (2002).

Hans van Wees
Reader in Ancient History at University College London, and author of *Status Warriors: war, violence and society in Homer and history* (1992) and *Greek Warfare: myths and realities* (2004). He is (co-) editor of a number of volumes, including *Archaic Greece: new approaches and new evidence* (1998, with Nick Fisher) and the forthcoming *Blackwell's Companion to Archaic Greece* (with Kurt Raaflaub).

Acknowledgements

A conference requires funding and organisation, as anyone who has held one knows. Lloyd and Mary owe a great deal of thanks to several bodies and individuals for supporting *The Clothed Body in the Ancient World*. We thank the Open University and the University of Birmingham for their initial support and funding; the British Academy for travel funding for overseas delegates; and *History Today* for sponsoring the production of the programme and advertising. We would like to extend special thanks to Dr Janet Huskinson for all her support at the OU during the preparation for the conference, and to Louise Mansfield, a secretary extraordinaire, who thought of, and implemented, many of the ideas that ensured the smooth running of the conference. Their help reduced the stress quota for everyone. We also owe a great debt of thanks to Liza, who has done by far the most work in editing the volume, and to the School of Historical Studies, University of Birmingham for making funding available for this final part of the project. Finally all three of us would like to thank all the delegates who attended the conference, both speakers and audience, as well as all those who have contributed to the volume, and the editorial and production teams at Oxbow. We hope you all enjoy the final product.

Liza Cleland, Mary Harlow and Lloyd Llewellyn-Jones
September 2004

After Lurie (1981)

of Birmingham), to whom we owe additional thanks for exhibiting part of her collection of Balkan Dress. Few of us will forget the image of Lloyd modelling the Minoan bull leaper's cod piece over his suit trousers!

INTRODUCTION

The 1990s witnessed a vogue amongst scholars for discussing the notion of the body in antiquity, with books and articles written by Egyptologists, Assyriologists, Hellenists, Romanists and Byzantinists.[2] The trend still continues. Such studies have focused on the body's interplay within ancient society as a whole, as well as on its ideological construction; in addition specific studies have looked at particular areas of the body – at hands, legs, heads, noses, eyes, feet; and at bodily functions – at blushing, weeping, smiling. Texts and images have been brought together with imaginative flair to provide new and sometimes startling insights into how ancient bodies presented themselves, allowing us to witness beautiful bodies, active bodies, passive bodies, political bodies, ugly and deformed bodies, sleeping bodies, mourning bodies, playful bodies and even bodies undergoing metamorphoses.[3] Nude bodies have commonly been discussed, but rarely has scholarship addressed clothed bodies.

Yet the clothed body was the civilized body, the yardstick by which social behaviour was measured. In ancient myth, Gilgamesh and Enkidu only become true, urbanised, heroes once they have clothed their bodies.[4] The same goes for that most heroic of all Greeks, Herakles: he is acculturated after his labours have ceased, and puts on a *peplos*, a robe, specially woven for him by the goddess Athene.[5] Dress articulates and defines an individual within his or her given society.

Strange then that so many studies of the ancient body have ignored the cultural importance of dress, the adornment that covers, hides, magnifies, augments, or changes the body. For the art historian Anne Hollander has gone so far as to argue that in the visual arts, painting and sculpture, the vital importance of dress in a society's consciousness leads artists to imprint the shadow of dress even on representations of the naked body. It is only by reading the invisible dress on the nude body that we can begin to understand that body's socio-cultural impact.[6] James Laver, the Twentieth century's greatest dress historian, wrote that: "Clothes are inevitable. They are nothing less than the furniture of the mind made visible."[7]

Of course, studies of ancient clothes have existed for many decades. An early example in English, Lady Maria Evans' *Chapters on Greek Dress*, was dedicated to the Oxford University Dramatic Society, in remembrance of their 1892 performance of Aristophanes' *Frogs*.[8] This tells us much about how early dress studies approached their subject: these were manuals for the re-creation of ancient dress, concerned primarily with how (classical) dress was draped and pinned in order to understand – or recreate – drama, sculpture or paintings. Even the influential works of Mary Huston are little more than studies in the construction of ancient dress; there is no attempt to offer a socio-cultural perspective to the discipline.[9] Larissa Bonfante's excellent and detailed 1975 study of Etruscan dress is modelled on the same approach to dress history, although a useful appendix of dress terms questions the semantics of ancient

Introduction

'I Wear This Therefore I Am': The Clothed Body in the Ancient World

The Clothed Body in the Ancient World, January 2002

This conference originated from a desire to engage with the interdisciplinary nature of the history of dress. The study of ancient dress and the clothed body encompasses the work of a very diverse range of scholars: textile conservationists, archaeologists, classicists, ancient historians, art historians, theatre costume designers and re-enactment enthusiasts, to name but a few. Each brings a particular angle to the discipline, and our intention was to bring experts, students and enthusiasts together to discuss all these aspects.

Interest in the conference was overwhelming, with delegates attending from all over Europe, the United States and the Middle East. The enthusiasm and interaction of both speakers and audience demonstrated that the history of dress is undergoing something of a renaissance at the moment. Forty-five papers were presented over three days across a broad range of topics. There was intense and stimulating discussion of methodological approaches and the relative validity of the diverse primary material available. This volume presents a representative survey of the original conference papers and ideas. The conference and volume inevitably reflect our own pre-occupations and interests, containing fewer papers on the physical remains of textiles and dress than on the literary and visual evidence. We recognise that textile historians, museum curators and those interested in reception theory have much to contribute to the subject. These contributions are implicitly recognised by all the authors: their omission here is simply a result of time and space constraints.

Historians of dress often approach their subject with little sense of the actual experience of wearing ancient clothing. However, the conference provided three entertaining and provoking insights into this area. Sally Pointer (National Gallery and Museum of Wales) presented a 'Roman makeover'. In her work Sally Pointer has, as far as is feasibly possible, recreated ancient cosmetics, and, although no more than a tentative reconstruction, the transformation of the model, Heather Jackson, was impressive. The application of the cosmetics, the accommodation of the false hairpiece and the traditional Roman *stola* and *palla* altered both stance and body language to a remarkable degree. Dan Shadrake, a professional re-enactor, came in the guise of a later Roman soldier and impressed delegates with his costume's attention to detail, and exposition of the various ways enthusiasts attempt to access authenticity in their dress.[1] Meanwhile, the complexity of mixing authenticity with the demands of modern textiles and the needs of film companies was discussed by Diana Wardle (University dress terminology and provides a useful bridge to more recent studies.[10]

By the last decade of the twentieth century scholars were becoming increasingly interested in the socio-cultural meaning of ancient dress, with Sebesta and Bonfante's *World of Roman Costume* deservedly establishing itself as the *grande dame* of recent socio-cultural dress studies.[11] Studies of the Persianization of dress in Athens, of social display through dress in Homeric and Archaic Greece, and of the cultural status of clothing in Late Antiquity have followed.[12] In 1999 a major conference on the theme of women's dress in Greece attracted a large audience and its papers, covering textual and art-historical approaches to Greek clothing, were subsequently published in one volume.[13] In 2001 a volume celebrating the career of John Peter Wild, a Roman textile expert, saw the publication of a number of papers dealing with the material evidence for ancient clothing, notions of dress in ancient societies, in ancient art and in the reception of ancient dress in later periods.[14] Scholars are now beginning to turn their attention to major studies of dress in its social environment and are stressing more than ever the importance of using dress, in ancient literary and visual representations, as a tool for investigating ancient life, ancient mores and ancient cultural responses. A recent study of veiling in the Greek world, for example, has thrown light on key concepts such as sexual and social segregation, and seclusion and status, in Greek society.[15] This interest is not only the preoccupation of British and American scholarship, as the attendance at the conference, and the chapters of this volume, demonstrate. For instance there have been two colloquia held in France in recent years (Nanterre, 2001; Lyons, 2003) resulting in publication of the papers presented by international groups of scholars.[16]

CONTENT

The individual conference papers presented here provide fascinating snapshots of works in progress on the clothed body in the ancient world. For the clothed body in Egypt and the Aegean, Joann Fletcher considers other aspects than garments, emphasising their independent importance in Egypt, and their relevance across gender and status roles, and arguing that modern conceptions of the gender and status relevance of such aspects of clothing the body must be discarded for their effective study. Lloyd Llewellyn-Jones discusses the reception and representation of ideas about ancient clothed bodies (in the context of concepts of historicism, authenticity, and location within contemporary aesthetics) by using the example of filmed biblical epic. Ariane Marcar provides a detailed critique of reconstruction as an investigative technique for dress, considering technical and archaeological context and issues of representation, providing a specific typology and geographical survey of Aegean dress, and outlining criteria for effective replication experiments. Finally, Hans van Wees argues for radical difference between Homeric and Early Classical forms of dress, particularly in social role and import, paralleled by a related change in the status and economic position of women, by surveying the types and characteristics of Homeric and later clothing.

For the clothed body in ancient Greece, Mirielle Lee considers the *peplos* in fifth-century Athenian life and art, arguing that its importance should be seen primarily as an historical construct of the time – expressing particular aspects and valuations of femininity – rather than as slavish representation of changing quotidian 'fashions.' James Robson discusses clothing in Aristophanic comedy – in terms of recreativity as opposed to realism – concentrating on instances of transvestism, and arguing for the transformative, rather than simply expressive, potential of Aristophanic clothing. Liza Cleland provides a survey of descriptions of fabric and colour in the Brauron Inventories, arguing that semiotic analysis can, in this case, provide valuable context for their linguistic complexities as records of clothing. Sylvia Milanezi examines the significance of *rhakos* in comedy, tragedy and epigraphy, widening her discussion from its appearances in Aristophanes, Euripides and catalogues of dedication, to consideration of theatrical masks and props, and its metaphorical importance in clothing the body politic. Finally, Emma Stafford outlines the types and depictions of ancient female undergarments, considering the questions of widespread or exclusive use, and erotic potential. These questions are traced in Greek, Hellenistic and Roman descriptions and depictions, in the context of 'missing' aspects of female life.

For the clothed body in Rome and Late Antiquity, Judith Sebesta elucidates the nature and contexts of the *toga praetexta*, providing the first complete survey of its adult wearers, and considering in particular its relationship to concepts of childhood and sexuality, *stuprum*, and ritual purity. Glenys Davies provides a comparable study of the toga (as *virilis*, and as an adjunct to gestural communication) discussing various aspects of its sculptural representation in terms of social contexts, gender roles, and social valuations. Shelley Hales surveys the importance of the adoption of divine costumes in clothing the imperial body. These are discussed in the context of definitions of 'good' and 'bad' emperors, and competition between literary and visual media of imperial representation and commemoration. Mary Harlow discusses the rhetoric of late Roman clothing, in terms of its presentation by the fourth century *Historia Augusta*. Liz James and Shaun Tougher consider the relationship between Byzantine dress as depicted, described, and worn, paying particular attention to gender, status, and colour, and using the latter as a link to the potential metaphorical significance of the clothed body. Finally, Orit Shamir gives a preliminary report on the excavated textiles from Kasr al-Yahud, concentrating, within the archaeological context of the site, on their origin and construction, and providing original pictures of some of the examples.

Once collected in a volume, such snapshots become something more: they reveal common themes in scholarship; they present methodological differences between disciplines and periods; and they provide contrasting definitions of the clothed body as received from various contexts. As such, the chapters of this book clearly reflect the characteristics of evidence from each period. Fletcher represents the richness of physical remains from Egypt; Llewellyn-Jones and Marcar describe different approaches to the centrality of art (and its reception) in Aegean evidence; and van Wees teases out the informative potential of Homeric epic. The second section elucidates the complexity of Greek evidence. Lee discusses the symbolic, rather than documentary, significance of garments in art, Stafford the potential of artistic evidence to obscure as well as illuminate particular garments. Both these chapters consider art in conjunction with literature, the primary focus of the remaining chapters. These move from Robson's consideration of Aristophanes' comedies, to Cleland's analysis of the semiotics of clothing, by means of Milanezi's wide ranging chapter on drama and inscriptions. The final section changes the focus to social symbolism in the Roman clothed body. Sebesta discusses literary evidence, Davies artistic representations, and Hales artistic and literary representations as agents of memory. This shift from simple symbolism to rhetorical significance in clothing is capped by Harlow's chapter on the late Roman rhetoric of clothing the body. The last two chapters take us back to our starting point. James and Tougher examine the reception of images of Byzantine clothing, and Shamir reports the physical remains of ninth century tunics.

In their varying focii, the chapters accurately reflect the different evidentiary characteristics and emphases of their periods. However, by their juxtaposition, they also suggest profitable avenues of cross-fertilisation. As the chapter on Byzantine images of clothing emphasises, issues of the reception and interpretation of clothing in art are by no means limited to the study of the Bronze Age Aegean, and indeed, Lee's discussion of historicism and archaism in the Athenian *peplos* is relevant to both areas. Similarly, the emphasis on ethnic and cultural identity as expressed through clothes – integral to the Roman chapters of Sebesta, Davies and Hales – is paralleled in van Wees' discussion of the shift from epic to early Greece. Lee's concern, to emphasise that sources do not necessarily simply document, but also often construct dress, provides a useful counterpoint. Stafford's paper reminds us of the areas of cultural continuity between Greek and Roman clothing, and in doing so, emphasises, by implication, the remarkably different attitudes of scholarship towards Greek and Roman dress: the social implications of the latter having long been regarded as established, if not fully defined.

The juxtaposition inherent in conference volumes also highlights areas that might be more fully explored in the future. From the very start, Fletcher's chapter on hair and cosmetics surely makes us wish for similar studies of Greece and Rome (by no means impractical, despite the relative lack of physical evidence). The clothing of Near Eastern bodies is under-represented in all three sections although the chapters of Llewellyn-Jones, van Wees, Lee and Hales make its conceptual and oppositional importance clear. Quite apart from their own inherent value, Persian dress has an undoubted importance for the study of Classical Greek clothing, as does Hellenistic dress for the relationship between the clothing habits of Greece and Rome. The centrality of Athenian dress to the study of the Greek clothed body, and of the toga to the Roman, are natural, but might well be profitably challenged in the future. The gendered nature of the literary and visual evidence also highlights the methodological difficulty of defining the different social symbolism in male and female clothing. Interpreting female and male dress present different problems and we need to develop a series of principles governing the relationship of one to the other.[17] Clothing the body is an inherently complex and integrally important aspect of human activity: we are only beginning to grasp its significance, but our attempts to do so can reflect and rejoice in this complexity.

Mary Harlow, Lloyd Llewellyn-Jones and Liza Cleland

NOTES

1. Dan Shadrake is a founder member of *Britannia* (late and sub-Roman re-enactment society: www.durolitum.ac.uk) and a designer at *History Today*.
2. For an overview see Montserrat 1998, 1–6.
3. See, for example, Porter 1999; Gleason 1995; Cohen 2000; Meskell 2002; Foxhall & Salmon 1998a; Bahrani 2001.
4. See George 1999.
5. Llewellyn-Jones forthcoming 2005.
6. Hollander 1993.
7. Laver 1932, 6.
8. Evans 1893
9. See Houston 1920; 1931
10. Bonfante 1975
11. Sebesta & Bonfante (eds.) 1994.
12. See Millar 1997; van Wees 1998; Harlow forthcoming 2005.
13. Llewellyn-Jones 2002.
14. Rogers, Jorgensen & Rast-Eicher 2001.
15. Llewellyn-Jones 2003.
16. *Antiquité Tardive* 12 forthcoming, 2005 Chausson & Inglebert (2003) *Costume et Société dans L'Antiquité et le haut Moyen Age.*
17. See Harlow 'Female Dress in the third to sixth centuries: the message in the media?' forthcoming, 2005b.

PART I
THE CLOTHED BODY IN EGYPT AND THE AEGEAN

Chapter 1

The Decorated Body in Ancient Egypt: Hairstyles, cosmetics and tattoos

Joann Fletcher

The vital role played by hairstyles and cosmetics in ancient Egypt, where clothing itself was, in most cases, little more than a simple piece of linen (Vogelsang-Eastwood 1993; 1994), is fundamental to any examination of the 'clothed body' within this society. Yet, such forms of adornment are regularly dismissed as mundane, frivolous, and relevant only to women (whether ancient Egyptians or modern audiences), despite their essential role in the Egyptians' daily life and afterlife.[1] Nevertheless, it is clear that elaborate hairstyles, accompanied by generous quantities of makeup and perfume, were worn by both men and women of all ages and social groupings, for a wide variety of reasons (Fletcher 1994b, 1995, 1998).

Such adornments, certainly employed for their practical qualities and as means of display, were also used for their erotic and ritual significance. Ongoing research into hairstyles, cosmetics, perfumes and tattoos continues to reveal further facets of this ancient culture, helping to redress the long-standing imbalance in Egyptological studies caused by over-emphasis on the ancient texts. Indeed, the textual evidence so thoroughly examined by generations of learned men is by no means the only way to understand ancient Egyptian society, which has for too long been represented by its 1% literate elite. The remaining population, having failed to leave a convenient written record, have been largely ignored, but recent advances in palaeopathology mean that the majority of ancient Egyptians can now begin to speak for themselves. Their well-preserved remains and extensive grave goods clearly demonstrate the importance of self-adornment to the 'average' ancient Egyptian, whether man, woman or child.

The widely varying ways in which Egyptians treated their hair reveal a fondness for ornate styles, influenced by religious beliefs and practical considerations. This is exemplified by the common use of false hair (recently shown to date to at least 3400 BC, the use of wigs and hair extensions continuing throughout the pharaonic period).[2] Egypt's extreme climate meant that all forms of dress had to provide protection from the heat whilst keeping the wearer cool. Although a shaven head might be the coolest option, the scalp and neck would then be exposed to the sun: head cloths or turbans to shield the head also trap body heat, whereas wigs provided protection whilst allowing heat to escape through their open-mesh foundation bases (Wilkinson 1988, 324; Winlock 1916, 238; Cox 1977, 67–71).

Given the number of mummies with abundant natural hair, the use of wigs seems to have been very much dependent upon personal preference, social status and occupation, wigs being obviously unsuitable for certain professions (eg. Turin Museo Egizio Inv.No.7052, Stevenson Smith 1984, 382, fig.379; No.55001, Fletcher 1995, 14, fig.406, and **Figure 1.1**). References to the 'Royal Wigmaker and Hairdresser' appear as early as 2500 BC (Speidel 1990; Fletcher 1995, 433–434; Riefstahl 1952; 1956). False hair also appears in artistic representations, the depiction of the natural hair beneath the wig clearly demonstrating its use as a mark of status (eg. female statue Cairo CG.4, Harpur 2001, 144–148, figs.126–132; male statue New York MMA.26.2.2, Hayes 1953 I, 111, fig.64.; male and female relief figures, Davies 1941, pl. X–XI, and **Figure 1.2**). In such cases, the natural hair has been smoothed down, cut short or even purposefully shaved (as distinct from being bald as a result of old age or illness, both conditions generally avoided by Egyptian artists, who tended to idealise the human form). The physical remains of individuals as diverse as royal women and military personnel clearly show receding hairlines and areas of baldness, which in certain cases have been supplemented with false braids (Cairo CG. 61055, 61056, 61061, in Smith 1912, 13, 14, 19; body no.70 in Winlock 1945, 9). Although an excessively hirsute appearance generally characterises manual workers (in contrast to the carefully depilated and bewigged elite) most Egyptians seem to have appreciated the cleanliness of hair cropped short or completely removed. This would also reduce the health risks associated with parasitic infection, since head-lice (*Pediculus humanus capitis*) can only thrive in the natural hair close to the host's blood supply, and a wig removed on a daily basis would prove an entirely unsuitable habitat.[3]

Figure 1.1. Detail of priestess/prostitute figures from the Turin Erotic Papyrus, Deir el-Medina c. 1250 BC, Turin Museo Egizio Inv. No. 55001 (line drawing copyright Joann Fletcher).

Figure 1.2. Detail of Nofret, Medum tomb of Rahotep and Nofret, c.2620 BC, Cairo Museum CG.4 (copyright Joann Fletcher).

In addition to their practical advantages, wigs and false hair have also been used throughout history as a means of communicating status in both social and sexual terms. Although the gender associations of short hair are arbitrary, the Western world is still very much influenced by the first century AD Christian doctrine that men's hair must be shorter than women's.[4] The application of such relatively modern attitudes to ancient Egyptian material inevitably causes problems, as clearly demonstrated by initial descriptions of a fragmentary limestone figure (**Figure 1.3**). Once hailed as the 'Mona Lisa of Ancient Egypt' and 'The Birmingham Isis', this figure is now recognised as a high status male official c. 1310 BC, wearing the typically elaborate 'double-style' wig fashionable at the time (Birmingham 69'96, Ruffle 1967, 39–41).

The Egyptians did not use either intricate styling techniques or hair length to differentiate gender. As in many cultures, long hair was often linked to male strength and virility as well as to sexuality in general. Certainly, hair (both real and false) featured heavily in the context of love and seduction in ancient Egypt, as is particularly apparent in representations of women during the mid-New Kingdom (c. 1400–1300 BC, Derchain 1975, 56–74; Manniche 1987, 42). Such artistic evidence is supported by literature, with the highly improper suggestion "Put on your wig and let us lie together!" in the Tale of Two Brothers c. 1300 BC.[5] In a love poem of similar date, a love-struck woman exclaims "My heart is once again invaded by your love when only half my hair is braided...I'll trouble myself no longer over my hairdressing and put on a wig to be ready". Here, the wig is employed as a metaphor for an impending sexual encounter.[6]

Figure 1.3. Fragmentary limestone dyad figure of male official, unprovenanced, c. 1310 BC, Birmingham Museum 69'96 (courtesy Birmingham Museums and Art Gallery).

The great emphasis on hair at this time has been interpreted as a visual reference to Hathor, the Egyptian goddess associated with sexual love and beauty, whose epithets included 'She of the Beautiful Hair' and 'Lady of the Lock' (Kozloff 1992, 335; Posener 1986, 111–117). This goddess is also portrayed with a number of elaborate coiffures, notably the curled bouffant style and the coloured layered style (Fletcher 1995, 67–68, 69–70). Her priestesses display similarly abundant hair, often supplemented with false braids and in particular the three-strand plait. Attached at the back of the head, this seems to have acted as a kind of 'badge of office', and is found in sculpture, painting and as part of surviving wigs (Posener 1986, 113; Fletcher, 1995, 67, 260–262, 388). Since religious ritual required the removal of all body hair for the sake of purity, priests and priestesses are portrayed both with shaven heads and with hair. It may therefore be assumed that wigs were worn by religious personnel when they were not undertaking ritual duties, with a large number of wigs discovered in a mass burial of clergy at the site of Deir el-Bahari (Cairo JE.26252.a–g, Lucas 1930, 190–192; Fletcher 2000, 498).

By examining both artistic representations and actual examples, it is possible to

Figure 1.4. Male double-style wig, Deir el-Medina, c.1400–1300 BC, British Museum EA.2560 (copyright Joann Fletcher).

trace the level of accuracy with which styles were portrayed, as compared to the surviving mummy hair, wigs and false braids. In the case of the mummy of Hatnefer (elderly woman, c. 1450 BC), numerous hair extensions had been used to create the curled bouffant style associated with the goddess Hathor (Qasr el-Einy Medical School No.1002, Lansing & Hayes 1937, fig.31, 20; Fletcher 2000, 498). Similarly the long wig belonging to the lady Merit (c. 1350 BC Turin Museo Egizio Inv.No.S.8499, Schiaparelli 1927, 101; Chiotasso *et al.* 1992, 99–105; Fletcher 2000, 497, fig.20.2) is typical of the abundant forms of coiffure found in representations of elite women at this time. Indeed, wigs were regarded as such an important part of dress that some burials contain several examples (e.g. Cairo CG.61062 in Smith 1912, 20–21, pl.16–17, second wig identified as Cairo JE.46913 Fletcher 1995, 387; Cairo JE.29681, Daressy 1907, 26, no.72).

The recent re-evaluation of hair fragments found in the tomb of Tutankhamen suggests that this king was originally buried with a short curled wig, whose original dimensions can be calculated from the proportions of his empty wig-box (Fletcher 1999, 67–68; Fletcher & Montserrat 1998, 206–207). Another wig (**Figure 1.4**) often described as 'a woman's wig' is actually a wonderful example of the double style, worn by elite men, made up of a curled upper section over an underpanel of long narrow plaits.[7] This tendency to associate false hair with women is also found in the descriptions of wigs in Cairo Museum, although it is correct only for the modestly proportioned wig of the royal woman Istemkheb, dwarfed by much larger examples displayed alongside it and once worn by Egypt's male high priests.[8]

The ancient wigmakers, whose tremendous skill is reflected in the wigs which have survived, seem to have been based in specialised workshops such as that discovered at Deir el-Bahari (Laskowska-Kusztal 1978, 84–120). Wigmakers and hairdressers are shown at work in both male and female tomb scenes, the hairpins used to secure hair having been found in both male and female burials, alongside combs and related equipment.[9] Small bronze implements seem to have been used to both wave and trim the hair,[10] and SEM analysis of hair ends indicates the incredible sharpness of blades as early as c. 3000 BC.[11] The Egyptians also coloured their hair, using the vegetable dye henna (*Lawsonia inermis*) to cover grey from as early as c. 3400 BC and throughout the pharaonic period.[12] This technique was still being employed over 2,000 years later, to recapture the original auburn hair of the elderly pharaoh Ramses II (Cairo CG.61078, 61061, Smith 1912, 59–65, 19; Musee de l'Homme 1985, 212–257, 389–390).

Contrary to reports that Egyptian wigs were made of wool or horsehair, analysis has shown surviving examples to be made of human hair, very occasionally padded out with vegetable fibre to achieve greater dimensions (Lucas 1930, 192–194; Fletcher 2000, 496). In most cases, the plaits and curls of hair were woven or tied on to a net foundation base made of finely plaited hair, the whole creation generally being coated in beeswax or a beeswax and resin mixture, which acted as a reliable fixative.[13]

Cosmetic preparations for the face were also an integral part of the daily life of both men and women from at least 4000 BC. Following daily bathing (either in the Nile or in purpose-made bathrooms, depending on status, Honigsberg 1940, 199–246; Brovarski *et al.* 1982, 31), the most important part of the toilet routine was a daily application of moisturising oil. Such oils seem to have been used by all sections of the population, but were especially necessary for those working outdoors. Indeed, the first strike in recorded history occurred c. 1152 BC, when men building the king's tomb failed to receive their oil supplies (Edgerton 1951, 137–145; Hughes, 1959, 165; Brovarski *et al.* 1982, 199; Fletcher 1998, 11).

Castor (*Ricinus communis L.*), was the most widely available form of oil for personal use, although a whole range of vegetable oils and purified animal fats were employed as moisturising agents, often enhanced by the addition of a wide variety of fragrances extracted from flowers, herbs and spices. Perfume production is portrayed in tomb and temple scenes, and complex blends were achieved by the careful combination of a wide variety of ingredients.[14] Numerous oil-based preparations are listed in the ancient medical texts, including a fenugreek oil recipe entitled "How to make the old young again….guaranteed to leave the skin beautiful and blemish-free, it is efficient a million times"(c.1500 BC, Edwin Smith Papyrus 21: 9–22, 10; Manniche 1989, 151–152).

Egypt's many perfumes were renowned throughout the ancient world for their quality, and were regarded as a high status commodity. The best known was *kyphi* which had a predominantly religious use (Manniche 1989, 57–58; Fletcher 1998, 30–

Figure 1.5. Detail of manual worker having eye paint applied, TT.217 Deir el-Medina, c. 1200 BC (line drawing copyright Joann Fletcher).

31). There were also a standard number of so-called 'Sacred Oils', namely festival perfume, *hekenu* perfume, Syrian balsam, *nechenem* salve, anointing oil, best cedar oil and Libyan perfume, with myrrh oil added by c. 2000 BC (Hayes 1953, 117, 243; Schoske *et al.* 1990, 83–84; Fletcher 1998, 9, 34). These seem to have been primarily employed for ritual purposes within temples, some playing a vital role in the mummification process (Buckley & Evershed 2001, 837–841), whilst others also served more general cosmetic purposes.

Further enhancement of the facial features was accomplished with eye-paint, the most familiar form of Egyptian make-up. Primarily used to make the eyes appear larger and more luminous, its effects are described in a love poem c. 1300 BC: "My longing for you is my eye-paint, when I see you my eyes shine" (Harris Papyrus 500, III; Lichtheim 1976, 192). Yet in practical terms, the use of eye-paint was almost as important as body oil in counteracting the effects of climate. Its application around the delicate eye area reduced the glare of the sun from desert surfaces, while its antiseptic qualities provided relief from eye complaints aggravated by sandstorms and flies (Brovarski *et al.* 1982, 216–218). This is reflected in the instructions for use given on a number of eye-paint containers, which are often inscribed with the names and titles of their male and female owners (Vandier d'Abbadie 1972, 55–91; Brovarski *et al.* 1982, 218–227; Schoske *et. al.* 1990, 158). It was clearly of equal importance to women and men, and scenes of its application include male manual workers whose eyes are shown being made-up as they work (Brovarski *et al.* 1982, 216, fig.57; Schoske *et. al.* 1990, 25, fig. 19, and **Figure 1.5**).

Figure 1.6. Detail of priestess/prostitute figure from the Turin Erotic Papyrus, Deir el-Medina c. 1250 BC, Turin Museo Egizio Inv. No. 55001 (line drawing copyright Joann Fletcher).

By c. 4000 BC, eye paint was being manufactured from the green copper oxide malachite and black kohl from the lead ore galena (Brovarski *et al.* 1982, 216; Hassan & Hassan 1981, 77–82; Jonckheere 1952, 1–12). Initially it seems that black and green were worn together, with green becoming the most popular colour during the Old Kingdom, when it was initially worn in a thick band across the eyes. Black then became the dominant colour: the beautiful almond shaped eyes found repeatedly in Egyptian art are a result of its widespread use.

Both lips and cheeks could be enhanced using crushed red ochre (Lucas 1989, 84; Brovarski *et al.* 1982, 200, and **Figure 1.6**) and the hands, feet and nails stained using a henna paste (Borchardt 1897, 168–170; Smith 1912, 60–61; Lucas 1989, 309–310; Brovarski *et al.* 1982, 200). Trained professionals performed manicures and pedicures. The office of 'Royal Manicurist' was held by a number of male dignitaries (Schoske *et al.* 1990, 21, 40; Fletcher 1994b, 108–109, fig.184), and female make-up artists were apparently employed by the wealthy (Posener 1969, 150–151).

The cosmetics portrayed alongside the men and women who used them often formed part of their tomb equipment, buried inside baskets, boxes or chests with multiple compartments for separate items. The casket found in the burial of the Middle Kingdom princess Sithathoryunet contained her gold and obsidian perfume jars, with matching kohl pot, silver rouge dish, razors, nail files (or whetstones) and a polished silver mirror. The cedar and ivory chest of the butler Kemuny held his mirror in the top section whilst his cosmetic pots were stored in a pull-out drawer beneath (Hayes 1953, 242–245, fig.155, 157; Lilyquist 1979, fig.61–64).

The Egyptians also employed a variety of equipment to administer more permanent forms of adornment, tattooing their skin with sharp flint points or bronze pins (**Figure 1.7**).[15] Used throughout history to express social values, mark rites of passage, or bestow protection through their varied symbolism (Brain 1979; Gröning 1997; Keimer 1948; Fletcher 1997, 28–30; Fletcher, forthcoming b), tattoos have come to be regarded as evidence of low social standing. They are certainly an adornment associated with men in the modern West. Yet ancient tattoos, whilst also regarded as something of a male preserve, were largely confined to the elite: the discovery of the 2,000 year old tattooed body of a Scythian ruler seems to confirm that "tattooing [was] a mark of high birth, the lack of it a mark of low birth" (Hdt 5.6; Brothwell 1986, 102, fig.81). The body of the Neolithic 'Iceman' reveals tattoo marks on his lower spine and knee joints corresponding to areas of strain-induced degeneration, suggesting that they may have been applied for therapeutic purposes to relieve joint pain.[16]

The earliest evidence for tattooing in Egypt dates back to at least 4000 BC (Keimer 1948, 1–6; Brovarski *et al.* 1982, 200). These female figurines decorated with dotted patterns on the abdomen and thighs correspond to the earliest tattooed remains dating from c. 2000 BC. Found within the royal necropolis at Deir el-Bahari, these include the mummified body of Amunet which has dotted tattoo patterns over the shoulders, chest, stomach and thighs and an extensive net-like design over the abdomen. Initially described as "probably a royal concubine", funerary inscriptions reveal that Amunet was a priestess of Hathor (Keimer 1948, 8–13). The bodies of two further women

Figure 1.7. Bronze tattoo pins, Gurob, c.1400–1300 BC, Petrie Museum UC.7790 (copyright Joann Fletcher).

discovered in a nearby tomb bore similar designs marked out in dotted lozenge patterns across their chests, arms, legs and thighs and abdominal walls, where there were also traces of light scarification. Despite their burial within the royal burial ground, the absence of any written evidence with the women led to their identification as 'dancing girls', their tattoos seen as indicative of dubious characters involved in an equally dubious profession (Keimer 1948, 13–15; Winlock 1923, 26).

Yet the repeated use of tattoo marks over the abdomen rather suggests a strong link with fertility and childbirth, the marks stretching and growing with the advancing pregnancy in a protective net-like design. Later examples also feature a small figure of the household deity Bes tattooed on the thighs, and although this has often been interpreted as a good luck symbol, a charm to ward off sexually transmitted diseases or even the mark of a prostitute (!), Bes was predominantly a protector of women in childbirth, and thus his portrayal on the thighs was surely a most appropriate location (Fletcher 1997, 29–30; forthcoming, b). In parts of modern Africa the tattooing of girls' abdomens and breasts is performed in recognition of their future biological role (Brain 1979, 50), and it seems highly likely that the ancient Egyptian practice of tattooing performed a similar function. The marks themselves may have acted as a kind of permanent amulet for women during the most dangerous part of their lives. It would also explain why there is as yet no actual evidence for the tattooing of ancient Egyptian men.

In short, it is quite clear that modern preconceptions have no place in interpreting the role of any of the cosmetic arts in ancient Egyptian society. This apparently mundane, even seemingly trivial subject in fact carries far more information than might at first seem to be the case. In attempting to understand the ancients' outlook on life as a whole, we must therefore begin to treat this subject as seriously as they so obviously did.

NOTES

1. Exemplified by the emphasis on the 'feminine' in: Capart 1907, Gauthier-Laurent 1938, Garetto 1955, Muller 1960, Haynes 1978, Hildesheim 1984, etc.
2. Earliest use of false hair, Fletcher 2000, 496, with subsequent pharaonic examples in Fletcher 1995.
3. "Egyptian priests shave their bodies all over every other day to guard against lice", Hdt. 2.36, 1954, p.143; see also Maunder 1983, 1–31 and Fletcher 1994a, 31–33.
4. 1 Corinthians 11:14–15; women's hair should nevertheless be covered, 1 Corinthians 11:10.
5. Papyrus d'Orbiney/Papyrus British Museum 10183, Derchain 1975, 56; Manniche 1987, 43; alternative translation in Lichtheim 1976, 203–211.
6. Papyrus Harris 500/Papyrus British Museum 10060 Iib.8, in Derchain 1975, 58; again an alternative translation, Lichtheim 1976, 191.
7. BM.EA.2560, Cox 1977, 67–70; 1989, 266, fig.248; Fletcher 1994a, 32–33; 2000, 496–497, fig.20.1. For similar style see Berlin AM.6911 in Schoske et al.1990, 112; Fletcher 1994a, 32.
8. Cairo JE.26252.a–g, Lucas 1930, 190–192; Fletcher 2000, 498, fig.20.3; compare to the similar sized wigs worn by fashionable European men a mere two centuries ago, eg. the 'Macaroni' c.1760–1800 in Cox 1989, 99 and frontispiece.
9. Gauthier-Laurent 1938, 673–696; Riefstahl 1952, 7–16; 1956, 10–17; Schoske et al. 1990, 21–23; Fletcher 1995, 434–439. Schoske et al. 1990, 112–115; Wilfong 1997, 65–67; Brovarski et al. 1982, 196–198. It is unfortunately the case that the presence of such equipment within a burial has often been taken as

evidence that the body is female, despite Lilyquist's assertion: "The least reliable means [of establishing sex] is probably the statement of the excavator: it is a fact that sex has often been determined by the mere presence of a mirror or a dagger in a grave, that is, objects which are traditionally associated with women or men respectively" (1979, 83). Yet in ancient Egypt, female burial equipment can include weaponry (e.g. Hayes 1953 I, 283), and male burials very definitely include 'cosmetic items'.

10 Brovarski *et al.* 1982, 189–195; Schoske *et al.* 1990, 116–117; for alternative if unlikely suggestion that small bronze implements were used in mummification process, see Kozloff & Bryan 1992, 428, No.115.
11 Fletcher 1995, 431–433, 442, fig.733, with thanks to Dr. Bill Cooke of UMIST for SEM analysis.
12 Fletcher 2000, 500, with thanks to Penelope Walton Rogers of Textile Research, York for dye analysis of ancient hair samples.
13 With the melting point of beeswax 60–63°C (140–145°F), this method of securing the hair would have been effective even in Egypt's extreme climate, see Lucas 1989, 31.
14 Lucas 1930, 41–53; 1989, 85–90; Forbes 1965, 1–50; Dayagi-Mendels 1989, 89–112; Fletcher 1998, 14–33; for analysis of contents see Chapman & Plenderleith 1926, 2614–2619; Gowland 1898, 268–269; Reutter 1914, 49–78; Serpico & White 1996, 128–139.
15 E.g. Petrie Museum UC.7790, Thomas 1981, no.472, pl.21; Booth 2001, 172–175; pins similar to tattoo instruments used in 19th century Egypt, Lane 1966, 42.
16 Spindler 1993, 167–173, with thanks to Prof. Don Brothwell for his comments.

Chapter 2

The Fashioning of Delilah.
Costume Design, Historicism and Fantasy in Cecil B. DeMille's *Samson and Delilah* (1949)

Lloyd Llewellyn-Jones

From its earliest inception, film has been fascinated with the world of the Bible. The Old Testament in particular offered a natural vehicle to filmmakers, perhaps because the narrative stories and larger than life characters were so familiar to cinema audiences. But Hollywood's biblical epics were not overly reverential: directors felt at liberty to embellish the Old Testament tales with a generous coating of eroticism, sensuality and Orientalist fantasy. The undisputed master of the genre was Cecil Blount DeMille (1881–1959), whose name has become the very byword for this style of religious epic. Now mostly known for his clichéd directorial riding crop, jodhpurs and megaphone, DeMille has become a figure of fun. But it is important to remember his role as one of the film industry's great pioneers: one of the few directors to survive the transition from silent to sound films, he maintained his popularity throughout his career.

Samson And Delilah was DeMille's first Technicolor epic, planned from the outset as visually opulent; taking advantage of the recent technological developments in colour film. This film delivered everything DeMille had come to represent: a Bible story with sex appeal; a big, brassy, gaudy, titillating extravaganza; "Manna for illiterates".[1] He commissioned Hollywood's leading designer, Edith Head, to create the costumes for the picture's female star, the ravishingly beautiful Hedy Lamarr.

In this chapter I want to concentrate on this 1949 biblical epic, paying particular attention to Edith Head's costume designs for the character of Delilah.[2] Costume, of course, plays a vital role in historical films, establishing, primarily, the appropriate feeling of another period: Hollywood costume designers worked hard to create the effect of a different time. While the costumes of epic films are important indicators of a film's 'period setting', they do more than just provide that information. In this chapter I want to investigate what costumes tell us, the modern audience, about the past and its reception. By examining the concept of historicity, I want to assess filmmakers' visualisation of the ancient world through the art of costuming.

I have opted to examine just one film out of the many hundreds of ancient world costume dramas produced in Hollywood between 1915 and 1965. The reason is straightforward: *Samson and Delilah* stands as exemplum of the biblical epic genre. Created at the mid-way point in epic film making (the first biblical epic in colour), it was crafted by the leading exponent in the field, DeMille, and the major costume designer of the day, Edith Head. Although the partnership of these two artists was productive, it was by no means pleasant; Head and DeMille had widely diverse viewpoints of what constituted historical 'authenticity.' This chapter investigates how both used costumes to conjure up a particular vision of the past. I will concentrate on the costumes of Lamarr's Delilah, because, generally speaking, leading ladies' costumes represent the apex of the designer's art in these films. The aim here is to examine the process of designing the historical costumes for Delilah and to examine the issue of Lamarr's body-shape, which influenced the design process itself, and the way in which the audience perceived the past through dress.

'PURE DEMILLE HOKUM': HOLLYWOOD'S INAUTHENTIC AUTHENTICITY.

The interaction between popular culture and historical representation is now emerging as an accepted area of academic debate.[3] Scholars question how historical films reflect the societies in which they were made, and speculate on how attitudes to the past are moulded by popular depictions of 'epic' history. It is increasingly realized that the historical veracity of the epic movie is not just a matter of narrative; scholarship is now debating how filmic concepts of the historical past are endorsed by visualisation, that is to say, set and costume designs (Tashiro 1998). In classic Hollywood publicity, the panorama of ancient Rome, the recreation of the hanging gardens of Babylon, the armour of Philistine soldiers, the veils of Ethiopian dancing girls, were all said to be faithful recreations – despite the fact that scholars did not necessarily know what the 'originals' looked like. Studio publicity departments were keen on stressing the laborious academic research that went into the recreation of ancient locations and costumes, and on claiming that what was being witnessed on the screen was an authentic recreation of ancient life. DeMille himself was obsessed with the idea of historical research and with the kudos to be obtained from persuading his audience that it was witnessing accurate recreations of the past on screen. However, his obsession with the *idea* of historical precision and his desire to realize lavish movies with mass appeal were contradictory: what DeMille claimed to do and what he actually did were two different matters.

When DeMille came to film *Samson and Delilah*, he had already gained a reputation as a big-budget director of historically-themed movies. *Cleopatra* (1934) was a secular epic based on the life of the infamous Egyptian queen, while *The Ten Commandments* (1923) *The King of Kings* (1926) and *The Sign of the Cross* (1932) were biblical extravaganzas. Even in his formative period of filmmaking, pre-1923, studio publicity already emphasized DeMille's army of research assistants and the years of background work that ensured historically correct re-creations of antiquity. DeMille claims to have developed his proclivity for historical research early on, when he routinely sent his secretary into public libraries to collect books on costume, architecture, armaments or whatever subject currently occupied his mind (1960, 105). Certainly, by the late 1920s his offices contained one of the biggest research libraries in Hollywood, and DeMille began to see himself as something of an academic, expert in Biblical history and Judeo-Christian theology.[4] When asked if DeMille was really concerned with research and accuracy, or if this was self-promotion, his scriptwriter, Charles Bennett responded:

> Oh yes, he had a research department working with him all the time. Everything had to be accurate, even to the kinds of plants that would be in a particular area. He was very thorough in that way …and very good (Server 1987, 28).

DeMille was to regard himself as the instigator of the concept of the 'research department', regarding the creation of the post of 'research consultant' as one of his most valuable contributions to moviemaking. In DeMille's philosophy, the research consultant was a lynch-pin in his production crew:

> [the research consultant] with scholarly objectivity …must often be a "No"-man to the wider fancies of producer, director or writers. …His most important function is to see that what goes into a picture is authentic for the time and place of the movie.[5]

In 1945 Henry Noerdlinger joined DeMille's Research Department and quickly established himself as a very able and patient co-worker. Earning DeMille's complete trust, he undertook the research for *The Unconquered* (1947) and then *Samson and Delilah*.[6] In 1956, when DeMille turned his attention to filming his second version of *The Ten Commandments*, Noerdlinger oversaw the publication of research notes compiled from the works of eminent Egyptologists, theologians and historians. DeMille then arranged to have the work distributed by the University of Southern California, and, in a wordy introduction to the volume, noted the lengths to which Noerdlinger had gone in order to compile the book, giving reasons for its composition:

> In our research …we have consulted some 1,900 books and periodicals, collected nearly 3,000 photographs, and used the facilities of 30 libraries and museums in North America, Europe and Africa. …Students will find here a distillation of materials for which otherwise they would have to search in many places, but which are here arranged and collated for ready reference. …consider it money well spent to bring to the screen the results of the work of so many patient and selfless scholars whose labours …have helped make [antiquity] live again. Research does not sell tickets at the box office, I may be told. But research does help bring out the majesty of [the past].[7]

Finding a specific historical period to locate the Biblical story of Samson and Delilah was problematic though, even for DeMille and Noerdlinger. Deciding on the chronological period of the tale was difficult. Moreover, they were forced to ask themselves just where "one of the greatest love stories in history or literature" was set (DeMille 1960, 364). The story of Samson and Delilah (Judges 16) is brief, but DeMille had once declared that he could make a film out of any two pages of the Bible. Yet, with so little to go on, he opted to pad out the plot with scenes taken from a little known novel, *Judge and Fool* by Vladimir Jabotinsky, which was set, like the biblical book, in and around Canaanite and Philistine cities of the Bronze Age Levant. However, this period, this locale, and these names meant very little to the average cinema-goer. The audience had no pre-conceived vision of ancient Hebrew and

Philistine life, but neither did DeMille. He sent Noerdlinger on a quest and, with some credibility (drawn from the latest scholarly research), Noerdlinger came up with a solution: the Philistines, he said, were an advanced northern Mediterranean race who swept into the Levant and Egypt during a great migratory period of the Late Bronze Age. They shared a cultural heritage with a very sophisticated island race, the Minoans; therefore, the 'look' of the film, of the Philistine scenes, at least, should be Minoan.[8] DeMille gave the go-ahead for the publicity department's blurb:

> The civilization represented in this particular biblical picture is known as the Minoan Civilization, about which not a great deal has been known until relatively recent times. … Mr DeMille [has] exceeded his own demanding nature by spending fourteen years in researching the manners, customs, flora, fauna, dress, habits and other indices of Minoan culture.[9]

The Minoans therefore became a convenient handle for Hollywood's recreation Philistine society, regardless of any sure historical evidence for such a close identification. The DeMille publicity machine assured the cinema audience that they were witnessing painstaking recreations of the original sites and sounds of the ancient Philistine-Minoan world, skilfully brought to life by an army of experts. Richard Condon, DeMille's Press Agent, noted, "We've got more on Minoan culture than Arnold Toynbee."[10]

But of course, by their nature, epic films do not show a completely honest view of ancient life. Ever since D.W. Griffiths' *Intolerance* (1916; Henderson 1972, 166ff) moviemakers had striven to get specific historical points right. However, on certain issues, epic treatments could be very lax, often way off the mark of historical authenticity, both in the details of narrative, script, sets and costumes, and in the whole generic ambience of films (Llewellyn-Jones, 2002; Solomon 2001, 25ff). However, it is important to remember that the shared reception of epic films by an audience is not (and can never be) uniform; received notions of what is historically right or wrong vary between audience members.

When it comes to film costume design, it should first be noted that the Hollywood epic generally presents a very conservative view of the ancient world, and that such design in Hollywood does not take risks. The epic movie's sense of the past is largely based on visual conventions inherited from Victorian historical paintings and early twentieth-century stage designs, so that the presentation of ancient life varies little in Hollywood filmmaking, relying instead on visual clichés: developed through repetition and based on audience familiarity.[11] Experienced moviegoers knew what Romans, Greeks and Egyptians were *supposed* to wear, and any film that seriously challenged this was not likely to gain popular acceptance or box-office success.[12]

DeMille was certainly familiar with the work of Victorian artists like Poynter, Alma-Tadema and Long, and it is clear that these romanticising visions of ancient life heralded the way for his filmic recreations (Dunant 1994; Robinson 1955; Christie 1991). At times, though, DeMille delved deeper back into art history: for *Samson and Delilah* he collected works by Baroque and Rococo masters too, being particularly taken with a painting of the shearing of Samson's hair by Rubens (Brown 1983, 78). Reliance on the old masters helps explain the dazzling baroque beauty of his vision of antiquity, with its rigorous denial of dirt and its elevation of the sumptuous. His take on the biblical past suggests a conspiratorial revision of historical truth: the typical *mise en scéne* of the DeMillian epic was too elaborate and too systematic to pass as an artistic vision of history, rendering DeMille's zealous claims of authenticity pointless. Besides, DeMille knew that audiences were not interested in the literal truth of the ancient world, but in *kitsch* and camp fantasies of pomp and luxury. These captured the early audiences of *Samson and Delilah*:

> Mr. DeMille has …here led his carpenters and actors and costumiers and camera crews into the vast manufacture of a spectacle that out-Babels anything he's done. There are more flowing garments in this picture, more chariots, more temples, more peacock plumes, more animals, more pillows, more spear-carriers, more beards, more sex than ever before. At least that's the sizable impression which Mr. DeMille has achieved by bringing together the Old Testament and Technicolor for the first time. (*The New York Times*, 22nd December 1949).

The *kitsch* grandeur of the film thrills and satisfies; the critic does not think to question its historical authenticity. The film historian John Cary goes some way towards explaining the dichotomy between DeMille's extravagant camp and painstaking historicity:

> If authenticity is brought into our conscious too laboriously, the drama suffers. DeMille, perhaps unconsciously, understood this… (1974, 91).

Other critics have been less understanding. Chabot questioned DeMille's historical source material more directly:

> Biblical accuracy? There was none. Oh wait, yes, there *was* a Samson, *and* a Delilah; other than that, it was pure DeMille hokum (2000).

DELILAH IN HIGH-HEELS: EPIC COSTUME DESIGN

Films are products of their time and even in the earliest silent pictures, elements of contemporary living were frequently incorporated into the 'look' of the film, to make the remote ancient world more palatable to the audience. One of the most interesting dilemmas in designing ancient spectacles was reconciling a modern perspective with the historical horizon of the period described: conflating the 'look' of the past with the 'look' of the present, without committing 'serious' anachronisms.

The notion of historicism contends that we should try to understand the past from its own perspective, attempting to totally eliminate our modern concepts of the past during the process of research. A historicist would therefore argue that the design of a historical film should be as authentic as possible. However, current issues in taste, perception, and reception are always and unavoidably present whenever history is narrated, whether in academic scholarship or imaginative fiction. Historical investigation is a process of dialogue in which our present-day thinking encounters the thinking of the past. The present-day cannot be denied or eliminated: in describing the past, the author simultaneously writes about his or her own world. This is very much the case with Hollywood epics, where a variety of voices (director, designers, stars) converge, merge, or clash over the re-telling. The result is not so much 'realist history' as 'designer history', in which:

> Historical references become secondary to design, although they are never totally absent. ...Designer history ...combines the apolitical focus of costume melodrama with the impersonal affect of the traditional History Film. The past becomes a movement of empty forms and exquisite objects... (Tashiro 1998, 95–6).

The Art Direction of an epic film must be particularly aware of creating historical authenticity which also appeals to contemporary taste. As Tashiro suggests, make-up, hairstyles, and costumes in the typical epic are particularly often adjusted to the period of filming, becoming the primary focus of Designer History. This is never more noticeable than in DeMille's biblical epics; it is no surprise to see Delilah in high-heels. These particular movies were major vehicles for important and influential female stars, and the Hollywood star-system allowed major actresses input into the look of their film wardrobes (Davis 1993, 205–32; Gaines & Herzog 1990). Consequently, there is an undeniable *contemporary* emphasis in the 'Minoan'-style costumes of Hollywood's Delilah.

The construction of the filmic images of Delilah was a collaborative effort, chiefly between director and costume designer, reflecting the particular concepts of beauty and sexual magnetism dominant at the time of filming. Costume designers were required to research the historical period of the film's location to give an aura of reality. However, they were then often free to interpret this in terms of the ideals of feminine beauty embedded in their own contextual culture, shared with the contemporary audience to whom they would 'sell' their products. Hollywood's 'historical' costumes always make a fashionable statement, although at the time, contemporary details might be hard to spot, since the audience themselves are so immersed in that 'look'.

> Every age remakes the visible world to suit itself and so has its own peculiar way of looking at the clothes which form its daily wear. The eyes of the beholders are so affected by their brains that they see not precisely what is before them, but what they wish to be there (Squire 1972, 17–18).

The contentious fashioning of Delilah is an essential aspect of the cinema audience's identification with the period and locale of the story and with the character herself. Delilah's costumes bridge the gap between past and present (Annas, La Valley & Maeder 1987).

All of Hollywood's directors, designers and publicity managers and marketing experts understood that 'historical' films were actually gimmicks used to exploit the notion of film glamour. The 'history film' placed top stars in fantastical situations, enabling their fans to see them acting in romantic or heroic ways while wearing revealing or flamboyant outfits. The star's personality or fashionable style could not, however, be subsumed beneath historical authenticity. Thus, the costumes of Lamarr's Delilah, had to suggest another time and place (pseudo-Minoan Philistia), but not at the expense of losing the unique and appealing features of Lamarr's own, Hollywood-manufactured, image.

DeMille was clearly aware of this; it was, after all, standard Hollywood policy. DeMille's methodology, however, is interesting in its continual use of the rhetoric of research integrated with the more commercial aspects of his filmmaking. Publicity campaigns ran prior to the production, and at the time of its cinema release, included cross-country lecture tours and scholarly articles on the historical authenticity of the film. DeMille insisted on keeping the myth of historical research alive.

PHILISTINE CHIC: DESIGNING DELILAH

Actually realising that research, in the film's costume design, created a noticeable dichotomy between the *historical* reality of Minoan dress and DeMille's vision of what Minoan clothing *should* be. Admittedly, in the late 1940s scholarship on Aegean clothing was still in its infancy: what did exist was often flawed – at least in terms of our *current* perception of Minoan dress. Mary Houston's influential work, originally published in 1931, was revised in 1947 when Noerdlinger was compiling his fact-file; there is little doubt that it was known to Noerdlinger and the Paramount Art Department. Somewhat naive readings of the Minoan artistic evidence led Houston to suggest that women wore an "elaborately cut, tight fitting bodice" and a separate flounced skirt worn over some kind of "crinoline" frame (Houston 1947, 8 ff; Marcar, this volume). This understanding of Minoan dress suited Hollywood's contemporary eye; the notion of Minoan women's clinched waists (emphasising the bust) and full skirts being perfectly in accord with the post-war 'New Look' couture influencing Hollywood's designers (**Figure 2.1**).

However, there were problems with accurately depicting Minoan female dress on screen. Breast-exposure, such an obvious hallmark of female Aegean dress, was obviously unacceptable, and accordingly, left out of Noerdlinger's publicity articles and the film's final costume designs. DeMille saw a certain amount of 'eastern', or biblical, glamour as necessary.[13] He wanted, in short, to make the female costumes (and Delilah's in particular) sexy:

> The men and women of the Bible [were] flesh and blood. Clothing in them in what we think is reverence, we have too often stripped [them] of their humanity. ...We [must] remember that Samson was swept away by a surge of passion ...by a slim and ravishingly attractive young girl. ...People will not come to see a picture in which Biblical characters walk around looking and acting like Biblical characters. ...They were men and women. And that is how I portray them (DeMille 1960, 364–5).

DeMille chose Victor Mature and Hedy Lamarr for the leading roles because they embodied the public ideals of manliness and sexiness, offering brawn and beauty. Mature, a clean-shaven saturnine hulk, was a straightforward piece of beefcake, handsome and dumb. Lamarr, in her 'Philistine' robes, embodied the late '40s vision of perfect womanhood. Ed Sullivan had called her 'the most beautiful woman of the century', and that endorsement was enough for DeMille.

DeMille appointed five designers to dress his cast.[14] The glamour assignment was passed onto to Edith Head, commissioned to dress Delilah and her sister, Semadar (Angela Landsbury). In the late 1940s, Head was one of Hollywood's most famous

Figure 2.1. Hedy Lamarr as a pseudo-Minoan Delilah, in a costume designed by Edith Head. Publicity still from the author's private collection.

and prolific costume designers. First working as an assistant designer on *Cleopatra*, she regarded DeMille as an egotist or "a freak trying to play God" (Head & Castro 1983, 81). She regarded DeMille's habit of overstaffing costume design as a ploy to maintain complete control over the films' visualisation; with several designers attempting to costume the film, he became the unifying factor.

Head's relationship with DeMille was strained, largely due to his rarely treating her with the deference due her position as Paramount's Head Designer. He would often demand twenty or thirty designs for one costume, keeping photostats of the approved design on file in his office, as points of reference to check on the completed costume. Head's memoirs, published after DeMille's death, are a valuable source for understanding DeMille's methods, and, despite his rhetoric, for grasping his less than authentic approach to 'historic' costuming. It is interesting to compare the official language of DeMille's publicity machine with her candid private memoirs:

Figure 2.2. Delilah's peacock gown, designed by Edith Head and made with over 2000 feathers. The image of Lamarr in Figure 2.6 is based on this studio portrait. From the author's private collection.

> *Samson and Delilah* is not a picture of which I am proud. ...I never thought I did good work for DeMille. ...I always had to do what that conceited old goat wanted, whether it was correct or not. He never did an authentic picture in his entire career, and in my opinion that made him a damn liar as well as an egotist (Head & Castro 1983, 81).

One particular clash occurred over a cape worn by Lamarr for Samson's destruction of the temple. DeMille demanded something extraordinary for Delilah's last appearance and wanted a costume with feathers: "for what reason, I don't know", recalled Head, "He never gave reasons". Having no idea of types of birds in 'Minoan' Philistia, Head asked the research department. *Perhaps*, they replied, there were peacocks: nothing more than conjecture. However, knowing DeMille would love the gaudy effect of peacock feathers, she designed a long, draping cape with the regal plumage (**Figure 2.2**)[15] Nevertheless, Head's memoirs stress that she saw it as a historical anachronism:

Figure 2.3. Hedy Lamarr's Delilah in a bias-cut silver metallic gown designed by Edith Head. Publicity still from the author's private collection.

I have always had the feeling that [the peacock cape] was entirely wrong. I doubt very much if there were any peacocks around or nearby in the days of Samson and Delilah. Nor would anyone, even Delilah, have worn the kind of cape that I designed – or any of the other costumes for that matter. I suppose that only scholars would know that the costumes were not historically correct, but it bothered me terribly. I was never able to find anything authentic to indicate what Samson and Delilah looked like, so I improvised. And I won an Oscar (Head & Castro 1983, 85).

Certainly, with hindsight, the designs for Delilah's costumes have an undeniable 1940s silhouette – squared shoulders, fitted skirts cut on the bias, tight cropped bodices, and uplift brassieres – all coupled with 1940s glamour make-up, elaborate hairstyles, and strappy platform sandals. This 'look' is well-captured in a surviving costume sketch (Annas, La Valley & Maeder 1987, 119) and movie stills (**Figure 2.1**). At one point, Lamarr wears a gown made from metallic fabric; draped over her bosom, the cloth resembling late 1940s Parisian couture (**Figure 2.3**). Many of the costumes comprised a tight fitting skirt – usually slit to the thigh – ending in a train, with a close-fitting bolero bodice, the 'harem top' of popular American fantasy. Added to this basic ensemble are jewelled headpieces which crown Lamarr's raven-black hair, fine chiffon or gauze veils and masses of chunky costume jewellery.[16] Having little to do with the reality of Philistine-Minoan dress, Delilah's costumes are pure *Arabian Nights* concoctions. What they skilfully do, however, is mark her a classic temptress.

It is not too surprising to find that in biblical scholarship Delilah is tagged "a temptress *par excellence*" or "extraordinary", a "*femme fatale* par excellence", the "classic *femme fatale*".[17] Hedy Lamarr (an actress notorious for being notorious) epitomises this aspect of Delilah's reputation. Even the fastidious Head admitted that Hedy looked like "the all-time *femme fatale*" (Head & Ardmore 1960, 9; Doniol-Valcroze 1989, 41–42).

There was one glaring physical omission: "she is certainly a little bit stringy for the taste of those who like their Delilahs plump" (Holt 1951, 251). Although there are no biblical descriptions of Delilah, within the tradition of classic biblical portraiture, she is portrayed as a voluptuous, big-bosomed woman. Indeed:

> The phenomenon of visualizing a textual figure is almost indispensable while reading a narrative that contains references to love and sexuality. The stereotypic temptress is good-looking, quite young, saucy, inviting, ripe to overripe, seductively attired, with big breasts – a playboy centrefold girl (Brenner 1993, 231).

This assessment was borne out by many old fine arts masters. Rubens (who had so influenced DeMille's vision) depicted Delilah with large naked breasts; exposed nipples squeezed into focused prominence by her tight clothing (Brown 1983, 2). Therefore, after consulting such historical paintings of Delilah with his usual research thoroughness, one would imagine DeMille choosing an actress with similar anatomical proportions (Wurtzel 1998, 40). Certainly, the pre-production artwork he commissioned showed a brawny athlete being eyed-up by a big-busted, slim-waisted siren (**Figure 2.4**). Yet, in the casting process DeMille chose the flat-chested Lamarr to star, provoking Grouch Marx's infamous quip: "First picture I've ever seen where the man's tits are bigger than the woman's."[18] Even contemporary reviewers bitterly noted this unmistakable Lamarr build: "All the revealing costuming lavished on her …left me desiring her to put some clothes on! There was really nothing to see! I've seen more curves on [a] 2-by-4" (Chabot 2000, 2). Indeed, DeMille was also chastised for *not* being a salacious cineaste. Harcourt-Smith complained:

> More serious perhaps is the slackness with which DeMille has allowed the strings of sex to sag. …Yet I suspect that *Samson and Delilah* will not make its money from its sexual appeal (1951, 412).

Somewhat ironically, Lamarr's agent urged her to do the film as a mixture of "muscles, tits, and sadism" or "muscles and tits sugar-coated with religion" (Lamarr 1966, 168–9). Some critics still see sex where none actually existed: "DeMille's spectaculars …gave legions of puritanical voyeurists a good excuse to watch Delilah romping in the near-buff. For one ticket, the audience got both sermons *and* tits!" (Greenberg 1975, 8). Although Delilah is never sexually exposed or in a near-buff

Figure 2.4. A big-busted Delilah from pre-release poster artwork. One sheet poster (1949) from the author's private collection.

state, this testifies to DeMille's incredible filmmaking powers in the art of 'sexless sex' and to the skill of Edith Head's costume designs.[19] Not only were the breast exposing garments of Minoan women censored at the research stage but, moreover, the strict morality code which had come into operation by the 1940s meant that Head was seriously compromised in her choice of designs. Victor Mature might be able to wear a short tunic or a skimpy loincloth, but Hedy Lamarr was not even allowed to show her navel. Consequently, Head was forced to come up with novel ways of concealing the actress' bellybutton, cleavage and protruding pelvic bones (**Figure 2.5**). With any focus on the pelvic area removed, attention naturally had to shift to the bust region.

Figure 2.5. "Minoan" dress: a silver lame split skirt with train and cut-off bodice designed by Edith Head for Hedy Lamarr's Delilah. Publicity still from the author's private collection.

> For *Samson and Delilah*, we had sketched costumes with a voluptuous bustline Hedy couldn't fill. ...So her costumes were not padded; we achieved a voluptuous effect by line, by drapery, and nothing could have been lovelier than the Delilah I took to Mr. De Mille in a costume of mesh and beaten silver, so lovely he actually *smiled*! (Head & Ardmore 1960, 99–100).

As Lamarr's agent confessed: "When [DeMille] sells sex ...people buy because he wraps it in fancy paper with pink ribbons" (Lamarr 1966, 173).

So, why did DeMille eschew the classical biblical portraiture tradition, his prescriptive pre-production sketches, and his own sexy film reputation by accepting a

Figure 2.6. Delilah advertises contemporary living: Lucky Strike Cigarettes. In this magazine advertisement (1950) Lamarr is depicted wearing the peacock gown. From the author's private collection.

flat-chested actress who needed specialist costume deceptiveness? DeMille was certainly aware of the Delilah of the old masters, but their centuries old definitions of plump feminine beauty did not jibe well with 1940s notions of 'attractive femininity', whose re-focused emphasis upon thinness is shown by surviving costume sketches for an anorexic Delilah (Annas, La Valley & Maeder 1987, 118).

Golden Age Hollywood exerted a profound influence on American and British design: film glamour was mimicked by women who aspired to resemble their favourite stars. In films set in the present, costume design obviously reflected contemporary modes; but historical films could also reflect contemporary fashion and aesthetic. Never the primary objective of film costume designers, the retail marketability of designs was nevertheless an important facet of the design. Elements of Hollywood's 'period costumes' were mass re-produced for department stores. Scarlett O'Hara's green sprig muslin dress in *Gone With The Wind* (1939), for example, was produced in dozens of variations which bore little or no resemblance to the original (LaValley 1987, Massey 2000).

The release of *Samson and Delilah* saw fashionable women going 'Philistine' with off-the-rack versions of the pseudo-Minoan robes and jewels. Delilah became a fashion icon. *Lucky Strikes* cigarettes used: "Hedy Lamarr says, 'A good cigarette is like a good movie – always enjoyable'" showing Lamarr lounging in the infamous peacock cape (**Figures 2.2** and **2.6**).[20] Delilah advocated a chic and sophisticated lifestyle to shoppers, an image far removed from the historical authenticity highlighted by DeMille's publicity machine, but one which he nonetheless fostered with equal care.

Despite DeMille's claims of historical dependability, in designing the costumes for Delilah, Head was compelled to interpret the ideals of feminine beauty embedded in contextual culture, to straddle DeMille's two major contradictory preoccupations, pandering to his notions of historicity while 'selling' a glamour-product in a major marketing strategy. DeMille ended up with a sexily chic, but morally acceptable, Delilah – the perfect artefact of 1940s Hollywood, but certainly not an image recognizable as part of the ancient Minoan world. The historical heroines of DeMille's movies, even the Philistine ones, always make a fashionable statement.

NOTES

1. Paul Rotha in Tanitch 2000, 50.
2. Released in December 1949, it played in cinemas throughout 1950.
3. For treatments of ancient history and cinema see Munn 1982, Babington & Evans 1993, Vidal 1992, MacDonald Frasier 1988, Elley 1984, Hirsch 1978, Cary 1974, Wyke 1997, Llewellyn-Jones 2002 and Solomon 2001.
4. A committed Christian, DeMille read the Bible on a daily basis, and delighted in inviting cardinals, bishops and rabbis onto his sets in order to debate some theological point. Billy Graham confessed that DeMille was a great Bible student who once corrected his scriptural error regarding The Ten Commandments. See Frost 1997, 137.
5. DeMille 1960, 106. DeMille's usual methodology was to have an artist sketch, and even paint, scenes in advance of shooting; all the historical components of the scene had to be included within the sketch and the final shot. See Davis 1993, 62 ff.
6. "Noerdlinger has been the most thorough and accurate research consultant I have ever had, making himself as much at home among the pyramids of the Pharaohs as in the tinsel and spun-candy world of the circus." (DeMille 1960, 360). He went on to research *The Greatest Show on Earth* (1952), and *The Ten Commandments* (1956).
7. Noerdlinger 1956, 2–3; Solomon 2001, 142–58; Orrison 1999. Despite (or because of) its spectacle, not all reviews of the film were favourable. *The Weekly Variety*, October 10th 1956 noted, "Emphasis on physical dimension has rendered neither awesome nor profound the story of Moses. The eyes of the onlooker are filled with spectacle. Emotional tug is sometimes lacking."
8. Evidence leaves little doubt that the Philistines came immediately, though probably not ultimately, from the Aegean. They were probably one of the Sea Peoples who, in the second millennium BC, uprooted by the collapse of the Mycenaean palace civilization, migrated from the Aegean, via Crete and Cyprus, to the Near East. For an interpretation of Philistine culture see Coogan 1999, 201–05.
9. *Samson and Delilah* press-book 1950.
10. Higham 1973, 289. Toynebee (1889–1975) was a British historian, known for his view of the past as a succession of civilizations rather than political entities. He published his 12-volume *A Study of History*,

a comparative study of 26 civilizations in world history, between 1934 and 1961.
11. For the Academic Painters and their recreations of antiquity, Liversidge & Edwards 1996, Ash 1989, 1995 & 1999, Wood 1983. Hollywood's debt to these artists is still felt today, Landau 2000, 64 ff. Influence of Victorian theatre design on cinema art direction: Finkel 1996 and Mayer 1994.
12. The 1954 film *The Silver Chalice*, set in late first century AD Syria and Judaea radically altered this design formula: its set and costume designs blend the semi-abstract and impressionistic, which, coupled with a poor script, made it a box office flop; Hirsch 1978, 34 ff.; Elly 1984, 117–18.
13. The Philistines get a better treatment, visually at least, in the 1985 film, *King David* and in the 1996 TV film *Samson and Delilah*. For an investigation of Bronze Age dress in Israel see King & Stager 2001, 146–62, 259–83.
14. Gile Steele and Elois Jenssen, male costumes; Dorothy Jeakins and Gwen Wakeling, extras. DeMille was always certain that his costumes demanded the work of several designers and that one or two would simply 'burn out'. Jeakins was also commissioned to design Delilah's costumes, Annas, La Valley & Maeder 1987, 118.
15. Peacock feathers were a mark of DeMille's films: in *Male and Female* (1919) Gloria Swanson, as a Babylonian princess, wore a headdress of white peacock plumes (a conceit Edith Head later used in Swanson's costumes for *Sunset Boulevard*). Lamarr's cape is still on view in DeMille's estate in Los Angeles; made from 2,000 peacock plumes, allegedly gathered from peacocks on DeMille's ranch. A standard Hollywood joke: 'no peacock is safe around DeMille.' Head & Calistro 1983, 84, 87–88 and Lavine 1981, 17.
16. Part of Lamarr's marketability was her dark looks: 'a red-lipped, tawny-eyed, black haired girl' which started a 'brunette trend'. Both Rita Hayworth and Joan Bennett were given Lamarr makeovers. Lamarr's dark hair certainly formed part of Delilah's Oriental appeal, Berry 2000, 121 ff.
17. Smith 1999, 113; Koosed & Linafelt 1996, 175; Fewell 1992. 73; Guthridge 1995, 22.
18. For a discussion of the remark see Babington & Evans 1993. 233–37.
19. A term used by Kozlovic 2002.
20. Victor Mature as Samson was also used in marketing: Samson-sized cornflakes were mass-produced by Kellogg, Higham 1978, 289.

Chapter 3

Reconstructing Aegean Bronze Age Fashions

Ariane Marcar

INTRODUCTION

This chapter considers garment reconstruction as a technique for investigating not only the physical reality of Aegean Bronze Age clothing, but also its relationship to artistic representations (and thus their evidence for various aspects of society). It discusses some of the issues which reduce the informative potential of the technique, arguing that effective replication must be founded on the available evidence for clothing construction, rather than on recreating particular images, and further that comprehensive cataloguing of garment depictions is necessary alongside such detailed technical considerations.

METHODOLOGICAL AND INTERPRETATIVE PROBLEMS

The clothing evidence for Crete, mainland Greece and the Cyclades during the BA is essentially pictorial, and dates principally to the LBA. In the absence of literary evidence and actual garment finds, we have traditionally attempted to learn more about Minoan and Mycenaean dress by trying to replicate the clothes illustrated in Aegean art. The principal aim of iconographic studies, meanwhile, has been to shed light on identity and social status, widely considered to be expressed by dress. Since the majority of the figurative frescoes are from palatial contexts, and frequently represent cultic and festive scenes, they have naturally been interpreted as pertaining to the elite. Some studies (Cameron 1974; Marinatos 1993; Morgan 1988, ch. 6; Kontorli-Papadopoulou 1996) mention garments as part of their overall iconographical studies, others concentrate on gendered dress.[1] Small differences in dress between the Mainland and Crete have traditionally been used to argue that the Minoans and Mycenaeans differentiated themselves through clothing. However, the extent of regional differences is difficult to gauge, since manufactured goods featuring figurative scenes were being regularly exchanged between LBA Crete, Mainland Greece and the Cycladic islands. Assessing and interpreting garment distribution patterns is therefore a complex affair. The changing identity of the kilt, associated with the warrior class, and LBA elites in general, exemplifies this well.[2]

An accent on replication is validated by the fact that the range of clothing depicted contains garments common to surrounding regions, or still in use today (loincloths, kilts, tunics, capes, mantles and flounced skirts) showing the legitimacy of depicted types. Despite stylisation, wall painters generally seem to accurately reproduce the basic shapes, colours, textures and construction of garments. However, costume depictions are not always straightforward to unravel: they are often only sketchily rendered, even fragmentary, and secondary seams are generally not shown. Clothing items are commonly superimposed, and not always easily separated. These interpretative problems are difficult to overcome, as is artistic ambiguity.

Consequently informative replication cannot be achieved in isolation: it needs to be placed in the wider context of scholarship on Aegean Bronze Age society. The apparent uniformity of the dress style (which seems to appear ready made with few antecedents on Crete at the beginning of the LBA, lasting until the fall of the Mycenaean palaces some 400 years later) has also, until recently, discouraged systematic analysis of the costumes as a group, or in any detail (Marcar 2001, 2004, and in press). This is shown by the continued use of generic garment terms (Rutkowski 1991, 45; Jones 1998, 46): 'loincloth' and 'kilt' are often used interchangably, while the parted kilt has sometimes been termed 'shorts' (e.g., Sakellariou 1974, 12–13; Xenaki-Sakellariou & Chatzilio 1989, 25 *'pantalon court'*; Morgan 1995, 243; 1998, 204; Rehak 1996, 44–45 fig. 2 G). Poor terminology and lack of detailed study have inevitably led to confusion about which garment types are depicted where, and about their construction.

Failing to take key aspects of textile fibre technology and the history of ancient garment construction into consideration has meant that many replicas bear little resemblance to the garments depicted in Aegean art, as Barber has recently pointed out (2000 with reference to Jones 2000). Simple construction methods, using the staple fibres (flax and wool, as shown by Linear B tablets) have certainly helped us obtain a better idea of how items such as the flounced skirt might have been constructed. However, the use of modern day synthetic fibres, or construction methods for which we have no evidence, means that some replicas only vaguely resemble the garments depicted in Aegean art (Jones 1998, 2000, esp. 39 for women's wear, showing apron with drawstring; Rehak 1996 and Sapouna-Sakellaraki 1971 for men's wear). In my opinion this is unacceptable, especially since garment shape is dictated by fibre type, not just the cut of the cloth. The use of Egyptian garments as prototypes is more justifiable, as there is some cross-over between the Aegean and Egyptian clothing range. However, the validity of this approach needs to be investigated further, given that substantial differences existed between the textile tool kits of these regions, including choice of fibre types (the Egyptians predominantly favoured linen). Reconstructions which replicate entire costumes from the outset, rather than exploring in detail the construction of individual garment types, and the variety of ways in which these were worn and made, are also problematic. A better understanding of the history of garment manufacturing and tailoring would rectify some of the misconceptions, and so improve our chances of proposing plausible replicas.

Such an understanding must surely be based on Bronze Age evidence for cloth production and clothing construction. Evidence for Aegean cloth production can be outlined as follows. Clay loom-weights of various forms and weights are by far the most common Aegean find: disc-shaped loom weights are characteristic of the region, testifying to the use of the upright warp-weighted loom. This contrasts with Egyptian and Near Eastern cultures (who predominantly used ground loom types: generally leaving no trace unless depicted). Although direct and pictorial evidence for these in the Aegean is lacking, it is probable that Aegean peoples also used horizontal and band looms.

A small number of weaving workshops have been identified within settlement and palatial sites thanks to groupings of loom-weights, principally found on Crete and in the Cyclades. Spindle whorls, fibre-wetting bowls, a handful of pins/needles and a small number of spools, constitute the remainder of the finds related to textile production (Barber 1991, 73–77 and figs. 2.41–42; Carington-Smith 1992, 687). Currently, the small number of identified dye-vats, along with vessels for fulling or washing cloth, represent our only direct evidence for the processing and finishing of cloth (Carington-Smith 1975, 55–69; Barber 1991, 239–41 for list; tubs linked to cloth: Kopaka & Platon 1993; Evely 2000, 485–511).

For fibre types, though the Linear B tablets list wool and flax (as well as referring to several cloth types, decorated bands, and to garments made of cloth and animal skins which are attested pictorially) precise information is lacking. The discovery of a single wild lepidopterous cocoon at the site of Akrotiri, Thera, has recently been used to suggest that transparent garments depicted in LMIA were made of silk, and that the fibre reached the Mediterranean before 500 BC (Barber 1991, 30–32; Good 1995; Panagiotakopulu *et al.* 1997; Doumas 1992, pls. 101, 105). However, despite one attestation in Egypt by 1000 BC, there is little else to suggest silk in the Aegean earlier. The Akrotiri find is an isolated one; there is nothing to tie this cocoon to silk production; and the garments could just as well be made of fine linen (Roehrig 1996: the much famed early XVIIIth Dynasty transparent textiles found in the tomb of Hatnofer, were the result of a loose weave of superfine linen thread, probably spun from young flax plants). In addition, transparent garments are rarely depicted outside of Akrotiri, suggesting that they were never commonplace in the Aegean.

Neither the use of felt in the production of accessories and outdoor wear, nor the identification of additional fibres have been sufficiently examined, while there appear to be no Linear B references to actual decorative techniques. Translation of terms remains general: i.e. 'multicoloured with variegated designs' (Barber 1991, 313). Consequently, we cannot at present correlate loom and loom-weight type with the cloth types depicted artistically, especially as the art of weaving lies principally in the skill of the weaver (Barber 1991, 126).

Turning to the pictorial evidence for clothing construction, the Aegean LBA clothing style appears fully developed in conjunction with the rise of the second palaces on Crete, and the flourishing of figurative art, during MMIII–LMIA. The bulk of this figurative art belongs to LMIA–B (c. 1600–1450 BC) and LMII–III (c. 1450–1200 BC). Images occur on a variety of media on the Greek Mainland, Crete, and in the Cyclades (under Minoan and Mycenaean artistic influence at certain times). The most detailed examples are found on large-scale wall-paintings, but smaller-scale clothed individuals occur regularly on the other major art forms (gold, ivory and stone). On Crete the largest group of wall-paintings – the sole example of a palatial source – is that of Knossos (dated to LMII–IIIA1, some to MMIIIB–LMIA and LMIA–B, Immerwahr 1990, 171–79). Others come from LMI houses. In the Cyclades the most famous wall-paintings are undoubtedly those of LMIA Akrotiri on Thera, which has produced the most complete range of large-scale pictorial scenes. Reasonably large numbers of figured frescoes have been uncovered at the mainland palatial sites of Mycenae, Pylos, Thebes, Tiryns and Orchomenos (most of these can be dated to LHIIIA–B, Immerwahr 1990, 190–94), but their overall state of preservation is poor. The Minoan-style figural frescoes found at Tell el-Dab'a in Egypt (early XVIIIth Dynasty, or LMIA, Bietak 1995, 2000; Bietak & Marinatos 1995) should also be considered.

Therefore frescoes represent our richest source of information on textiles and garments. Unfortunately, their wide date range, especially the Knossian, means that fashion developments can only be situated generally. On the other hand, garment identification is facilitated by the artists' general adherence to the same basic artistic conventions (irrespective of the medium or minor variations in style, i.e. in the way the garment was worn) when depicting costume. The flounced skirt and the associated collarless open fronted bodice with fitted sleeves are the most prevalent and longstanding female items.

A single costume seems often to have comprised several clothing items and cloth types decorated with a distinctive range of multicoloured motifs. More often than not decoration consists of a single repeated geometric motif, concordant with pattern weaving, as Barber has demonstrated (1991, 316–330) against the traditional view that many motifs were embroidered. The rare finds of needles throughout the Aegean certainly argue against the widespread use of embroidery during the BA. Moreover, the dating and extent of the adoption of embroidery and tapestry in the Aegean remain undetermined (Barber 1991, 314, 320–21, 352–53; 1999, 65–66 – tapestry c. 1350 BC). Finds of beads and metallic attachments (designed to be sewn to cloth) highlight that motifs should be related not only to pattern weaving, but also to beading; a popular technique well attested in BA Egypt and Anatolia (Persson 1931, 77, 79–80, 106; Barber 1991, 171–73 n. 11, 312 for Dendra and Mycenae; Marcar 2004, 234). Analysis of individual garments should therefore entertain the possibility of multiple decorative techniques (Barber 1991, 140, fig. 4.20 Switzerland c. 3000 BC; col. pl. 4 right, mid-1st millennium BC Pazyryk, Altai Mountains; also 189–90 and fig. 7.3 Hallstatt). The pictorial evidence for other techniques remains slim: even leather decorating (e.g. embossing or stitching of cut-outs) or painting on cloth are only very rarely hinted at by the evidence (Barber 1991, 343). While a number of simple motifs can be classed as conventions for depicting animal skins, others (tricurve arch, crocus) appear to be symbolic in nature (Barber 1991, 316–330; Marcar 2004).

THE QUESTION OF TAILORING

Although precise details of Aegean cloth types, including their decoration and weight, are lacking, we need to consider the question of tailoring in terms of both its characteristic traits, and its place in our evidence for ancient garment manufacturing techniques. There are two prevailing views on the construction of the more fitted Aegean items, such as the bodice. The first favours sophisticated tailoring techniques, and is reinforced by the periodic use of the word 'tailor' in contemporary scholarship

(Wardle 1988; Tzachili 1997; 2000), principally due to 'tailors' being used to translate the Linear B word *ra-pte-re*. The second favours simpler techniques, often modeled on ancient Egypt (Jones 2000) since, unlike the Aegean, Egypt has yielded numerous examples of fragmentary and complete garments.

For the purposes of this discussion it is useful to define the word 'tailor' or *tailleur* (cutter). It is now applied to men's wear, designating someone who makes close-fitting clothes through careful cutting and seaming (female counterpart dressmaker). Traditionally the tailor-dressmaker also acts as the designer. Having decided upon the garment style the tailor must select an appropriate fabric, which is decisive, as different types possess different properties. Wool is stiffer and heavier, possessing elastic and waterproof qualities, and can therefore be used to produce warmer, more rigid garment shapes that do not cling so readily to the body. Conversely, linen is generally used to create lighter and even transparent fabrics, which make less structured or shapeless garments unless otherwise tailored.

As there are often several ways of making a single item, even simple ones, the tailor must also decide which method is the most suitable, and then cut the garment out of the fabric. This involves cutting the fabric into several precisely shaped pieces, generally relatively small, some requiring further pleating, gathering or facing. Such garments are customarily made according to the individual's specific measurements. Tailoring is therefore an expensive and time-consuming technique, which requires training, and unlike the production of draped garments, results in a considerable amount of wasted cloth. As we know that textiles and garments were valuable items, cloth wastage deserves careful consideration with regard to the Bronze Age. The frequent mention of repairs in the Linear B texts, and the finds of mended items in Tutankhamon's tomb and elsewhere, show that we cannot apply modern-day notions of mass-production and consumerism to the ancient world (Hall 1986, 59–60 on mending).

Sleeved garments appear in Egypt around 3000 BC and are known from the early 2nd millennium BC onwards in Europe. In both regions construction remains simple (Vogelsang-Eastwood 1993, 119–20, 136–37; Barber 1999, 39). Shaped armholes are most conspicuous in their absence from Aegean depictions: the lack of the shaped armhole seam running from armpit to shoulder, and occasional depictions of underarm side seams, suggest that the chest piece and sleeve were generally formed from one piece of folded cloth. Also illustrated in Syrian art, and notably at Akrotiri, this practice was clearly the most widespread. In contemporary Egypt we also find simple tubular shaped pieces of cloth used as sleeves, some apparently detachable. Garment makers were therefore making sleeves in a variety of simple ways.

Aegean bodices need not have been consistently sewn to a skirt at the level of the waist, to form a loose fitting tunic, as has recently been proposed (**Figure 3.1**, Jones 1998, esp. 264 and pl. 8.20b; Harrison 1991, 224–225). Although, in the rare cases where the waist is not hidden by the flounced skirt on the more detailed Akrotiri examples, we find no seam line, pointing to tunics (Doumas 1992, pls. 10, 12 for flounce skirt resting on hips) there are several points that go against this suggestion. First, the overall pictorial evidence for a separate bodice remains strong: a variety of lower garments were worn with the bodice, and are often distinctly decorated, some even

Figure 3.1. Bodice worn with a sheepskin-shaped skirt. (Line drawing copyright Ariane Marcar.)

apparently worn over tunics (**Figure 3.2**).[3] Second, though the fitted look may have been exaggerated somewhat by the artists, there is technologically no reason why Aegean peoples could not have created a tight fitting bodice without the use of elaborate tailoring. This could have been achieved in a number of ways; the determining factors being cloth type and weight. Indeed it is quite possible that wool and flax were combined to create a finer cloth with greater elasticity. After all cloths of mixed fibres were being produced in Europe from the mid-3rd millennium BC onwards (Jørgensen 1992, 102, 114–16, 118).

Barber has also shown (on technical grounds, as the iconographical evidence remains very slim) that cloth may have been cut on the bias to produce a stretch effect (1991: 315 with reference to Crete, 317–18 note 6). The ties and laces that were occasionally used to gather the front sides of the bodice (see Knossos faience figurines) would also account for the figure-hugging aspect of the bodices. Combined, the evidence suggests that the tight-fitting aspect should therefore be perceived as accurate, rather than as an artistic convention to highlight the form of the underlying body.

The other item generally regarded as tailored is the parted-kilt, which has often been labeled 'shorts'. It is principally known from a handful of small metal artefacts and seals, illustrating sketchily drawn running men with parted legs (e.g. **Figure 3.3**; Matz & Biesantz 1964, nos. 16 and 290 seal from Pylos [Tholos tomb *D*], gold ring from Mycenae). The tightly belted waist, and the two lines that cut sharply across each thigh denoting the hemline, customarily designate this item. On first impression the resemblance to shorts is strong, as a loose-fitting fabric does appear to encase the legs individually. However, on closer inspection, we find that there are several indicators

Figure 3.2. The Mykenaia, showing a 'v' neck tunic. (Line drawing copyright Ariane Marcar.)

to the contrary. First, the typical construction traits that characterise most styles of trousers, which we would not expect artists to have readily overlooked, are absent. Generally speaking, such items require a seam to join the two halves: running from the navel down, passing between the legs and running up between the buttocks to hip level. Furthermore, side seams running from the outside or inside leg to the knee or ankle are generally a necessity, though these can be placed at the front and back instead. A common, but not obligatory, feature is the opening generally left in the front, the fly, which needs to be brought together or fastened in some way. One of the simplest methods is to use a drawstring, which creates a pyjama-type trouser. Alternatively, to minimise cutting and shaping, shorts can be made from sewing small rectangular pieces of woollen cloth together, onto which an asymmetrical diamond-shaped gusset is added at the crotch (Barber 1999, fig. 2.11 for short pants from Cherchen, c. 1000 BC, front rather than side seams).

Surely the absence of most of the above features, notably of primary seams on the better-preserved depictions, makes it extremely unlikely that such items existed during

Figure 3.3. Reproduction of the 'Lion Hunt Dagger', Mycenae. (Photo courtesy of the Ashmolean Museum, Oxford.)

the 2nd millennium BC. Certainly there is no evidence that drawstrings were used to help secure Aegean garments. Nor did the Greeks ever adopt the trouser: literary evidence shows that they connected trousers with the Medes and Persians. During Roman times trousers were associated with mounted northerners, though Roman soldiers eventually adopted them under Trajan and Aurelian. The strong connection between trousers and horse riding ties them to the Eurasian steppes, the primary homeland of the horse (Renfrew 1996, 82–84; introduction by mounted nomadic pastoralists in the first millennium BC suggested by Barber 1999, 37, 39: leggings with diamond gusset noted above).

Taken as a whole the Aegean iconographical data goes against true tailoring. The majority of the items consist of loose fitting or draped cloaks, mantles, robes, loincloths, kilts and wrap-around skirts, types seen in Egypt and elsewhere. The absence of relatively simple techniques used in the production of ready-to-wear and tailor-made clothes (i.e. back seams, commonly used on fitted items such as jackets or blouses) on clay and bronze Aegean figurines, our only three dimensional artistic category, further reinforces this view. So does the evidence from Linear B records, which make no reference to cloth cutters or garment sizes; two categories we would expect if a class of tailors existed. Indeed, Barber finds little to no evidence for elaborate cutting or tailoring, especially of Greek mainland garments (1991, 315).

This brings us back to *ra-pte-re*. On first impression the equation with 'tailor' appears convincing, as it is etymologically related to the Greek word *rapto*. However, several other translations have been offered. One strongly links it to leather, the word being thought to designate 'saddler' ('sewing-man [for armour?]' Lindgren 1973, 133–134). The adjective *rapterija* describes "(reins) with stitching work" (PY Ub 1315), a further connection with leather, rather than with the textile industry (Ventris & Chadwick 1973, 578). *ra-pi-ti-ra* (female) is generally interpreted as 'sempstresses, clothes-menders' or 'sewing women' (Lindgren 1973, 133–134; Chadwick 1988, 82). Consequently, the term 'sewer' seems the most appropriate translation, especially as the *raptere* do not occur in any directly occupational contexts.

So the evidence overall points to a tradition of draping and wrapping with only minimal cutting and shaping, as found in Egypt, Anatolia, Mesopotamia and the Levant at this period. The shapes of ancient garments echo the shapes of cloth, generally rectangles or squares, many coming directly off the loom, and subsequently sewn down some or all of the edges, a consistent feature throughout the BA in neighbouring cultures. Further shaping was probably limited to cutting or rounding the lower or upper corners of rectangular cloths.[4] As far as I am aware, we have no conclusive pictorial evidence from the LBA (in the Aegean or elsewhere) for fitted garments using darts, godets, gores, separate collars, lapels, cuffs and pockets. Nor is there evidence for the use of interlinings, placed between the fabric and the lining to create varying shapes, or for padding (e.g. of the shoulders, to raise and extend the shoulder line).

The use of belts and ties, often shown with knots or bows, to gather or secure garments in the Aegean further points to wrapping and draping, as fitted and tailored garments rarely make use of these. The limited evidence for the sewing of supplementary pieces onto garments upholds this: in the main these consist of strengthening or decorative bands, hem and waistbands. Decorative bands occur along the neck and shoulder line, and down the front or sides of lower garments where primary seams are traditionally located.[5] (Actual depictions of primary seams without banding are rare, but do occur, notably on the better-preserved frescoes at Akrotiri, Thera, and at Pylos on the Greek mainland, see Doumas 1992, pl. 10 for underarm seam.) For the bodice, the decorative borders consistently run from the shoulder down the sleeve, and along the edge of bodice openings, acting not only as reinforcement but to give the garment a structured shape.

Overall, the manufacturing methods are typical of those found in pre-industrial societies before mass production became cost effective. Sewers concentrate on finishing rather than seaming. This probably explains why finishers, rather than sewers, are relatively well represented in Linear B, as in the texts of surrounding regions.

Appropriate garment construction techniques, which I have discussed here in detail, are clearly fundamental to informative reconstructions. However, it is also necessary to have a clear idea of which garment we are attempting to investigate, not just of which depiction we wish to recreate. Chronological and regional differences come to light through cataloguing dress motifs and male and female garments, according to simple fashion terminology, by region and period (Crete, Mainland Greece and the Cyclades, see **Figure 3.4** for garment distribution). Notably, the evidence suggests a number of important alterations in the range during and after LMIB (Marcar in press). More detailed investigation also exposes further differences between the LMIA Theran and Cretan costume ranges, suggesting that though the style may have originated in Crete, these styles should be separated according to geographic region, rather than grouped under the heading "Revealing Minoan fashions" (Jones 2000). Indeed, I have documented thirty-four garment types: many being variations of core types already known (**Figure 3.5**), showing the range to be considerably wider than originally thought. It is, however, still a narrow one.

What we appear to have is a clothing range made up of a restricted number of core types, altered or styled in a number of ways to form sub-types. This is characteristic of most ancient and pre-industrial societies, and so need not be interpreted as atypical (e.g., Anawalt 1981 on Mesoamerican clothing; Vogelsang-Eastwood 1993 for the ancient Egyptian range). For instance, at Akrotiri, women are often depicted in one of two tunic types: one with loose tapered sleeves, the other with narrow tubular sleeves (see **Figure 3.5** and Doumas 1992, pl. 101 and pls. 12, 120, 123). On the Greek mainland long and short tunics with horizontal neckline appear typical. Several cape types varying in length and texture are also featured at Akrotiri (Doumas 1992, pl. 27 and pl. 38 top right).

CONCLUSIONS

In sum, limited understanding of ancient garment construction (and of the inherent limitations of the Aegean BA textile evidence) combined with a premature focus on replication over garment classification, has resulted in a number of misconceptions about the Aegean clothing range. It has also prevented us from asking more salient questions about the social needs, attitudes and wider economic considerations that went into forming it.

This chapter has shown that the evidence strongly points to a tradition of draping and wrapping (with little seaming, the bodice being the most fitted item of the range). Given how little we know about cloth types, it is important to ask ourselves what we hope to gain through reconstruction. Currently, given the gaps in our knowledge, I believe that we should focus on estimating fabric weight, dyes and decorative techniques before setting out to reconstruct entire costumes. Naturally, it is only by using fibre types and decorative techniques for which there is convincing evidence that we will propose more plausible replicas. Since garments are only known through basic representations the cut of the garments will always be difficult to establish – we will always be faced with several options. One way to avoid creating a confusing range of look-alike types, which will only distance us further from the original portrayals, is to apply a strict set of criteria for replication.

I would therefore suggest the following. Firstly, and understandably, the most important criterion is to have a sound understanding of garment construction and its history. Secondly, since garment shape is not only determined by how the cloth is cut, but by the choice of fibre and its weight, ideally only known Bronze Age garment construction techniques and fibre types should be used. Thirdly, we must be precise about the type we are attempting to recreate, as even simple garments were made in several styles; hence the need for a basic garment typology like that proposed above and in the figures. Finally, and naturally, in the interest of greater accuracy, every known illustration of a given garment type should be examined before replication is attempted.

NO.	GARMENT TYPE	1ST PALACE PERIOD	2ND PALACE PERIOD	3RD PALACE PERIOD
1	DOUBLE BELT WITH HANGING ENDS	X	X	–
2	STRAPS	X	–	–
3	SASH	X	X	X
4	MALE FRONTAL FLOUNCES/FLAPS TYPE 1	–	X	X
	TYPE 2 (LONG)	–	X	SHORT TYPE ROUNDED EDGES?
5	APRON	–	X	–
6	CODPIECE: BAG-SHAPED	PROBABLY	PROBABLY	–
	RIGID	MMIII-LMIA	X	POSSIBLY
7	HIP-CLOTH OR HIP-BAND	X	POSSIBLY	–
8	LOINCLOTH TYPE 1	X	X	X
9	LOINCLOTH TYPE 2	X	X	X
10	BREECHCLOTH	POSSIBLY	X	X
11	KILT	MMII-III (1 e.g.)	X	X
	TASSELLED KILTS	–	–	X
12	A-LINE SKIRT: A) ORDINARY CYCLADIC	–	X	POSSIBLY
	B) SHAGGY TUFTED	–	X	–
13	A-LINE, CONTINUOUS PLAIN HORIZONTAL STRIPES: TYPE A	–	X	X
	TYPE B	–	X	X
14	WIDE, FLAT SIDE PLEATED SKIRT	X	X	–
15	SO-CALLED SHEEP-SHAPED SKIRT	–	X	X
16	A) FULL-LENGTH TUBULAR FLOUNCED SKIRT	–	X	X
	B) WRAP-AROUND FLOUNCED SKIRT	–	X	X
17	SKIRT MADE OF STRIPS	–	X	–
18	ANIMAL SKINS/PELTS	PROBABLY	X	X
19	SLEEVELESS 'V' NECK PONCHO	X	–	–

Figure 3.4. Distribution of Garment Types.

GARMENT TYPE	1ST PALACE PERIOD	2ND PALACE PERIOD	3RD PALACE PERIOD
SHAWL	–	–	X
VEIL	–	X	–
A) ORDINARY MANTLE	–	X	–
B) OFF-THE SHOULDER MANTLE FASTENED AT THE SHOULDER	–	X	X
DIAGONALLY WRAPPED MANTLE	–	X	X
ROBE OR COAT-DRESS	–	–	X
THE UNBELTED CLOAK/ROBE WITH STAND-UP COLLAR	X	–	–
TWO STYLES OF STAND-UP COLLAR, ON WAISTED ROBES OR BODICES WITH BELL-SHAPED SKIRTS	X	–	–
A) MID-LENGTH CLOAK	X	X	–
B) SHORT CAPE	–	–	X
LONG CLOAKS OR CAPES	–	X	X
FULL-LENGTH TUNIC WITH SHORT TUBULAR SLEEVES AND 'V' NECK	–	X	X
OPEN FRONTED TUNIC WITH TAPERED SLEEVES	–	X	–
FULL-LENGTH TUNIC WITH SHORT TUBULAR SLEEVES AND HORIZONTAL NECK	–	CYCLADES LIKELY	X
SHORT TUNIC WITH SHORT TUBULAR SLEEVES AND HORIZONTAL NECK	–	–	X
MALE 'V' NECK SHIRT WITH SHORT SLEEVES	X MM-LM	–	–
COLLARLESS SHORT-SLEEVED BODICE	X MMIIB-MMIII	X	X
TASSELLED KILTS	–	–	X
SLEEVE BORDERS WITH HANGING TASSELS	–	X	X (two e.g.)

Figure 3.4. continued.

Small items
1 Belts
2 Straps
3 Sashes
4 Male frontal flounces and flaps
5 Front and back apron
6 Bag-shaped and rigid codpieces

Lower garments
7 Male hip-cloth or hip-band
8 Loincloth: type 1 (cloth covering the genital area, buttocks uncovered in part)
9 Loincloth: type 2 (buttocks always covered, item resembling the Indian male *dhoti*)
10 Breechcloths (type of back-apron covering the buttocks)
11 Kilts
12 A-line skirts: a) ordinary types and b) shaggy fleece or tufted wool types
13 Full-length A-line skirts with continuous plain horizontal stripes & other variants
14 Wide and flat side-pleated skirts
15 So-called sheepskin-shaped skirts, known also to have used as capes.
16 Flounced skirts:
a) The full-length tubular flounced skirt
b) Wrap-around flounced skirts
17 Skirt made of strips (seen only once at Akrotiri)

Upper and full length garments
18 Animal skins or pelts
19 Sleeveless 'v' neck poncho
20 Shawls
21 Veil
22 a) Ordinary mantle and b) Off-the-shoulder mantle fastened at the shoulder
23 Diagonally wrapped off-the-shoulder mantle and plain unwound, but draped variants with wing-shaped ends.
Robes or coat-dresses
25 Stand-up collars featured on unbelted cloaks/robes, and 26, also found on waisted robes and bodices matched with bell-shaped skirts
27 Mid-length cloaks and short capes
28 Long Cloaks or Capes
29 Tunic A: full length with short tubular sleeves and 'v' neck
30 Tunic B: open fronted with tapered sleeves
31 Tunic C: full length with short tubular sleeves and horizontal neck
32 Tunic D: Short with short tubular sleeves and horizontally neck
33 Male 'v' neck shirt with short-sleeves
34 Collarless short-sleeved bodice

Figure 3.5. Basic Aegean Bronze Age Garment Range, by types.

NOTES

1 Construction of women's wear: Jones 1998, 2000; Tzachili 1997; Televantou 1982; Marinatos 1984 and Wardle 1988. For men's wear: Sapouna-Sakellaraki 1971; Giesecke 1988 and Rehak 1996.
2 Kantor 1947, 44; Sakellaraki 1971, 224–35; Wachsmann 1987, 104–5; Barber 1991, 336; Matthäus 1995, 183; Rehak 1996, 48, 50; 1998, 44–45; Marcar, 2004.
3 Marinatos 1986, colour pls. XXX, XXXII top for Ayia Triada sarcophagus scene showing a bodice worn over a 'v' neck tunic, cf. **Figure 3.2**.
4 As in the case of v-neck items (Orlandou 1977, fig. 124 terracotta male figurine, Juktas); the aprons found on the Knossian Snake Goddess faience figurines; and the borders of men's breechcloths (e.g., Sapouna-Sakellarakis 1995, pl. 10 no. 162 portly male bronze figurine from Hierapetra, pl. 41 no. 1 part of a clay figurine from Knossos, pl. 48 no.5 and pl. 47 no. 1–2 Vapheio and Chieftain cups, or Marinatos 1986, pl. 206 and 102 respectively).
5 Doumas 1992, pl. 12 for tunic with central band running down front of garment presumably hiding and strengthening the seam underneath; Lang 1969, pl. 120 8–9 H 5 for processional figures and pl. 121 16 H 43 for hunter.

Chapter 4

Trailing Tunics and Sheepskin Coats: Dress and status in early Greece[1]

Hans van Wees

Apart from giving birth, only one female activity rates a mention in Hesiod's almanac: weaving (*Works and Days* 779). Textile work was, of course, prominent in women's lives throughout antiquity, but this has tended to obscure a highly significant difference between the roles of cloth in the world of the epics and in later Greece. To Homer, an abundance of high-quality home-produced cloth and clothing was a major status symbol, and women's weaving was essential to the prestige of their families. By the end of the archaic period, the most prestigious forms of cloth and clothing were bought and imported. This development entailed a drastic change in the symbolism of dress, and a significant decline in the significance of weaving and the status of women in Greek society.

THE HEROIC DRESS CODE

In Homer and Hesiod, both men and women wore two layers of clothing. The primary garment for men was a simple sewn tunic (*chitôn*), usually worn under a cloak (*chlaina*), consisting of a thick rectangular piece of cloth fixed with a single pin. Tunic and cloak were worn by everyone, from aristocrat to slave; it was the mark of a beggar to have no cloak, and make do with an old deerskin (see Milanezi, this volume). Instead of a *chlaina*, a man might wear a *pharos*, a lighter wrap, loosely draped around the shoulders. This wrap, described as 'delicate', is less often mentioned; it was evidently more exclusive. The primary garment for women, the *peplos* or *he(i)anos*, has aptly been described as a 'blanket-dress': a large rectangle of cloth folded around the body, fixed with two or more pins at the shoulders, and gathered around the waist with a belt (see Lee, this volume). A wrap known as *krêdemnon*, 'head-binder', *kalyptra* or *kalymma*, 'veil', was worn on top, draped over the head and shoulders. Again, these two garments were worn by everyone from aristocrats' wives and daughters to slaves.[2]

The basic uniformity of dress meant that differentiation of status was achieved mainly through quality and size rather than different types of clothing. Homer gives very few indications of fabric, but 'curly' (*oulios*) cloaks must be woollen, and wool is the only material which women ever card, spin or weave in the epics.[3] Linen was also known, however, and probably used for some *peploi*, which are described as made of 'smooth cloth' (*lis*) and 'fine cloth' (*othonê*).[4] Linen yarn takes about three times as long to produce as woollen yarn,[5] and was accordingly regarded as a luxury (Thucydides 1.6.3). Since in the Homeric world this luxury remained confined to female dress, it was a marker of gender as much as a marker of social status among women.

An obvious indicator of status was the coarseness or fineness of cloth. The literary evidence shows that 'delicate' (*leptos*) fabric was highly valued, and archaeological evidence from Euboea, c. 1100–700 BC, suggests that the finest fabrics used three times as much yarn as the coarsest pieces and were proportionally more labour-intensive.[6] Much more conspicuous, and more labour-intensive still, was patterned cloth. Women's robes were "multicoloured" (*Iliad* 5.735, 8.386; *Odyssey* 18.293), decorated with "many devices" (*Il.* 14.179), or indeed "multicoloured all over" and "most beautiful in coloured decorations" (*Il.* 6.289, 294; *Od.* 15.105, 107). Only the *peplos* is ever said to be so woven in Homer, and the audience would have understood that the two great purple webs (with "colourful flower patterns" woven by Andromache, *Il.* 22.440–1, and scenes from the Trojan War woven by Helen, *Il.* 3.125–8) were also *peploi*.[7] Hesiod, however, mentions a patterned veil as well (*Theogony* 574–5). Quite apart from the cost of the various dyes used, the extra labour-cost of weaving patterned decorations, especially non-repetitive figurative scenes, is incalculable. In classical Athens, dozens of women, presumably working in rotation, took nine months to weave a richly decorated *peplos* for Athena.[8] Like the use of linen, the application of patterned weaving was confined to women's dress and thus a marker of gender as well as status.

Another striking feature of Homeric female dress was its size. In male costume, size did not matter much and was rarely a sign of status. Only one cloak is described as 'big' by Homer, and this belongs to a swineherd who reserves it for very cold days; only one tunic is described as 'long', and this is matched by the long tunic worn for warmth in winter by an ordinary farmer.[9] The Athenians and their fellow-Ionians wore tunics which were not merely long but 'trailing', an exceptional style for which they remained famous throughout the archaic period.[10] The one male garment often called 'large' is the *pharos*: a knee-length wrap would require some 2 m^2 of cloth and an ankle-length wrap about 3 m^2, by contrast with c. 1 m^2 of cloth for a knee-length cloak and c. 1.5 m^2 for an ankle-length tunic.[11]

By contrast, the guiding principle in female dress was 'the larger, the better' (*Il.* 6.90, 271, 293; *Od.* 15.107, 18.292). The veil, reaching from the top of the head to well below the waist, must have been about 2 m^2 in size, the same as a knee-length *pharos*.[12] Women's belts were very long, as the epithet 'deep-girdled' indicates and early Greek art illustrates (*Il.* 9.594; *Od.* 3.154; *Homeric Hymn* 2.95, 161, 201, 304; van Wees, forthcoming). The *peplos* was the largest garment of all. It reached far below the wearer's feet, so that it was hitched it up over the belt in front, leaving deep overhanging folds (hence 'deep-bosomed'), while at the back it was left to trail along the ground (hence the epithet '*peplos*-trailing').[13] Another way of adding length to the *peplos*, not explicitly attested in Homer but often represented in art from the eighth century onwards, was to fold down excess material at the top of the garment so as to form a flap (*apoptygma*) covering the chest. Originally perhaps only a small strip of material was folded, to prevent the cloth from tearing where the pins were fixed, but very soon the flap was far longer than necessary for this purpose – adding to the length of the garment clearly became an end in itself.[14] The *peplos* was also much wider than necessary to cover the body, and the adjective 'with stretched *peplos*' hints at extra-wide garments, gathered with a belt to form a multitude of vertical folds.[15] A *peplos* was thus some 2 m tall and anywhere between 1.5 and 3 m wide, i.e. up to 6 m² in size – four times as large as a man's tunic.

Taking into account the different sizes of garments, the varying qualities of cloth, and the time needed to spin wool and linen, we can calculate that a short, coarse woollen cloak would probably have taken only 24 hours or 3 working days to make, while the largest, finest, plain linen *peplos* might take 1,200 hours or 150 working days. An elaborately patterned *peplos* might well take twice as long, which explains why no one was surprised that a masterpiece like Penelope's great shroud should take three whole years (*Od.* 2.106–9; 24.141–5).

Large garments were prestigious not only because they required a great deal of labour and fabric, and much effort to keep clean and in good repair, but also because they hampered movement – especially trailing tunics and robes, but also loosely draped wraps and veils, which were liable to slide off. They thus signalled exemption from strenuous labour, and a leisured lifestyle. Yet again, it was primarily female rather than male dress which exploited size to display wealth and leisure.

THE CONSUMPTION AND PRODUCTION OF CLOTHES IN HOMER

The amount of cloth and clothing that a household could use was almost infinite. Frequent 'changes of clothing' were a feature of the elite lifestyle (*Od.* 8.248–9; cf. 6.64–5), and to have no changes of clothing at all was a feature of the lives of slaves (*Od.* 14.513–14). More importantly, clothes were a staple of gift-giving, especially at marriages, but also whenever a household entertained visitors. Guests were given clean clothes to wear after bathing, and even the least honoured guest could expect to receive a tunic and cloak as a parting-gift. More lavish gifts might include dozens of tunics, cloaks and wraps.[16] Cloaks doubled as blankets and were complemented by an array of woven sheets, wraps, rugs, and cushions used as bed and chair covers. An abundance of soft furnishings was another integral part of the elite lifestyle. Nestor insists that he cannot allow his guests to spend the night elsewhere:

> as if you were visiting a pauper who has no clothes at all, who does not have many blankets and sheets in his house, nothing for himself and his guests to sleep in comfortably – but *I* do have a store of beautiful blankets and sheets (*Od.* 3.345–51).

In addition to plenty of covers to accommodate guests, a rich household needed a surplus for gift-giving purposes: gifts of hospitality to Odysseus (*Od.* 24.276) and the ransom for Hector (*Il.* 24.230) each included a dozen 'rugs' (*tapêtas*).

Finally, much cloth was burned and buried to honour the dead, who were cremated fully dressed and covered with one or more wraps or *peploi* as shrouds; ash urns were also wrapped in one or more *peploi*.[17] "A man who has much property" absolutely required a large, specially woven shroud for his funeral (*Od.* 2.97–102, 24.132–7). Andromache lamented that, unburied, her husband would be:

naked – and yet clothes are laid up in store for you at home, fine and elegant, made by the hands of women. Well, then, I shall incinerate them all in a burning fire, not for your benefit because you will not lie in them, but to be a source of fame among the men and women of Troy.[18]

It is worth noting that the gender divide in clothing was crossed in these funerary rites, insofar as the bodies and ashes of dead men were covered with linen *peploi*, garments worn in life only by women. Status display clearly took precedence over gender on these occasions. In short, any self-respecting Homeric household needed large quantities of cloth of the highest possible quality. The storerooms of the rich were packed with boxes full of cloth: in Menelaus' house, Helen stood "beside the clothes-chests in which she kept the highly decorated *peploi* which she made herself" (*Od.* 15.104–5; cf. 2.339; 21.51–2; *Il.* 6.288–90).

Helen was no exception: *all* cloth was normally made by the women of the family and their female slaves, rather than bought.[19] When domestic labour did not suffice, one might hire women to spin and weave as day-labourers (*Il.* 12.433–5), rather than rely on barter to obtain ready-made clothes from an outside source. Even the most exotic garments in the epics, the *peploi* in Priam's storeroom described as "the work of Sidonian women" (*Il.* 6.289–92) were not imports, but woven by Priam's own Phoenician slaves.[20] Men were thus wholly dependent on the labour of their wives, daughters and slave women for the abundance of fine clothes and furnishings they needed to play a part commensurate with their status in community life.

This vital contribution to household resources was acknowledged in a number of ways. First, spinning and weaving skills were a source of personal reputation for a woman, especially among other women. The censure of other women punished failures to meet standards: Penelope worried that "some Greek woman in this community might be indignant with me" should she fail to weave a suitable shroud for her father-in-law (*Od.* 2.101–2; 19.146–7; 24.136–7). Conversely, the praise of other women confirmed weaving skills. "I noticed the shiny tunic he wore: it was as soft as the skin of a dried onion and bright as the sun", said a man describing Odysseus' outfit to Penelope: "I tell you, many *women* admired it".[21]

Secondly, as we have seen, the greatest efforts and the greatest prestige were reserved for the women's own clothes, much larger than the men's and often elaborately decorated when men's clothes were at best dyed in a single colour, red or purple (red: *Il.* 10.131–5; *Od.* 14.500, 21.118–19; purple: *Od.* 4.115, 154, 19.225–7, 241–2). Not coincidentally, almost every single *peplos* in Homer has a named weaver, while the weavers of other clothes are never mentioned.[22] The *peplos* was the garment to which women applied their greatest skills, and it made the reputation of its maker, whose name was remembered. On presenting her favourite *peplos* as a gift, Helen called it "a memento from Helen's hands" (*Od.* 15.130).

Another piece of Helen's handiwork, the *peplos* adorned with scenes from the Trojan War, represents "the struggles which Greeks and Trojans suffered on her behalf" (*Il.* 3. 125–8). For some, this is "a pathetic symbol of the omnipresence of war" (Kirk 1985, *ad loc*), but perhaps we should see it in a more positive light. Helen's chosen motif might be seen as both self-expression and self-glorification, since the war was for her simultaneously a cause of guilt and a source of future fame, as she was keenly aware

(*Il.* 6.357–8). It is tempting to see a parallel in a scene of lamentation on a Middle Protoattic mug from Athens, dating to c. 660 BC (Kerameikos 80; van Wees 1998a, fig. 1.11). Here, the robes of at least two of the mourning women are decorated with images related to death: one has a sphinx, the other a picture of a mourning woman. She is drawn, not in the Protoattic style of the rest of the painting, but in the old Geometric style, perhaps in deliberate imitation of what woven patterns still looked like. The scope for creativity in women's work, it seems, extended to tailoring designs to particular occasions, to personal interests, and indeed to personal experiences.

Finally, Homeric husbands and wives jointly engaged in gift-giving, just as they jointly presided as hosts over feasts at home (van Wees 1995, 154–63). Women's gifts, however, remained distinct from their husbands'. They were presented only to other women, and consisted of a limited range of items, either wool-working tools or finished pieces of cloth. When his Egyptian host gave Menelaus rich gifts, "his wife separately presented very beautiful gifts to Helen: a golden spindle and a woolbasket on wheels, made of silver with a golden rim" (*Od.* 4.125–35). In turn, when Menelaus presented Telemachus with a golden cup and silver mixing-bowl, Helen gave him a *peplos*, but specified that her gift was not really for him: it was destined for his future wife, and he should leave it in the care of his mother (15.126–8). Aphrodite's wedding-present of a headdress for Andromache (*Il.* 22.468–70) is surely modelled on a type of gift common between women. Women's dedications of cloth to goddesses, such as Hecabe's *peplos* for Athena (*Il.* 6.286–311) were clearly also common. The existence of a female sphere of gift-exchange, almost entirely separate from the male,[23] afforded women a degree of independent control over the products of their own labour, and is further testimony to the high respect accorded to their skills in the Homeric world.

INTRODUCING 'THE LYDIAN EXPERIENCE': CHANGES IN DRESS IN ARCHAIC GREECE

The glamorous world of Homer's heroes is not, of course, the real world of early Greece, but the evidence of art and archaeology suggests that its material culture, at least, corresponded quite closely to what the Greeks knew in the late eighth and early seventh centuries BC, and this is also true of Homeric dress.[24] One notable trend from the mid-seventh century onwards was that forms of display in clothing which had previously been confined to female dress were extended to male costume as well. Large wraps, a rare luxury item in Homer, almost drove out pinned cloaks as items of civilian dress. In artistic representations from c. 650 BC onwards wraps are shown wound around the body in the elaborate and restrictive way standard throughout the archaic and classical periods. Complex decoration also became a feature of male dress: Sappho pictured Jason in an amazing technicolour cloak (F 152 L-P), and archaic vase-paintings show many men dressed in tunics with figured decoration. By the late sixth century, the most richly dressed men in Greek art wore such voluminous and elaborate outfits that some modern scholars have interpreted them as transvestites – or indeed as women wearing false beards (van Wees 1998b, 347–52, 358–62).

Clothes became much more varied. Alongside the basic types of garment, archaic poetry features such obscure items of female dress as the *cherromaktra*, a headdress, and the *lados*, a 'summer dress', and introduces items of male dress such as the *kypassis*, a short tunic, and the *chlamys*, a short cloak. Extremely fine 'see-through' cloth is first attested in Sappho's reference to the *beudos*, 'a short diaphanous tunic' (F 177 L-P). With the development of the culture of the symposion, the range of cloth accessories and soft furnishings displayed at dinners and drinking parties grew to include *hemitubia* (napkins), *lasioi* (linens), and *tula* (cushions) (Sappho FF 46, 54, 100, 101, 119 L-P; Alcaeus F 140 L-P; Alcman F 117 Page).

A sign of increasing sophistication in dress was the emergence of a notion of 'rustic' attire. Whereas once the dress code was the same for everyone, Sappho mocks a 'rustic girl' in a 'rustic outfit' (*agroitin stolan*), "who does not know how to pull her rags down to her ankles" (F 57) and the huge 'five-oxhide sandals' of an attendant at a rural wedding (F110). Hesiod's farmer had no qualms about wearing a goatskin on top of his high-quality "soft cloak and ankle-length tunic" (*W&D* 537–46; cf. *Od.* 14.529–30) and Homer's heroes covered their chairs with combinations of simple fleeces and ornamental woven rugs,[25] but by the sixth century the use of fleeces and goatskins was associated with extreme rusticity and poverty.[26] Around 570 BC, Cleisthenes of Sicyon was said to have humiliated the rural population of his country by making them wear the *katônakê*, a leather cloak with sheepskin trim (Theopompus *FGrH* 115 F 176, 311). In fact, those forced to adopt this sheepskin coat, which in classical Athens was regarded as typical of slaves, were a rural serf population much like Sparta's helots, who were also made to wear distinctive low-status dress, including animal hides and dog-skin caps.[27]

While demand for high-quality cloth rose, demand for large quantities probably declined. Clothes and cloth appear to have played a much reduced role in gift-giving in archaic and classical Greece, and the burning of large amounts of cloth at funerals may have been curbed. A law attributed to Solon forbade anyone to be buried with more than three pieces of cloth.[28]

Above all, the most prestigious textiles were no longer produced by domestic labour but imported from abroad. Milesian cloaks, for instance, were imported in large quantities by the Greek cities of southern Italy well before the end of the sixth century. The Sybarites, a byword for luxurious living until the destruction of their city in 510 BC, imported these cloaks on such a scale that they formed a close friendship with the Milesians. In Syracuse a drive to limit conspicuous consumption led to a ban on 'Milesian-style cloaks' for men (Sybaris: Timaeus *FGrH* 566 F 50 [Ath. 519b]; Syracuse: Diodorus 12.21.1). Scythian dye, Scythian shoes, and cloaks of Scythian wool, all mentioned by archaic poets, indicate substantial imports from the Black Sea area.[29]

Above all, the dress style of the famously wealthy Lydians was adopted, as we know from Sappho's reference to Lydian sandals (F 39) and, more interestingly, from her contrast between an ornate headband (*mitra*) imported from Sardis and a plain headband made in her home town of Mytilene (F 98, see Stafford, this volume). This foreign piece of headgear appears to have been the height of fashion across Greece, since her contemporary Alcman has a girls' chorus in Sparta sing of luxuries including "a Lydian headband, show-piece (*agalma*) for violet-eyed young women" (F 1.67–9 Page). Sappho reminisces about the simplicity of her mother's generation, when girls wore simple wreaths of flowers in their hair (F 125). Such nostalgic sentiments need have little historical foundation, but it is conceivable that the adoption of more elaborate and exotic attire was indeed a new phenomenon around 600 BC, part of the creation of a new, 'luxurious' elite lifestyle which Anacreon was soon to label 'The Lydian Experience'.[30] By definition these new fashions could not be created by women at home: the fact that Milesian cloaks and Lydian headbands needed to be imported was essential to their prestige value.

As a result, where men had once depended on women to provide them with enough high-quality cloth to keep up with the neighbours, women now became dependent upon their husbands and fathers to provide them with the high-status outfits they wanted. Where clothes and furnishings had once served to advertise women's weaving skills, and men's control over skilled female labour, they now primarily displayed wealth pure and simple. Women continued to weave, but their skills became less significant and accordingly less appreciated.

NOTES

1 This chapter is an adapted and expanded section of 'The invention of the female mind', forthcoming on-line for the Center for Hellenic Studies, Washington DC, in *Women and Property in the Ancient World*, edited by D. Lyons and R. Westbrook.
2 For this interpretation of Homeric dress, see van Wees (forthcoming) defending the views of Studniczka (1886) against those of Helbig (1884), Abrahams (1908), Lorimer (1950) and Marinatos (1967). Exceptions to the female dress code are two 'nymphs' (*Od*. 5.230–3; 10.543–5) and two female personifications (Hes. *W&D* 198–200) who wear *pharos* instead of *peplos*. Slaves: *Od*. 6.100 (veils; see Llewellyn-Jones 2003, 124–8); 14.513–14, 520–2, 528–32 (cloaks, tunics); cloakless beggar: *Od*. 13.434–8.
3 'Curly' cloaks: *Il*. 24.646; cf. 10.131–5; *Od*. 4.49–50, 299, 7.338, 10.451, 17.89, 19.225. Wool-working: *Od*. 4.135, 18.316, 22.423; *Il*. 3.387–8; 12.433–5.
4 *Lis*: *Il*. 18.352–3, 23.354 (*heanoi*); 8.441 (covering a chariot, cf. *peplos* at 5.194–5); *Od*. 1.130, 10.352–3 (to cover seats, cf. *peplos* at 7.95–7). *Othonai*: *Il*. 3.141, 18.595 (female dress); *Od*. 7.107 (nature unclear). Linen (*linon*) is otherwise used for sheets (*Il*. 9.661; *Od*. 13.73, 118) and corslets (*Il*. 2.529, 830). References to 'lustre' or 'delicacy' of cloth cannot be taken to imply that it is linen, *contra* e.g. Helbig 1884, 125–8; Lorimer 1950, 371–2.
5 Carr (2000, 164–5) reports that yarn can be spun at 100 m/hr for wool and 36 m/hr for linen.
6 *Leptos*: e.g. Od. 2.95, 7.95–7; *Il*. 18.595. Archaeological evidence: Popham *et al*. 1980, 227–9 (Lefkandi) and Bloesch and Mühletaler 1967 (Eretria); the coarsest material has 10 x 12 threads per cm, i.e. 2,200 m of yarn per square metre; the finest has 26 x 40 threads per cm, i.e. 6,600 m/m².
7 Not wall-hangings: *contra* Barber 1994, 153, 211; 1991, 358–82. At *Od*. 1.130–1, it is the chair rather than the cloth which is 'ornate' (*daidalos*; cf. 1.132, 19.55–8): *contra* Wagner-Hasel 2002, 22.
8 Dillon 2002, 57–8; and on patterned weaving in general, see Barber 1991, 358–82; 1994, 153–4.
9 Tunic: *Od*. 19.242; Hesiod, *Works and Days* 537. Cloak: *Od*. 14.520–2.
10 *Il*. 13.685: that the 'Ionians' here are Athenians is clear from the catalogue which follows (685–700). Other 'tunic-trailing Ionians': *Homeric Hymn* 3 (Apollo) 147 (Delians); Asius F 13 (Samians).
11 Assuming the following dimensions for a wearer c. 1.60 m tall: 1 × 1m for a cloak; 2 pieces of 1.25 × 0.60 m for a tunic; 1 × 2 m for knee-length wrap; 1.25 × 2.5 m for an ankle-length wrap.
12 The veil worn by Ino must have reached well below the waist, because it is long enough to be wound around a man's chest: *Od*. 5.346, 351, 373, 459).
13 Deep-bosomed: *Il*. 18.122, 339, 24.215; cf. *Homeric Hymn* 2.5, 5.257. *Peplos*-trailing: *Il*. 6.442, 7.297, 22.105; cf. Alcaeus F 130B.18 L-P. For this interpretation, see van Wees, forthcoming, with Losfeld 1991, 226–8, *contra* Helbig 1884, 132, 136; cf. Studniczka 1886, 102–4, 120; Abrahams 1908, 16; Marinatos 1967, 12, 48.

14 The usual explanation is that the flap helped keep the upper body warm (Studniczka 1886, 6; Abrahams 1908, 30; Pekridou-Gorecki 1989, 82; cf. Losfeld 1991, 218–20). Yet in Homer warmth is never a concern in female dress, whereas the importance of size is much stressed.
15 Stretched *peplos*: *Il.* 3.228, 18.385, 424; *Od.* 4.305, 12.375, 15.171, 363; interpreted as 'wide' by Studniczka 1886, 116–17, *contra* e.g. Helbig 1884, 131–5 ('tight'), Abrahams 1908, 32 ('long').
16 Tunic and *pharos* after bathing: *Odyssey* 3.467; 6.214. Tunic and cloak or *pharos* on departure: e.g. 13.67; 14.516. Lavish gifts of cloth: 8.392–3; 24.275–7; *Iliad* 24.229–31.
17 Hector's body was dressed in a *chiton* and white *pharos*, with a white *pharos* for a shroud (*Il.* 24.229–31, 580, 588); his ash container wrapped in 'soft purple *peploi*' (plural: *Il.* 24.795–6). Patroclus was covered with a linen *heanos* and a white *pharos* on top (18.352–3); his urn covered with a linen *heanos* (23.254). Laertes' shroud was to be a *pharos* (*Od.* 2.94–102, 19.139–47, 24.129–37).
18 *Il.* 22.510–14. Gods provide divine cloth for their favourite warriors: *Il.* 16.670, 680; *Od.* 24.67–8.
19 All the cloth owned by Alcinoos was likewise made by his wife and her maids (*Od.* 7.234–5 with 6.74 and 7.105–11; it is perhaps notable that his daughter appears to do no weaving). That this was the norm is evident from the constant references to women spinning and weaving, and the complete absence of reference to cloth being bought.
20 Kirk (1990, ad 290–2) rightly stresses that Homer says unambiguously that the *women* were brought to Troy, and that there is no justification for emending the text to refer to the *peploi* instead.
21 *Odyssey* 19.232–5. It is possible to translate 'admired him' (*auton*), but 'it', the *chitôn*, makes much better sense in context: it is covert praise for Penelope, who would be the weaver of this fine tunic (although she claims no more than that she selected the outfit from their storeroom, 19.255–7).
22 Named weavers: *Od* 15.105–8 (Helen); *Il.* 5.337–9 (the Charites); 5.734–6 and 8.385–7 (Athena); 6.289–95 (Sidonian women); 14.178–80 (Athena); also Helen and Andromache (*Il.* 3.125–8; 22.440–1), which must be *peploi* (see above). The only individual *peplos* (as opposed to the generic *peploi* mentioned in stock-epithets) without a named maker is the one presented as a gift to Penelope by a suitor (*Od.* 18.292–4). The only garments other than *peploi* with named weavers are a tunic and *pharos* worn by Odysseus: the plot requires identification of Arete and her maids as their makers (*Od.* 7.234–5).
23 Only Penelope proposes to give a gift to a man: evidently acting as *de facto* head of household, she offers a beggar a tunic and cloak (*Od.* 17.530); when she later offers not only clothes, but also sandals, spear and sword (21.339–41), Telemachos feels bound to assume his place as head of household, telling her to leave such matters to men and go back to her spinning and weaving (21.350–2). The only *peploi* given as gifts between men are part of Priam's ransom for Hector (*Il.* 24.229).
24 For the date of the Homeric world in general, see van Wees 2002; West 1995; Crielaard 1995. For the date of Homeric dress in particular, see van Wees, forthcoming.
25 Fleece seat-covers: e.g. *Od.* 17.32; 19.58; 20.95–6; *Homeric Hymn* 2.196 (contrast the ornate woven covers *Od.* 1.130–1, 20.150–1); as bedding: *Od.* 23.180; *Il.* 9.661.
26 Theognis 55–6; Anacreon F 388 Page. Cf. the *sisyrna*, a fur wrap: Semonides F 31b; Alcaeus F 379.
27 Slave dress: Aristophanes *Lysistrata* 1150–6. See van Wees 2003 for Sicyon's serfs, and Myron of Priene *FGrH* 106 F 2 for helot dress.
28 Plutarch *Solon* 21.5. The story of Periander of Corinth, c. 600 BC, burning large numbers of female garments in honour of his dead wife (Herodotus 5.92η) may reflect this funerary custom and, given the hostile twist in the tale, changing attitudes towards it.
29 Cloaks: Hipponax F 2 West. Dye: Sappho F 210 L-P. Shoes: Alcaeus F 318 L-P. On archaic trade in luxuries and 'semi-luxuries', see especially Foxhall 1998.
30 Anacreon F 481: *lydopatheis*. For the new 'oriental' lifestyle, see esp. Morris 1996; Kurke 1992.

PART II
THE CLOTHED BODY IN CLASSICAL GREECE

Chapter 5

Constru(ct)ing Gender in the Feminine Greek *Peplos*[1]

Mireille Lee

The Greek historian Herodotus tells an extraordinary story in which the women of Athens use their dress pins to kill a man, the sole survivor of Athens' attack on Aegina:[2]

> Even the one man . . . did not survive but ended in the following way. He came back to Athens and told what had happened, and the womenfolk of the Athenian men who had fought against Aegina, furious that he alone of all should have escaped, encircled the man and stabbed him with the brooch-pins with which they fastened their robes, each one asking him, "Where is my man?"
>
> So he too died; and to the Athenians this deed of the women seemed even worse than the defeat itself. They could think of no way to punish the women but to change their mode of dress to the Ionian mode; for before this the Athenian women wore clothes of the Dorian fashion, which is very like that of Corinth. The Athenians now changed this to a linen tunic, that the women might use no pins. In truth, this women's clothing was not originally Ionian but Carian, for in Greece all the older sort of women's dress was what we now call Dorian (5.87–88).[3]

This remarkable story of murderous women is conventionally cited as textual confirmation for the dramatic changes seen in the sculptural representation of feminine garments in the middle of the Archaic period, around 550 BC.[4] Among the statues of maidens (known as *korai*) dedicated on the Athenian Acropolis, the earliest (dating to the early sixth century) wear a garment that appears to have been pinned on the shoulders like the early Dorian garment described by Herodotus (**Figure 5.1**). As seen more clearly in the diagram (**Figure 5.2**), this garment is an untailored rectangle of wool that is draped around the wearer and fastened at the shoulders with pins. Modern scholars refer to this garment interchangeably as Dorian *chiton* or *peplos* (plural: *peploi*). It can be worn with or without an overfold (also known as the *apoptygma*)[5] which could either be worn loose, or belted over or under the overfold. The little pouch-like fold of fabric sometimes created by the girding is called the *kolpos*. By the later sixth century, *korai* from the Acropolis wear a different garment (known as the Ionian *chiton*) which, as Herodotus describes, was not pinned but buttoned or sewn on the shoulders. This garment is frequently worn with an over-garment called

Figure 5.1. Early Archaic kore, Acrop. Mus. #593. (Photo courtesy of the Acropolis Museum).

a *himation*. The *chiton* appears in Greek art in the mid-sixth century and essentially supplants the earlier garment (with a few notable exceptions) until the Early Classical period, ca. 480–450 BC, when the Dorian *chiton* or *peplos* again becomes the predominant mode of feminine dress.

The *peplophoros*, a female figure wearing the pinned garment known as *peplos*, becomes so ubiquitous in the period following the Persian Wars that it is considered a hallmark of the Early Classical style of Greek art.[6] The change from the Ionian linen *chiton* back to the pinned Dorian garment seems to be explained by Thucydides (6. 3–5), who tells us that in the early fifth century BC, Athenian men stopped wearing the luxurious linen *chitones* favored by the Ionians and adopted the more modest dress of the Dorian Lacedaemonians. Although it is unclear to what extent Thucydides' testimony applies to women's dress as well, it does support the notion of a change in Athenian dress sometime in the fifth century from a luxurious garment to a more modest style of dress. This transformation in feminine dress is conventionally thought to indicate a rejection of Eastern luxury in the years following the Persian Wars, as was proposed by Franz Studniczka over a century ago in his study of ancient Greek dress (1886, vii).

Figure 5.2. Diagram of the arrangement of the peplos. *(Reproduced with the permission of the artist.)*

Although the historical evidence for the *peplos* and its artistic representations seem to support one another, their relationship is in fact quite complex and problematic. Perhaps the most serious issue is that, although archaeologists and art historians understand the pinned garment in the iconography as *peplos*, Herodotus refers to it only as *himation* and *esthes*. The *peplos*, which appears in Greek literature as a feminine garment as early as Homer, was equated with the pinned Dorian garment in the late nineteenth century by Studniczka. As I have demonstrated elsewhere, we cannot be sure that the *peplos* is indeed the old Dorian garment worn by the early Greeks (Lee 2003). An additional problem with the literary evidence is that the testimonia of both Herodotus and Thucydides refer specifically to the city of Athens, while the iconographic changes are broadly Pan-Hellenic. Both large and small-scale sculptures of *peplophoroi* have been found from Magna Graecia in the west to Lycia in the east (which is, ironically, even farther east than Caria, the supposed source of the Ionian *chiton*). Finally, although Herodotus was writing in the middle of the fifth century, he makes no mention of the pinned garment having been re-adopted by Athenian women, though the *peplos* is ubiquitous in art of that period.

Sculptural representations of *peploi* indicate further inconsistencies. Although Herodotus' testimony implies that the early Dorian garment was completely abandoned in favor of the Ionian *chiton*, it continues to appear in monuments throughout the Archaic period (such as the so-called 'Peplos kore', **Figure 5.3**, dating to c. 530 BC). The 'Peplos kore' is especially vexing because she wears both *chiton* and *peplos* together, calling into question the exclusivity of the two garments.[7] Conversely, in the Early Classical period, when the *chiton* is replaced by the *peplos* in virtually all sculptural representations, it persists in certain contexts, most notably the temple of Zeus at Olympia, where figure "O" of the west pediment wears a *chiton* and mantle while the other female figures in both pediments are *peplophoroi*.[8] Finally, there is the

Figure 5.3. 'Peplos-kore', Acrop. Mus. #679. (Photo courtesy of the Acropolis Museum.)

problem of consistency in the representations of the pinned garment we call *peplos*. Although Herodotus defines the Dorian garment as pinned in contrast to the sewn Ionian *chiton*, dress pins are rarely represented on *peplophoroi*. The few dress fasteners that are represented on the sculptured examples in no way resemble the shaft-style pins implied by Herodotus' testimony; they are exclusively round brooches or buttons. Some scholars have suggested that in most cases the Early Classical *peplos* was sewn rather than fastened with pins, but this solution contradicts Herodotus' definition of the Dorian garment as a *pinned* garment.

The underlying assumption of most scholarship on Greek dress is that the garments represented in the monuments accurately reflect the dress styles of the period. There is no *a priori* reason that this should be the case, especially since figurative art during the period in question primarily represents mythological and heroic stories and events. Furthermore, although the testimony of the ancient authors seems to explain changes in dress among the monuments, we have seen that their accounts are problematic and cannot be taken at face value. Certainly Herodotus' account of vengeful Athenian women killing a man with their dress pins is a remarkable tale, and should tell us more than why one type of garment was exchanged for another. If, as Carolyn Dewald suggests, the story is derived from a series of popular misogynistic folk stories about maddened women attacking defenseless men, it can certainly elucidate a more nuanced meaning of the garments represented, especially in terms of gender ideologies (1981, 98).

But although the literary evidence cited to explain the change in women's fashion from the *peplos* to the *chiton* and back again is problematic, the fundamental conception of the *peplos* as a traditional feminine Hellenic garment still holds. We need not depend on literary sources for this interpretation; it can be read directly from the iconography. The most likely interpretation of the Early Classical *peplophoros* is that it is an iconographic construct of a female figure wearing a historical garment that was remembered from earlier times, perhaps through its continued ritual use. Evelyn Harrison has suggested such an interpretation for the *peplos*-clad maidens on the east Parthenon frieze. Those on the southern side of the procession wear a sleeved *chiton* under the *peplos*, while those on the northern side do not.[9] Harrison believes that the southern maidens are "contemporary" Athenians joining their ancestors on the north (1989, 53). The *peplos* was therefore worn as a ceremonial garment in the Panathenaia, and was understood as symbolic of the ancient Hellenic identity of the Athenians.[10]

Harrison's interpretation of the *peplos*-clad figures in the High Classical Parthenon frieze neatly explains the appearance of both *peplos* and *chiton* among the Archaic *korai* and Early Classical *peplophoroi*. If the *peplos* was a ceremonial garment worn over the *chiton* in ritual contexts, we should identify those *korai* wearing both garments as representing human figures, perhaps priestesses or participants in a sacred ritual such as the Panathenaia. *Peplophoroi* wearing the *peplos* alone should be understood as heroic or divine figures, clad in the most ancient form of Greek dress. The iconography of dress in the Early Classical period therefore does not reflect contemporary dress practices, as has been assumed since Studniczka despite the absence of archaeological and epigraphic evidence.[11] Rather, the *peplos* represents an old Hellenic garment that was worn only in ceremonial contexts (perhaps only the Panathenaia?).

The idea that the *peplos* might have been a traditional garment that was resurrected in the Early Classical period for iconographic purposes was put forth in the late eighteenth century by Böttiger (1794, 62) and supported by both Barker (1923, 1–3) and Heuzey (1922, 195) in the early twentieth century.[12] In his *Charicles*, Becker notes: "If there was originally a particular garment called by this name, it must have become obsolete" (1866, 428). Both Harrison and Ridgway have expressed doubt that the *peplos* was worn as an everyday garment in the fifth century.[13] Review of the historiographic, literary, and archaeological evidence confirms their suspicions: the *peplos* was not a garment in general use in the Early Classical period: its appearance on the monuments represents an iconographic construct of Hellenic identity.

The historical connotation of the *peplos* is supported by the fact that the garment is worn by Pandora in Early Classical Athenian vase paintings representing her adornment by Athena.[14] In **Figure 5.4**, the central scene on the top register shows Pandora in a frontal pose wearing a *peplos* fastened with straight pins at the shoulders.

Figure 5.4. Red-figure krater by the Niobid Painter, BM E467. (Photo courtesy of The British Museum.)

A white-ground kylix by the Tarquinia Painter represents Pandora (labeled Anesidora, her alias) being adorned by Athena and Hephaistos. Here she seems to be wearing a *peplos* fastened with pins, although the vase is severely damaged. Berczelly suggests that "this robe, *the first peplos*, might have been understood in the widest sense of the word as the archetypal peplos, given by Athena to the primordial woman. …Thus the peplos of Pandora could have represented the mythical pattern or prototype for all the peploi in the world."[15]

The fact that Pandora is represented wearing a *peplos* connects her symbolically to all other *peplophoroi*, and demonstrates the significance of the garment for the Greek construction of gender. Pandora served as the archetype for "the prevailing popular sentiment that women were by nature lustful, irrational, immoderate creatures who needed constant restraint, and that the stability of the state depended upon keeping them under strict control."[16] But, despite her shortcomings, man could not deny the necessity of woman's roles in both biological and social reproduction. Of primary importance was her ability to weave, a skill taught to Pandora by Athena and passed down through the generations. All these values, both positive and negative, are represented in the *peplos*.

The *peplos* is usually depicted as made of a heavy material, presumably wool, that obstructs the contours of the body, especially the sexual organs (**Figure 5.5**). The

Figure 5.5 (left). Figure K, "Hippodamaia," east pediment, Temple of Zeus at Olympia. (Photo courtesy of the Archaeological Museum, Olympia.)

Figure 5.6 (right). Photograph of woman wearing traditional Bedouin women's dress. (Photo courtesy of Prentice Hall.)

asexual appearance of the Early Classical *peplophoros*[17] is in stark contrast to the typical thin Archaic drapery that conforms to the shape of the body, accentuating breasts, buttocks, hips, and legs.[18] Although the girding of the *peplophoros* does in part emphasize the breasts and hips, it also serves to cut the body in half visually, as does the overfold.[19] The fact that the garment is pinned on the shoulders suggests that it may be easily unfastened, as in the west pediment of the Temple of Zeus at Olympia: a consequence of the centaurs' violence against the Lapith women (Cohen 1997, 66–92). While such an arrangement might suggest a certain vulnerability, a beneficial aspect is that it is particularly adaptable for breast-feeding an infant, as suggested for traditional Bedouin women's dress (**Figure 5.6**), which is identical in structure to the *peplos* (Storm 1987, 127, fig. 5.2).

The dialectical relationship between the *peplos* and the female body is significant in terms of the Greek construction of gender in the early fifth century.[20] The heavy drapery envelops and conceals the 'lustful, irrational, immoderate' female body, effectively negating feminine sexuality. This suggestion of control is reinforced by girding (sometimes more than once on the same figure),[21] which visually dissects the body into two regions: above and below the waist.[22] The division is emphasized by the overfold, which covers the chest with a double thickness of fabric. But while the breasts are obscured by the thick material, their accessibility is implied by the fact that the lappets are merely pinned, not sewn, shut. The ease with which a woman wearing a *peplos* might nurse a child suggests a celebration of women's nurturing, maternal, role.[23] Finally, the fact that the *peplos* is created from an uncut, unsewn, piece of fabric exactly as it came off the loom suggests a particular respect for this product of women's labor.[24]

The ideological association between women and weaving cannot be overemphasized. Weaving is particularly identified with feminine *metis* (cunning) in the Greek tradition, and its dangerous aspects are a significant theme in Greek tragedy (the poisoned *peploi* of Medea and Deianeira, the *peplos* used by Clytemnestra to kill Agamemnon).[25] Women's weaving, and, by extension, women themselves, have the potential to do tremendous damage, to men in particular. In order to mitigate such negative capacities and foster positive qualities, both women and women's production must be brought under social (patriarchal) control. The requirement that women weave garments for cult purposes, such as the famed Panatheniaic *peplos*, is one way of codifying their production and putting their labor into the service of the community.[26] The formerly dangerous textile is thus transformed into a symbol of social order, and women's production of cloth is understood as the means of binding society together.[27]

The *peplos* as a historical garment may thus be understood as an embodiment of traditional Greek values regarding both women and textiles. The garment appears in the iconography of the Early Classical period as a means of communicating those values, whether women actually adopted the garment themselves. A similar argument has been made for the Roman toga (Vout 1996, 204–20; Stone 1994, 13–45), the national garment of the early Romans, worn by both men and women. By the time of Augustus, however, the garment was rarely worn except on ceremonial occasions (Stone 1994, 13; Sebesta, Davies this volume). Nevertheless, Roman men consistently represented themselves as *togati* in art and literature to communicate their identity as Roman citizens. The toga thus became a symbol of Roman-ness. As traditional garments, both the toga and the *peplos* became a "badge, a kind of 'collective representation' which distinguishes groups and characterizes them in reference to other related and unrelated groups" (Hamilton & Hamilton 1989, 20). The *peplos* also represents, however, a prescription for femininity; the ubiquitousness of the *peplophoros* in the Early Classical period suggests a strictly defined role for women in the years following the Persian Wars.[28]

The fact that only women are represented wearing this historical garment suggests that they were viewed ideologically as repositories of tradition.[29] Throughout Greek literature good women are portrayed as treasurers of the household, from Penelope in Homer's *Odyssey* to the young wife in Xenophon's *Oeconomicus*.[30] Women's responsibility for the maintenance of the wider community was likewise demonstrated by their prominent roles in religion and ritual, including the Panathenaia at Athens, which celebrated the mythical past (Just 1989, 277–78). At Athens women were understood:

> as the guardians of family, kinship, and religion, a portrayal that stressed their commitment to the domestic sphere in which society situated them. Exiled from civic affairs, placed within the protection of the *oikos*, assigned the role of reproducing society as legitimate wives and mothers rather than of participating in it as citizens in their own right, they become in their "domesticated" state the representatives and symbols of society's continuity, embodying quite literally the natural processes on which that continuity rested, and concerned with what were perceived as the equally "natural" laws by which that continuity was sanctioned (Just 1989, 212–3).

The *peplophoros* may be seen as the embodiment of these traditional values: she is sober, modest in dress, restrained in gesture, a 'good woman' who occupies herself with weaving traditional garments such as the *peplos*. The *peplophoros* is a domesticated woman, her clothed body, tamed.

NOTES

1. This paper is based in part on my dissertation, *The Myth of the Classical* Peplos (Bryn Mawr, 1999). I wish to thank my advisor, A.A. Donohue, for her continued guidance and support. Versions were presented at Yale University, Cornell University, Rhodes College, and the Annual Meeting of the Archaeological Institute of America in Dallas (1999). I thank these audiences, as well as the participants at *The Clothed Body in the Ancient World*, for their comments and suggestions.
2. Coldstream suggests the date of this expedition might have been as early as the eighth century (1977, 135), while Morris proposes a date in the early seventh century (1984, 107–116).
3. Translation adapted from Grene 1987.
4. This study focuses on the representations of feminine dress in Greek sculpture of the Archaic and Classical periods. The evidence of vase-painting represents a different iconographic tradition, and as such will be addressed only tangentially.
5. The term *apoptygma* persists despite Thompson's persuasive arguments that its identification stems from a misreading of the epigraphic evidence (1944, 198).
6. Rigdway 1970, 8. The corpus of Early Classical original *peplophoroi* is collected in Tölle-Kastenbein 1980.
7. Indeed, the early *peplophoroi* from the Athenian Acropolis (including **Figure 5.1**) likewise wear sleeved garments under their *peploi*. The combination of the two garments will be discussed further below.
8. *Peploi* and *chitones* appear together also in many red-figure vases of the Early Classical period.
9. This point was first noted by Beschi 1984, 8–9.
10. Harrison (1898, 44, 41) proposes that Early Classical style as a whole stemmed from a desire to express Greek ethnic identity.
11. Dress fasteners all but disappear from the archaeological record after the seventh century BC; likewise, *peploi* are absent from temple inventories recording dedications of garments in sanctuaries. For a complete discussion of the archaeological and epigraphic evidence for the *peplos*, see Lee 1999, Ch. 4.
12. For a full discussion of the historiography of the *peplos*, see Lee 2003.
13. Ridgway notes: "Although some *peplophoroi* can undoubtedly be recognized as divinities ... the great majority of extant examples remains uncharacterized and unidentifiable. Only the deliberate imitation of the severe form of the *peplos* in later times may suggest that the costume (or the style) carried a meaning that could be considered symbolic at least by the time of the revival. It is therefore impossible to know whether the *peplos* was actually worn by the Greeks of the early fifth century B.C. ..." (1984, 46). Ridgway also questions the contemporaneity of the *chiton/himation* combination worn by the Archaic *korai* (1985, 7). See also Ridgway 1993, 172, n. 4.61.

14 The myth of Pandora is told by Hesiod in both the *Theogony* (570–610) and *Works and Days* (57–105). Zeus commanded Hephaistos to make the first woman out of earth, in retaliation for Prometheus' having stolen fire and given it to mortal men. In both versions of the story Athena adorns her with finery; in neither version are the garments called *peploi*. Athena is also credited with teaching Pandora to weave. Pandora lifts the lid from the *pithos* scattering its contents, the evils that plague men, across the earth; only Hope remained inside the jar.

15 1992, 61. Berczelly further suggests that Athena's gift of the 'first *peplos*' was commemorated annually by the reciprocal gift of the Panathenaic *peplos* given by the women of Athens. Hurwit suggests that the representation of Athena dressing Pandora in the *peplos* can be read allegorically as the goddess teaching the first woman the art of weaving (1995, 183).

16 Hurwit (1995, 180, 184) notes that along with 'know thyself' and 'nothing to excess', visitors to the Temple of Apollo at Delphi were instructed to 'keep women under rule'.

17 Childs (1988, 11) notes that the fronts and backs of Early Classical *peplophoroi* are "hardly distinguishable".

18 Gopnik notes: "It is clear that the sensory stimulation provided by the peplos is very different from that provided by the chiton. Therefore, a change from a peplos to a chiton would change the information provided to us about our body" (1983, 1323).

19 Rubinstein notes that modern women's skirt and blouse combinations "cut the body in half, dwarfing the person and intimating a figure of less significance," while men's business suits create a unified appearance (1995, 84).

20 On the relationship between the body and dress, see Arthur 1999, 1–7.

21 For example, the kneeling figure "O" in the east pediment of the temple of Zeus at Olympia, usually identified as a handmaiden, wears an over-girded *peplos* with a *kolpos*, indicating the presence of girding underneath the overfold.

22 A similar notion of the human body as divided into upper and lower parts exists among Gypsies living in North America. The body below the waist is associated with great shame; fear of pollution is so extreme that after washing lower body clothes the hands must be washed before handling upper body clothes. On the other hand, the upper body is without shame, and women's breasts may be exposed or even touched by others without pollution. The dichotomy between the upper and lower parts of the body is reflected in Gypsy dress: women's blouses are frequently left unbuttoned or simply pinned, while their heavy skirts cover the legs to the floor: Sutherland 1975, 264.

23 The positive value ascribed to lactation is not at odds with the overall negation of sexuality of the figure.

24 Barber calculates that the *peplos* would have measured roughly five feet by six on the basis of representations of the garment, taking into account the average height of Greek women at the time. The size of the *peplos*, she asserts, was determined in part by the capacity of the warp-weighted loom (1992, 110). See also van Wees, this volume.

25 Lee 2004; See also Duigan 2004, 78–84, on *metis*.

26 The ritual and political appropriation of women's textile production has been argued also for the Aegean Bronze Age (Lee 2000, 111–123) and Aztec Mexico (Brumfiel 1991, 224–251; McCafferty & McCafferty 1991, 19–44).

27 On weaving as a symbol of social cohesion, see especially Scheid & Svenbro 1996, 9–34. The ideal model for weaving was decidedly feminine, despite evidence for professional male weavers in Classical Athens: Thompson 1982, 217–22.

28 One might compare Christian Dior's 'New Look' in the years following World War II: Pochna 1995, 72–77. See also Llewellyn-Jones, this volume.

29 Only one male figure has been identified as possibly wearing a *peplos*. A small bronze statuette from Euboia of the river god Acheloös is represented as a bearded man wearing multiple garments. Gais describes the figure as "heavily dressed," without identifying the types of garments (1978, 359 and fig. 8). Ridgway classifies the figure as wearing a *peplos* with a *kolpos* in addition to a *chiton* (1984, 46). The statuette is not included by Tölle-Kastenbein in her corpus of original *peplophoroi*.

30 duBois 1988, 100–103. Xenophon specifically uses forms of the word *phylattein* 'guard' in reference to the responsibilities of the wife, Pomeroy 1994, *ad* 7.25, 7.36, 7.39, 9.15.

Chapter 6

New Clothes, a New You:
Clothing and character in Aristophanes

James Robson

From the spectacle surrounding the costumes of the choruses of *Birds* and *Clouds* to the paratragic use of disguise in *Acharnians* and *Thesmophoriazusae*, clothing plays a potent role in the plays of Aristophanes. No extant ancient author seems so readily – nor, perhaps, so inventively – to have exploited clothing to artistic ends. In this chapter I shall investigate some hitherto neglected aspects of Aristophanes' use of clothing and outline what I believe to be the basis of the special relationship which Old Comedy has with costume.

I start by exploring the important position that clothing holds in Aristophanes' plays, considering in particular the role of clothing in the realisation of humour. Subsequently, I shall go on to look at scenes in which Aristophanic figures appear wearing clothing inappropriate to their character-type, focusing on scenes of transvestism. Finally, I shall aim to draw some conclusions about the way in which clothing is represented in such scenes, touching on the fascinating interrelationship between clothing, character and stagecraft.

THE SEMIOTICS OF DRESS

When we watch a dramatic performance – be it in the form of a play, television programme or film – we commonly expect the characters' clothes to inform us in some way about their wearers. An audience can usually rely on clothing – regardless of the extent to which it is stylised – to convey information about the gender, age, relative social standing, and even personal history, of the characters we meet.[1]

It seems reasonable to infer that clothing conventions in ancient drama followed similar patterns: that is, that the clothing worn by characters on the ancient stage would also have conveyed to the audience information concerning gender, age, social status and other information besides.[2] However, an interesting situation confronts us when we begin to consider the potential of the semiotics of dress in Aristophanes' plays, which I shall outline now.

ARISTOPHANES AND 'RECREATIVITY'

In Aristophanic drama, as in other ancient dramatic performances, characters' clothing would also, no doubt, have conveyed the kind of information I have just outlined – gender, age, status – and in addition to this, species and even object, too. It is interesting to note, though, that the clothing worn by a character would have consistently reflected age, gender, status and so on in a way that the words uttered by a character would often have *not*. The reason for this is that in Aristophanic comedy we find what Michael Silk has recently termed 'recreative' characters (2000, 221).

It will be important to consider briefly what is meant by 'recreative', a term best understood by reference to its opposite, 'realist'. Silk describes the 'realist' characters which people the vast majority of Western literature as follows:

> The people presented have what we may see as a constant relationship with 'reality' – with the world outside as we perceive it or might be presumed to perceive it – because ... they are seen to stand at a constant distance from that real world. They impinge as sentient beings, each with a tendency to be (in Aristotle's language) 'appropriate', 'lifelike' and 'consistent ... .' (2000, 213–4)

Silk goes on to argue that Aristophanic figures often do not belong to this 'realist' tradition, and that whilst "some Aristophanic characters ... lend themselves better than others to realist interpretation" (2000, 216) it is nevertheless the case that "the people of Aristophanes *per se* are not strictly containable within any realistic understanding of human character at all"(2000, 212). Silk calls the mode of representation of which most of Aristophanes' characters partake 'recreative', and suggests that their "distinctive and essential feature is discontinuity, linguistic or otherwise" (2000, 221); "if and when they change, they change abruptly and, perhaps, entirely" (2000, 223).

The kind of phenomenon which Silk is describing may usefully be represented by some simple examples. Recreativity can work on a number of levels. At one extreme, a character may alter radically, such as at *Thesmophoriazusae* 211–2 when Euripides' Inlaw volunteers to dress as a woman and attend the all-female Thesmophoria.[3] In real life – or in a 'realist' work of literature – we would ask what has motivated his decision to put himself forward; we would ask why he had not volunteered before and how he thinks he will manage the deceit. But these questions are unanswerable and essentially inappropriate in the context of Aristophanic comedy. Instead, we can point to the Inlaw's decision as being a recreative high point in the play, a turning point in the sequential, but not logically *con*sequential plot.[4]

Recreativity is also discernible in a more subdued form at the micro-level of the text. For example, characters may use words or allude to concepts which would be inconsistent with, say, a real-life figure of their social class or education. This phenomenon – which Gregory Dobrov refers to as 'ventriloquism' – can be seen, for example, in the speech of characters such as Dicaeopolis and Trygaeus who, Dobrov posits, "most certainly exceed their 'natural' competence as common-sense rustics when they base their speech and behavior on tragic models in a sophisticated and critical way" (1995, 56).

As a last example of recreativity, let us look at one of the numerous asides which characters often make – interrupting their own flow or that of others – which would either be out of place in realist drama or at least reacted to differently by other characters. At the beginning of the *Lysistrata*, for instance, our eponymous heroine is prompted by Calonice to say why she looks so worried and Lysistrata begins to explain (*Lys.* 9–15):[5]

Lysistrata:	My heart's burning, Calonice, and I'm feeling very sore about us women: because in men's opinion we're thought to be such utter rascals (*panourgoi*) –
Calonice:	And so we are, by Zeus!
Lysistrata:	But when they've been told to meet here to have a discussion about a far from trivial matter, they lie asleep and don't come.

In a 'realist' or real-life exchange, we should either expect Calonice not to make such a crass comment or for Lysistrata to question Calonice as to her precise meaning. Indeed, in a realist drama, Calonice's comment might prove psychologically revealing, whereas in the context of the *Lysistrata* it is better accounted for as an instance of recreativity.

It will prove interesting to examine this last example of recreative behaviour further. What we have here in Calonice's utterance – "And so we are, by Zeus!" – is an instance of humour. The relationship between humour and recreativity is a fascinating one and certainly merits more attention than I am able to give it here: suffice to say, however, that the presence of recreative characters in a play has important consequences for the realisation of humour.[6] In a comedy populated by realist figures, we may legitimately expect a proportion of the humour to stem from the way in which these figures are characterised, and their subsequent interaction and individual responses to the situations which they confront. In a recreative genre such as Old Comedy, though, where only some of the figures we meet have consistent 'characters', humour relying on subtle characterisation can hardly be expected.[7] That is certainly not to say that an author working in a recreative genre will be at a loss when it comes to finding ways to make his audience laugh – Aristophanes' plays are, after all, rich testimony to how humorous a non-realist play can be. However, what we only rarely find in Aristophanes is humour predicated on an individual's 'personality'; and what we find more often is humour based on character-*types*: types such as women, old men and foreigners.[8] And, of course, it is their *clothing* which allows character-types to be easily perceived by an audience.

One way of viewing the case of Calonice, then, is this: since she is defined as female by her clothing, Aristophanes is free to use one of his favourite humorous techniques – that is, to have her conform to a traditional comic stereotype. In the case of women, the stereotype involves being bibulous, sex-mad and a scourge to men. And in a non-realist drama, there is nothing to stop a character-type freely admitting to living up to stereotypical traits, as Calonice does here – "And so we are, by Zeus!"

From this discussion, we can see that clothes play a key role for Aristophanes in the creation of humour: a fairly straightforward role maybe, given – and yet perhaps because of – the complexities that his recreative comedy presents. Clothes help establish a social identity for the personage on stage along with which is connected a set of expectations which Aristophanes may choose to exploit – and it is this role of clothing which I shall now explore further.

INAPPROPRIATE CLOTHING: TRANSVESTISM

Following this preliminary look at the role of clothing in Aristophanic comedy, let us move on to what will be my focus for the rest of this chapter, namely Aristophanic scenes where we come across characters wearing clothing inappropriate to their character-type. Aristophanes has his characters assume inappropriate clothes for a number of reasons: characters may adopt a deliberate disguise, such as Dicaeopolis' transparent beggar's disguise in the *Acharnians*, or the Inlaw's disguise in the *Thesmophoriazusae*, which allows him to penetrate the festival where Euripides' fate is to be decided. Alternatively, new clothes may accompany a transformation, either permanent, such as that of Demos in the *Knights* when he is rejuvenated (1316ff.); or temporary, like the short-lived transformation of Philocleon into urbane sophisticate in the *Wasps* (1122ff.).[9]

Owing to confines of space, I am unable to tackle all instances in Aristophanes of inappropriate clothing being adopted and so shall limit my discussion to a sample drawn from a substantial sub-group of such scenes, namely those featuring transvestism. In looking at these scenes of transvestism – both male characters adopting female clothing and *vice versa* – I shall attempt to bring out a number of key features that they share and subsequently explore the implications of the patterns that emerge from my analysis. The two plays of Aristophanes on whose scenes of transvestism I shall focus are the *Thesmophoriazusae* and the *Ecclesiazusae*.

Thesmophoriazusae

To take these two plays in the order in which they were first performed, the *Thesmophorizusae* – produced in 411 – contains a series of cross-dressing scenes, the two most extensive, which I shall examine here, being those involving the poet Agathon caught in the act of composing one of his tragedies, and the dressing up of the Inlaw.[10]

The first male figure we meet in female clothing is Agathon, who eventually emerges from his house at line 95 of the play. Before conversing with Euripides and the Inlaw, Agathon sings a lengthy and mannered tragic-style lyric (101–29).[11] The Inlaw comments on Agathon's clothing both when the latter enters the stage – "I don't see any man here at all; what I see is Madam Cyrene" (97–8) – and then at greater length, and in paratragic style, once Agathon's song is finished (136–40).[12]

> Whence comes this epicene (*gunnis*)? What is its country, what its garb? What confusion of life-styles is this? What has a bass to say to a saffron gown? Or a lyre to a hair-net? What's an oil-flask doing with a breast-band? How incongruous! And what partnership can there be between a mirror and a sword?

Thus the Inlaw emphasises the incongruity between the male poet and his female attire and does so to humorous effect.[13]

In the sequence that follows, Agathon makes a series of comments which have been much discussed by scholars, since they form the earliest set of explicit statements we have from the ancient world concerning the act of composition.[14] The relevance here is that these comments also concern the way in which the adoption of new clothing can affect the wearer. In the first of these, Agathon claims that his reason for adopting female dress is to allow him effectively to compose female parts in his tragedies. At 148–52, Agathon says:[15]

> I change my clothing accordingly as I change my mentality. A man who is a poet must adopt habits that match the plays he's committed to composing. For example, if one is writing about women (*gunaikei'* ...*dramata*), one's body must participate in their habits (*tropoi*).

He adds (154–6):

> If you're writing about men (*andreia* [*dramata*]), your body has what it takes already; but when it's a question of something we don't possess, then it must be captured by imitation (*mimêsis*).

These views on the process of composition and the role of clothing are both embellished and somewhat changed at 164–7, where Agathon comments:

> And Phrynichus – you must have actually heard him sing – he was an attractive man and he also wore attractive clothes, and *that's* why his plays were attractive too. One just can't help creating work that reflects one's own nature (*physis*).

One problem which Agathon's comments have posed for critics is his seeming confusion between imitation (*mimêsis*) and nature (*physis*): in the first two comments (148–52 and 154–6) Agathon advocates the *imitation* of women, by adopting female dress and habits, to facilitate composition (*mimêsis*), but in the third statement (164–7), he suggests that a poet's work is a product of his/her internal *state* (*physis*).

In looking for consistency in these statements, scholars have also been puzzled at how Agathon as a man manages successfully to compose a lyric for female parts (as he does on stage at 101–29) if, indeed, "one just can't help creating work that reflects one's own nature" (167).[16] The solution of Cantarella and Zeitlin is that Agathon, although a man, is in fact female by nature.[17] If this is how we are to understand this scene, however, we are faced with the task of explaining why Agathon dons female clothing, since strictly it is unnecessary. A number of solutions suggest themselves. Perhaps the clothes are to be viewed as providing Agathon with extra inspiration; perhaps they are an expression of this female *physis* of his – and/or perhaps we are to see Agathon *kômôidoumenos* as trying to cover up his transvestite proclivities by claims of artistic *mimêsis*.[18] Any of these explanations is possible, of course, and given that we are in the world of Old Comedy we may be well advised not to look to favour one to the exclusion of the others. But let us add to these a further possible interpretation of the views Agathon expresses in this scene which, I believe, adds an intriguing perspective to the play; namely that Agathon's statements can be understood as comprising a theory that the donning of female clothes effects an *internal change*. Thus it can be argued that it is Agathon's *mimêsis* of a woman which has provided him with a female *physis*,[19] and his comment of 148 can therefore be read both ways: not only does Agathon change his clothing along with his mentality, but also changes his mentality along with his clothing.[20] What is more, this interpretation of Agathon's views has profound implications for our understanding of the rest of the play since we can view this theory of *mimêsis* as being put to the test, first by Euripides' dressing up of the Inlaw and then by Eurpides' own experiments with female disguise.[21]

When Agathon eventually refuses to go to the Thesmophoria on Euripides' behalf, the Inlaw volunteers his services in, as we have discussed, a recreative moment *par excellence* (*Thesm.* 209–214). In the action that follows, the Inlaw's face is shaved (221ff.) and his nether regions singed (240) – both of which processes are drawn out into lengthy humorous sequences. The Inlaw is then dressed up in clothes which Euripides requests from Agathon, mentioned one by one as they are handed over – a saffron gown (253), a breastband (255), a head-piece (258), a mantle (261) and shoes (262).

It will prove interesting to note what features these two transvestite scenes from the *Thesmophoriazusae* have in common. First, attention is drawn to the new clothing in the script. This may partly be explicable through the practical need to relay the nature of the clothing to an ancient audience, many of whom may have been sitting a long way from the stage. Second, humorous capital is made of the new clothing. In the case of Agathon, humour stems from the elaborateness of both Agathon's clothes and his reasoning for wearing them, whereas with the Inlaw the focus is on his transformation and the humour of the scene stems from the process of dressing as a member of the opposite sex, most notably the need for the Inlaw to be shaved and singed (the latter element, we should note, being unnecessary and nonsensical in 'realist' terms). A third common feature is the fact that the adoption of new clothing has an effect on its wearer. As we have seen, Agathon makes explicit statements about the connection of clothing with the process of composition – 'I change my clothing accordingly as I change my mentality' – and in one reading at least his female clothing can be viewed as acting as a facilitator allowing him to compose female parts in his tragedies. Indeed, as I have suggested, his statements may be underpinned by a theory that women's clothing can allow a man to acquire a female *physis*. We may note in comparison that the Inlaw also takes on various female characteristics after he dons women's clothing.[22] Not only is he, at first, able to attend the Thesmophoria undetected, but he is also able to deliver a shocking, yet seemingly informed speech to the women in which he enunciates female vices and such deceits as Euripides has so far failed to reveal (*Thesm.* 486–519). Whilst the Inlaw does assume a certain knowledge of the female realm, his adoption of new clothing certainly does not allow him to talk like a woman consistently in the way that Agathon could when composing his tragedy. Rather, it would be more accurate to say that he displays both female and male character traits when in disguise. Indeed, Aristophanes makes good capital of the fact that, just like his phallus at 644 during his unmasking, male characteristics continually 'peep out' (*diakuptein*).[23]

It is tempting to judge the successes and eventual failure of the Inlaw's disguise as a examination of Agathon's theory of *mimêsis* and *physis*. It is a theory which, when tested, provides mixed results, and so which, it would appear, is essentially flawed. Imitating a woman may well have allowed Agathon to compose female parts for his plays, but the Inlaw only manages to deceive up to a point and is eventually found out. Perhaps Agathon's *mimêsis* is successful because it is better than the Inlaw's; or, as some scholars have suggested, perhaps the point is that Agathon's *physis* was actually female all along. Or perhaps we are to conclude (and this requires us to merge the identities of the stage Agathon and the real-life Agathon) that since the theory is flawed, Agathon's *mimêsis* is not really successful either, and for all the efforts he dedicates to cross-dressing the parts he writes are essentially unconvincing.

At this point, we should also note that the 'peeping through' of the Inlaw's masculinity from his female garb sits well with the exploration of theatricality that lies at the heart of the play.[24] Aristophanes is playing with the fact that, in reality, the Inlaw is a character played by a male actor. On the one hand, in the context of theatrical performance there is no barrier to his becoming a convincing woman despite his masculinity – in tragedy, after all, female parts would regularly have been played convincingly by men. On the other hand, in Old Comedy a theatrical illusion may in an instant be turned – recreatively – into its binary opposite: thus a male actor's dress may suddenly be exposed as the imperfect disguise which, in real life, it would no doubt be.[25]

Ecclesiazusae

At the heart of the plot of the *Ecclesiazusae*, first produced in 393, is the seizure of power by the women of Athens. The reversal of gender roles is represented visually in two scenes of transvestism – the first where the women of Athens, led by Praxagora, don male clothes before heading for the assembly and the second at lines 311ff. of the play, where Praxagora's husband Blepyrus emerges from his house wearing his wife's clothes.[26]

To take the Blepyrus scene first, most of the humour in this sequence stems from a combination of his inappropriate attire and the fact that Blepyrus is desperate to defecate. Presumably his dress was such as to raise an initial reaction from the audience: one would guess that masculine characteristics – say his gait, shape and hairiness – were juxtaposed with his outlandish female clothes. What we can glean with more certainty is that clothing is both a focus of attention and exploited as a source for humour. Blepyrus, his unnamed Neighbour and Chremes all comment on his attire, namely his dress (*hêmidiploïdion*, 318) and his Persian slippers, (*persikai*, 319). The Neighbour asks – with a sideswipe at the Dithyrambic (and thus 'floating', 'airy') poet, Cinesias (329–30):[27]

> What's this yellow all over you? Surely, Cinesias hasn't shat all over you from somewhere?

And Chremes, too, draws attention to the clothes (374):

> What's this? Are you wearing your wife's shift (*chitônion*)?

The attention given to Blepyrus' clothing – and its exploitation to humorous ends – finds a parallel in the first episode of the play where Blepyrus' wife Praxagora and her acolytes don male clothing in preparation for their visit to the assembly.[28] The women require items such as beards, cloaks, shoes and walking sticks. At various points during the scene the women have difficulty adapting to their new sex roles. For example, one woman has difficulty moving in men's clothing: "Look, there's Smicython's wife Melisiche trying to run in her old man's boots" (46–7). Others find adopting male habits a challenge – one woman brings some wool to card to fill in time before the assembly begins and several swear by female rather than male oaths: "by the two goddesses" (*ma tô theô*,155); "yes, by Aphrodite" (*nê tên Aphroditên*,189).

As in the *Thesmphoriazusae*, new clothing appears to effect alterations in the characters of this play, albeit in a different way. Blepyrus is rendered passive by his clothing – a passivity which is reflected by his constipation – whereas the adoption of male clothing has allowed his wife and her acolytes to become active.[29] Praxagora's progression is an interesting one: at the start of the play, she alludes to herself as a wife in her domestic sphere having sex in the bedroom (8–9), practising depilation (13) and stealing food from the pantry (14–5) – all typical female pursuits in Old Comedy. However, she soon reveals herself as first an active figure in the wider world – she arranges and takes charge of the women's meeting – then shows herself to be an accomplished orator and is finally elected leader of the city. The women, too, make unconvincing men at the outset what with their carding and inappropriate oaths, but after disguising themselves according to Praxagora's instructions are revealed to be sufficiently competent in their new role as to notice and rectify the one mistake that they do make as they make their way to the assembly: they correct a feminine *philas* to a masculine *philous* (298–9). In the *Ecclesiazusae*, then, the connection between clothing and behaviour may not be as much of a focus of interest as in our earlier play, but it is nevertheless true to say that the effect that clothes have on their wearers is discernible in both plays.

CLOTHING AND RECREATIVITY

The changes undergone by different characters upon the adoption of new clothing are instructively different from each other, and this difference is best accounted for in light of the level of recreativity displayed by the characters concerned. The largest contrast is to be found between the Inlaw on the one hand and the characters in the *Ecclesiazusae* on the other, a play which can boast figures which are recognisable as realist creations, their moments of recreativity being occasional and relatively slight.

To be sure, in both the *Thesmophoriazusae* and the *Ecclesiazusae*, the donning of new clothes can be seen to have an effect on their wearers, and regardless of whether a cross-dressing character is essentially recreative (such as the Inlaw) or realist (such as Blepyrus and Praxagora – and, arguably, Agathon),[30] clothing of the opposite sex has the power to transform. For a recreative figure such as the Inlaw, however, the adoption of female clothing is contemporaneous with a sudden and dramatic change in behaviour and the knowledge to which he has access. But both a symptom and cause of his recreativity is that his new female persona is itself undercut, with the result that masculine characteristics are intermittently discernible. In contrast, the more-rather-than-less realist, less-rather-than-more recreative characters of the *Ecclesiazusae* still suffer changes through the potent force of clothing of the opposite sex, but these changes are gradual, more subtle and, most importantly, *linear*.

Praxagora's capability for activity and leadership, for example, do not disappear when she removes the clothing of the opposite sex; nor does Blepyrus' passivity.

Perhaps we have reached a rather obvious conclusion: that the recreative power of clothes is greater – yet also, of course, less stable – the more recreative the characters are. Thus there is a certain inevitability in the way in which the Inlaw, for example, is able to change radically with the adoption of new clothing and further, to have this new identity stand subject to further rapid change.[31] And to make a connection with comments I made towards the beginning of the chapter, Aristophanes may be said to be playing with the way in which clothing projects identity to a dramatic audience. The less 'personality' a character has, the more he or she is defined by the clothing worn – and thus the more readily a change of identity can occur, and the more unstable identity can be shown to be.

In a characteristically Aristophanic twist, it may be possible to discern in the *Thesmophoriazusae*, though, our playwright toying with the audience's expectations as to the nature of his recreative world. After all, at first glance the implication of Agathon's comments that an alteration of appearance can cause an alteration of *physis* might be thought to suit recreative drama well, since it is a reality of staging that what defines a character most clearly is the clothes he or she is wearing. But playfully, Aristophanes shows Agathon's theory to be wrong. In Aristophanes' brand of theatrically self-conscious, recreative drama nothing is so straightforward.

NOTES

1. Of course, it is always open for a director to unsettle or challenge his or her audience's assumptions in various ways, but it should be borne in mind that, for its effect, such a conceit depends on the existence of – and an audience's awareness of – certain conventions connected with dress.
2. Saïd (1987, 226) postulates that comic costume is "strictement codé et manifeste clairement le sexe et le statut social des personnages".
3. This is an example which Silk himself uses to demonstrate recreativity (2000: 208–9).
4. The contrast between 'sequential' and '*con*sequential' is one made by Silk (2002, 224).
5. The text and translations in this chapter are based on Sommerstein 1980 (*Ach.*), 1990 (*Lys.*) 1994 (*Thesm.*) and 1998 (*Eccl.*).
6. As I have argued elsewhere (1999, 50–2), whilst 'recreative' highpoints are certainly not always humorous, instances of humour *are* usefully be described as 'recreative', displaying as they do qualities such as discontinuity, binary reversal and apparent absence of logical consequentiality.
7. There are, of course, problems with ascribing personalities to any fictional figure, however realist they might be. Even if we adopt Barthes' distinction between a real-life 'person' and a fictional 'figure' (1975, 178), we can nevertheless, like Silk, make useful distinctions between more-rather-than-less and less-rather-than-more realist 'figures'. See also Gould 1978 and Goldhill 1990.
8. The discussion of Ehrenberg (1951, 40) is still useful on this point, positing that there are 'types' rather than individual 'beings' or 'characters' in Aristophanes' plays. I should add the *caveat* that such 'typicalisation' is still always liable to be momentary or subsumed within recreative premises: Aristophanes is not like Menander, many of whose *dramatis personae* are to all intents and purposes simply 'types'.
9. For discussions of the clothes changing in Aristophanes see Saïd 1987 and Bowie 1993 (s.v. 'clothing' and 'transvestism').
10. Through confines of space, I am unable to consider the scenes of Euripides' paratragic cross-dressing as Helen (850ff.), Andromeda (1009ff.) and Echo (1056ff). For discussion of these, see Rau 1967, 53–89; Saïd 1987, 218–23 and Taafe 1993, 95–9.

11 On which, see Muecke 1982, 48. See also Rau 1967, 103–8 and 1975, 341–3 and Slater 2002, 155.
12 The parody is of Aeschylus' *Edonians*: cf. Aesch *fr*. 72 (Mette). See Moulton 1981, 118 and n.31 and Rau 1967, 108–11.
13 Saïd (1987, 237) suggests that "travestissements trassexuels sont toujours 'manqués'", since actors wear the padding and mask and so on of their character's original sex.
14 And perhaps the first technical use of *mimêsis, pace* Muecke 1982, 43.
15 See Muecke (1982, 53) on the phrase *hama tê gnômê* (148).
16 In the discussion that follows, we should bear in mind that few members of an audience are likely to notice this slide from one position to another. See Stohn 1993, 199–200 and Slater 2002, 155.
17 Cantarella 1967, 13–4; Zeitlin 1981, 177–8. Cf. Muecke 1982, 54. Like Moulton (1981, 95), critics seem to understand *drama gunaikeion* as simply being one which features female characters.
18 This is the suggestion of Muecke (1982, 43) who also posits, however, that by *mimêsis* we are to understand "disguising oneself as a mime artist" (1982, 55).
19 Stohn (1993, 199) suggests that Aristophanes, aware that "[d]er Versuch, sich mit einer Rolle zu identifizieren, vollzieht sich vor allem in seelischen Bereich", has reworked this idea "in bühnwirksamer Form." The relationship between appearance and reality is, of course, central to the play. See Muecke 1982 and Zeitlin 1981. For feminist readings of the play, such as those of Ferris (1989, 26–8) Taafe (1993, 74–102) and Bobrick (1997) the major significance of scenes of transvestism seems to be the ease with which men can imitate women.
20 It is perfectly in keeping with this view to argue that Aristophanes is also having fun at the expense of either some or all of the following: (i) the real-life Agathon; (ii) Agathon's poetry; (iii) other poets; (iv) current theories of poetic composition; although ascertaining the exact nature of any satire is complex. For different views, see e.g. Muecke 1982, 55; MacDowell 1995, 256–7; Gelzer 2002, 362–3 and Stohn as summarised by von Möllendorff 2002, 149.
21 Of course, this theory can in turn be read as an 'excuse' for cross-dressing, especially given its subsequent failure (see below).
22 Zeitlin (1981, 178) talks of the "transfer of Agathon's persona" to the Inlaw.
23 The ostensible reason for the Inlaw being found out, for instance, is just such an example of the 'peeping out' – a linguistic slip centering on the difference between a male and female chamber pot (*hamis* and *skaphion*, 633).
24 See note 31 above. Zeitlin (1981, 180) comments that the "contradictions inherent in the mimetic process ... between what you play and what you are, are tested again and again in the play".
25 On which see Saïd 1987, 224–5.
26 For discussions of this scene, see Ussher 1969, 23–7; Saïd 1979, 38; Stone 1980, 413; Bowie 1993, 259; Taafe 1993, 113–4 and Slater 1997, 107–11 and 2002, 216–7.
27 On fifth-century views of dithyrambic poetry, see Zimmermann 1992, 119–20 and Dobrov & Urios-Aparisi 1995, 164–6.
28 For discussions of this scene, see Ussher 1969, 27–9; Saïd 1979, 37–41; Stone 1980, 410–2; Bowie 1993, 257–8; Taafe 1993, 109–13 and Slater 1997, 98–107 and 2002, 209–16.
29 See Bowie 1993, 258 and 260–1 and Slater 1997, 107. Feminist readings of the play, such as those of Saïd (1979; 1986) and Taafe (1993) emphasise the failure of the women's disguise. To be sure, Aristophanes dramatises moments where the women make slips, but this is what we should expect from a comic drama. Further, the emotional direction of the scene and, most importantly, the women's success in gaining power, would suggest that they do manage a credible 'illusion'.
30 The dramatic aims of the Agathon scene can only be met if he is shown to have a stable character (i.e. more-rather-than-less realist): otherwise his 'theory' that *mimêsis* begets *physis* could not be expounded effectively. Nor, if his character were not relatively 'realist' would critics argue that he in fact displays a female *physis*.
31 But this is not to say that there is anything less inevitable about the presence in the *Thesmophoriazusae* of a figure such as Agathon whose extraordinary character remains relatively constant – for all his gender-bending theories.

Chapter 7

Beauty in Rags.
On *rhakos* in Aristophanic theatre

Silvia Milanezi

It might seem absurd in a book on the clothed body to propose a chapter on rags and raggedy garments. In Ancient Greece these are usually associated with people of low political, social, and economical condition: outcasts or beggars. From epic poetry onwards, *ptochoi* are perceived as bellies in rags: going from town to town, their tearing hunger matching their torn garments. Rags and raggedy garments are not suitable costume: they do not make someone particularly special, beautiful, desirable or sexy-appealing. Yet in Greek texts, rags or tattered garments have a peculiar relationship with women. I shall try to highlight this quite astonishing association, concentrating on theatrical costumes and inscriptions. The vocabulary of rags and tatters will be studied in Aristophanes, Euripides and epigraphy: firstly to understand the relationship between women's garments and theatrical costumes and then the relationship between rags and political ideology.

ON THE VOCABULARY OF *RHAKOS*

From epic onwards, the generic term for rags, tattered shabby or torn garments, is *rhakos* – usually associated with beggars' outfits.[1] Other words also convey similar ideas: Aristophanes (*Ach.* 410–79) provides good examples of this vocabulary. Tired of the war, Dikaiopolis decides to sign a private peace with the enemy (130–2), provoking the wrath of his fellow demesmen (280 ff.). He therefore needs to give a convincing speech to justify his political position, and seeks Euripides' help, looking for "the rags of an ancient drama" (415). Euripides is at home composing, wearing rags himself (*ta rhaki' ek tragoidia echeis*, 412): he has formed the habit of creating wretched, beggary kings (Ar. *Ra.* 842) and therefore has too great a choice of rags. (Between 445 BC and 425 BC, when this play was produced, Euripides had written a great number of tragedies dealing with unfortunate kings). Dikaiopolis can not remember the name of the character or tragedy he is looking for, so Euripides, like a salesman in the agora, describes his merchandise. He offers Oineus' or Phoenix's rags (*truché*, 418–22), Philoctetes' shred of raiment (*lakidas peplon*, 423–4), Bellerophon's loathy gabardine (*spargana*, 431; *duspiné pelomata*, 426–7), Telephos' swaddling clothes (*rhakomata*, 433–

4), and finally Thyestes' and Ino's rags (*rhakea*, 433–4).²

Although all the dramas mentioned above are lost, Aristophanes seems to be parodying the very vocabulary and elocution employed by Euripides in creating and describing his tragic characters and their theatrical costumes, as in *Telephos*.³ Other tragic poets also employ such terms, but for Euripides they seem essential to the creation of the pathetic.⁴ For the sake of humour, Aristophanes recreates the atmosphere of Euripidean drama by using neologisms as *rhakoma*⁵ or diminutives as *rhakion*, in order to show his poetry bouncing between high and low speech.

Scholars face a linguistic difficulty in dealing with these terms: should they be understood as passive or active? Here, and perhaps in Euripides also, they are presented as the results of a life of illness, dispossession, abandonment and wandering: matching the inner sorrow of their wearers. In fact, Telephos excepted, these characters "are all victims of an implacable fate" (Aélion 1983, 163). But, in their phonetic structure, *rhakos*, *truché*, *lakis*, *rhakoma*, and *sparganon* are onomatopoeic of decaying fabrics: their liquids and gutturals mimic the sound of tearing in the interrupted action of decay.

As well as examples of vocabulary, this passage also provides their context, but it is somewhat more difficult to unravel. Why does Aristophanes present Euripides as the inventor of a new tragic type, the king in rags (*Ra*. 842)? The beggar-king, Odysseus, was created by Homer, while Aeschylus brought Xerxes to the stage in rags (*Pers*. 834–6): symbolising his failure at Salamis, since he was hardly completely destitute. Yet Aristophanes seems to be stressing the real novelty in Euripides' theatre, more striking because tragic costumes had become particularly lavish and ornate.⁶ Lacking textual or iconographical confirmation, we should not assume that all Euripides' kings were in rags, but nor can we consider Aristophanes' lines purely exaggeration, misinterpretation of Euripides' tragedy, or a comic accumulation of names of tragic characters for the sake of laughter.⁷ No one knew Euripides, perhaps no one will ever know Euripides, better than Aristophanes.⁸ These characters may have worn different costumes whose common point was nevertheless their shabbiness. Such rags were undoubtedly associated with ritual lament, with mourning for a loved one and for oneself: Euripides' paradigm was a female one, first brought to the stage by Aeschylus in *Choephoroi* but developed by Euripides into a 'poetic of sorrow.' This brings us to Euripides' treatment of women's rags and tattered garments.

WOMEN'S TRAGIC RAGS

Scholars prefer to study the kings' rags, largely ignoring Ino's *rhakea*. Athenians knew Ino's story well – Aeschylus and Sophocles had written on this theme – but only a few fragments of Euripides' *Ino* are extant, so we rely on Hygin, *Fable* 4. Ino was the wife of Athamas, king of Thessaly, and mother of his two sons. Delayed in her return from Parnassos, Athamas thinks her dead, and marries Themisto, giving her two sons. Discovering Ino alive, he makes her nurse for the four children. Themisto, knowing of Ino's existence, but not her role, and fearing for her own position, decides to kill her rival's sons, sharing her plans with the nurse. Ino betrays Themisto into killing her own sons and therefore committing suicide. Despite Ino's regrets (she probably begged Athamas' pardon, Ar. *V.* 1413, Eur. Fr. 399 N2) her sad fate was written: struck with madness Athamas and Ino kill their own sons (Apoll. 3.4.3). Ino throws herself into the sea. The drama perhaps finished with a *deus ex-machina* announcing her transformation (Webster 1967, 98–101; Luppe 1984, 41–59).

Ino's sorrow was proverbial, but only Aristophanes alludes to her *rhakea*.[9] As an eternal bacchant, wandering exiled and dispossessed from town to town, Ino's once-bright tragic costume would surely be shabby as her pitiful condition. Ino may have appeared on-stage only as the nurse, her wandering in the prologue, but her costume would still be tattered or shabby (slaves and servants wear and sleep in rags)[10] expressing her pathetic condition to underline the disorder in Athamas' house. Euripides would have worked on the pattern of the wrecked *oikos* as in *Medea* and *Herakles*. The ageing Ino was abased, deprived of her most important titles: wife and mother. Trapped, Ino, step by step, joins the list of Euripides' trademark wicked, unhappy women.

As a servant, Ino probably wore a shabby garment, although women seldom wear rags in theatre, even if they often evoke them.[11] Tragic women could be exuberantly dolled up (Clytemnestra, A. *Ag.* 855 ff., celebrating her husband's return, Hermione's golden diadem and shimmering, diaphanous garments, Eur. *Andr.* 147–53), but also wore mourner's dress, changing clothes between the first and second part of the play, like Atossa or Helen.[12] These are not precisely rags. Even Hecuba, the sorrowful mother in Euripidean drama only stresses that she will soon be wearing rags (*Tr.* 497).

We must be cautious when facing dramatic texts, but need not think that poets only describe "something because it cannot be seen" (Pickard-Cambridge 1988, 179). When tragic characters perform funeral ritual for their loved ones, we can imagine the actors letting their veils fall or tearing them. Such violent gestures were not only spectacular, but imitated actual ritual lament. On stage, these gestures were absolutely necessary to match the *katastrophé*. Text and choreography help spectators to reach the empathy necessary for the final *katharsis*, joining the lament: tragedy, the poetics of sorrow, gave the opportunity to shed public tears without shame (Di Benedetto 1971, 223–38; Segal 1995).

Garments were torn on-stage, but perhaps could only assume the status of rags by continuous wearing. In this sense, Iocasta is not yet a ragged-queen like Telephos, having just begun the process of lamenting; her garments just beginning to decay. Electra seems the only woman really in rags in extant Euripidean tragedies. From the start, she calls attention to her dress: rags that go with her filthy hair. Superficially, this expresses her social condition, but on a deeper level, it calls divine attention to her situation, to the perversity of her wicked mother, which compels Electra's social condition as a witness. Above all, Electra's *truché* is the memory of her father's murder, the decaying *oikos* of the Atreides. Like Demeter in mourning, Electra does not change clothes, or wash.[13] "Her father's daughter" (*El.* 1103–4), she does not want to ease her pain or forget vengeance to come, because she is also a kind of Erinys (Loraux 1999, 54). As such, she is associated with Penia (the only woman certainly wearing rags in Aristophanes) described as a tragic Erinys (*Pl.* 423–4). Like Electra, Penia is shabby and filthy, her condition persistent, her costume the memory of her *geras*. Electra presents herself as a continuous mourner, her torn outfits representing not only a passage from life to death, but a journey from death to death, revenge being her only possible path back to life. Ino is not an Electra, but, like Iocasta, might have torn her garments when faced with her own misfortune, coming back on-stage in mourning, her shabby servile garments torn in madness or grief. In this sense she is a queen in rags, giving a basis for the Aristophanic joke: however, it must also have a basis in reality, so it is useful to consider the association of *rhakos* with women in daily life.

OLD GARMENTS, MENSTRUAL CLOTHES OR RAGS?

Rhakos is readily used for daily life: associated with women, it seems the antithesis of feminine 'coquetterie'. Analysis of the fourth century BC Attic inventories of Artemis Brauronia (*IG* II² 1514–1531, cf. Demeter and Koré, Tanagra, third century BC: Michel 832; Reinach *REG*, 1899, and Hera, Samos: Schwyser 462 B) shows many clothes dedicated by women clearly designated *rhakos*. Remembering, perhaps, Hecuba's choice of the most beautiful, most magnificent, garment to placate Athena's wrath, (*Il.* 6.286ff.), scholars are reluctant to admit that *rhakos* in these texts means tattered garments or simply rags. Mommsen (1899, 353 ff.), suggests that *rhakos* in the Brauron inventories stands for a menstrual cloth offered to Artemis on first menstruation. Linders criticises this interpretation – based on magical agrarian ritual (*Geop.* 1.14.2) – pointing out that this is "nowhere attested in ancient sources" (1972, 58). Brulé accepts it, regarding such offerings to Artemis as unsurprising since the most polluted is also the most holy (1987, 233–236). He adduces other offerings associated with blood (1987, 235), but cannot produce a text associating menses with offerings to the gods. Purity of menstrual contamination became a condition for entering a temple only in later periods (Parker 1990, 101–2; Mills 1984, 255–65).

Rhakos is often used in medical texts, sometimes in association with women. From the fifth century it is a metaphor for decaying flesh (A. *Pr.* 1023), and becomes almost a technical term in medical texts, for coverings of flesh or organs (Sor. 2.40). In poetic and medical texts *rhakos* is a bandage used to protect infectious wounds, (S. *Phil.* 39, 274; Hp. *Morb.* 2.36; *Peri Syriggon* 9.1) or an envelope used to protect medicinal mixtures (linked to menstruation, *Peri Syriggon* 10.1 *Peri Epikyesios* 42). *Rhakos* can also be a sort of tampon made with wool or linen (*Peri Epikyesios* 33). Illness at menarche was medically regarded as treatable through defloration and pregnancy, being a physiological matter dependent on the passage from *parthenos* to *gyné* (*Peri Epikyesios* 33; King 1983, 109–27; 1994, 108; Brulé 1987, 235). Doctors criticised the related custom of offering the virgin's most splendid garments to Artemis (*Peri Parthenion* 1.13). Nevertheless, women continued dedicating such garments (*polutelestata tôn himatiôn*, see Cleland, this volume) to their patroness; but these need not be associated with *rhakea* or menstrual cloth. Although menstruation is understood in medical texts as a physical purgation, *katharsis* (*Peri Diaites* A.30.1, 34.1) we cannot be sure that menstrual blood is *katharos*, pure, in the religious sense. Women may just as well have dedicated their garments purified of the *miasma* of blood by washing (*Il.* 6.267; Ginouvès 1962, 234–428). Indeed, Brulé has recently abandoned his hypothesis (1990, 74–76).

Returning to the Inventories, Linders argues that, if Mommsen is right, the earliest inscriptions (343 BC, *IG* II² 1525) ought to contain impressive numbers of *rhakea*. In fact, *rhakos* is more frequently used in the later inscriptions, and is also added in the annual updates.[14] The lapse between *IG* II² 1525 and 1524 is only one year, and Brulé argues that garments in good shape would not become raggedy so quickly (1987, 234). However, garments soiled with blood would be more attractive for moths and mice.[15]

Linders points out that in *IG* II² 1524 "items are sometimes more fully described" (1972, 58). The Athenian officials were perhaps more attentive in 342 than in 343, not contenting themselves with reiterating previous descriptions, but stressing the ageing gifts which may have been in bad shape long before. Linders regards 'tattered' as the only possible reading for *rhakos* in these inscriptions, and argues that women dedicated to their goddesses new, old, unfinished and even defective garments, as thanksgiving gifts (mostly for passing from childhood to adolescence, weddings, and childbirth, *AP*.6.201–2 [Artemis] 6.200 [Eileithyia]).[16] Yet 'used' or 'old' are not precise synonyms of 'raggedy.'

One might attempt to relate these *rhakea* to the social condition of their donors, but these capricious inventories keep their secrets. Some dedicants are anonymous (offerings *anepigraphos, agraphos*).[17] In other entries, women's names appear without other designation: only a few have their place of residence, or their husbands or fathers (Linders 1972, 7–8, n.5; Brulé 1987, 226). Some dedicants can be associated with the Athenian elite.[18] But the great majority of dedicants remain a mystery.

The situation seems clearer at Tanagra, where, around 250 BC, "the 'bourgeoises' of Tanagra" (Reinach 1899, 68) dedicated garments to Demeter and Kore on the construction of a new temple (Reinach 1899, 53–115; Migeotte 1992, 75–81). As both the dedicants' names and those of their husbands or fathers are indicated in the subscription list, they were probably the local elite. In fact, some names appear in both subscription and dedication lists, like Philokko, whose offering is the only one defined as *rhakos* (*Philokkô tarantinon rhakinon*). Reinach interprets this as worn out, tattered, comparing it to the Samian inventory, and with the Brauronian inscriptions (1899, 97). Yet this inventory is not a revision of the ancient properties, but a new list, under a new archon, following that of the previous year.

As *rhakana* is the name of a later garment (*Edict.Diocl.* 7.60, 22.4) *rhakinon* could be a noun designing a sort of feminine outfit, an *epiblema* or a veil made of a diaphanous material.[19] *tarantinon* would then be an adjective form stressing the origin of the fabric. However, the Attic inscriptions use *rhakos* as an adjective, and, grammatically speaking, as an apposition to the entries. At Samos, *rhakinon* is an adjective form, associated with different types of garments like *halourgis* or *periblema* (Michel 832, 18, 21, 26). *tarantina*, in the inventories mentioned above, are often designated as *rhakos*, but other garments receive the same qualification (e.g. *IG* II² 1514.28, 38, 49, 67 etc.). We should consider it as an adjective derived from *rhakos* even if in other contexts it is a variant of *tribonion*,[20] and, with Linders, conclude that *rhakos* or *rhakinon* in these texts can only mean tattered, worn out, and, in the most advanced cases of decay, rags.

Women's garments were equally important valuables as tripods, basins, cattle and slaves: in pre-monetary society they played a fundamental role in commercial and friendly exchange.[21] In the fifth century, women could sell the products of spinning or weaving (Ar. *Ra.* 1346–51), and salesmen ran a prosperous business trading old garments (Ar. *Pl.* 1063 and *scholia*). Garments are objects of exchange, setting in motion a particular kind of relationship satisfying both sides (donors-receivers; sellers-buyers). By dedicating garments in sanctuaries, women deprived themselves of their most valuable possessions.[22] It is possible that they were deliberately spoiled as complete consecrations.[23] Far from being irreverent, this would prevent their use, stressing the privileged relationship between goddess and dedicant. New, old or spoiled, the offering stood for the dedicant forever with the goddess.[24] Although such offerings were spontaneous (Pl. *Leg.* 909e; Burkert 1987, 44), they did not loose their exchange values. Women, by their offerings, aimed at obtaining the goddess' faithful, sweet protection in their future lives, as wives, as mothers. Fathers and husbands permitted the consecration of garments because, as mothers, or mothers to be, the dedicants were more valuable: they paid their share to the city (Ar. *Lys.* 651) giving birth to citizens, assuring the continuity of their *oikos*.

Philokko's shawl would eventually figure in another list of the old, useless, worthless (*palaios, palaios achreios, katakekommenos,* etc.) dedications to the goddesses, as in the Milesian inventory of Artemis Kithonia (Gunther 1988, 215–37, esp. 229–32): transferred to a deposit in the sanctuary, making room for the new ones. But new or old, bright or faded, these gifts still conserved the memory of generation after generation of piety.

But what about Ino? She was worshipped in many cities (Schachter 1986, 62; Apollod. 3.4.3; Paus. 3.26.1), but, although certain aspects of her cult can be associated with Artemis as *kourotrophoi*, she is not, in Greek texts, associated with female ritual, or female *rhakea*. Her cult at Thebes is linked to collective, citizen mourning: an opportunity for political reproach (Paus. 3.26.1; Plu. *De Sup.* 13). As the examination of rags or raggedy garments in Greek daily life and religion cannot fully explain Ino's *rhakea*, we must return to the theatre.

FROM TATTERED CLOAKS TO MASKS

In Aeschylus, the Danaids, in their helplessness, lacerate their Sidonian veils (*Supp.* 119–21) and their cheeks (69–70), destroying the beauty that incites love. These lines allude to veils but also to masks, the linen mask that would be furrowed by their nails. The *Choephoroi* (22–31) and other women in tragedy also call attention to their masks, *prosopa*, washed or dyed with tears, bloodied, furrowed by sorrow as in funeral lament.[25] Far from appealing to the imagination, tragic masks were realistic, marked with paint indicating wounds, or other peculiarities of the characters (Poll. 4.141; Pickard-Cambridge 1988, 185). Gestures accompanied words, making the action clear for audience members far from the stage. Such references to the mask can be understood in relation to conflict between oral and written in the fifth century (Green 1994, 22).

Does Aristophanes allude to Ino's *prosopon*? This hypothesis is reinforced by *Vespae* 1412–1414. Threatened with trial, Philokleon addresses the woman he has wronged and her witness this insulting remark: "And you Chaerephon, will testify for her, like pale Ino hanging at Euripides feet". Here Aristophanes makes a meta-theatrical joke. First of all, he clearly alludes to Euripides' *Ino* (perhaps to a scene in which she begged her husband's pardon before the *katastrophé*), criticising Euripides' 'madness' regarding Ino's story – he was probably working on his *Phrixos A* and *B* (Webster 1967, 131). Aristophanes is also mocking Chaerephon, Socrates' friend (*Nu*. 144, 1465), who he associates with death as a 'child of Night' (*Ra*. 486a) and a bat (*Av*. 296; Eup. Fr.129). This yellowish-face or deathly complexion were easily compared with Ino's. In Philokleon's tirade Aristophanes calls attention to masks, particularly Chaerophon's. Perhaps Chaerephon wore a portrait mask (Stone 1980, 37). Repetition of his name might also stress the ridiculous situation of the wronged woman, whose hope was put into an almost womanish man, as pale as Ino.

The scholiast (Ar. *V*. 1413) relays that Euripides represented Ino pale with pain. Taillardat (1965, 214) takes for granted both these plays allude to Ino's mask and suggests that she wore the mask *katakomos ochra*, "pale with long black hair, a vision of pain".[26] Ino might have worn *mesokouros ochra*, differing only slightly with shorter hair: as a servant she could also wear the *oiketikon mesokouron*, half-shorn, having moderately long hair, partly grey, a low *onkos* and pale complexion (*leuke*, *parochros*). Finally, she might have changed masks. I agree, however, that at *V*. 1413 Aristophanes is alluding to Ino's mask.

How can Ino's *rhakea* (*Ach*. 434) be a *prosopon*, mask? *Prosopon*, mask, derives from *prosopon*, face (Calame 1986a, 85–100; Frontisi-Ducroux 1995, 39–63) because the mask covers the face like a veil, transforming it: their drawings make "a face in fine linen" or "a veiled face" (Pl.Com. Fr.151 K–A; Suida s.v *thespies*, Pickard-Cambridge 1966, 69, 79; 1988, 179). *Rhakos* recalls the very fabrication of masks: wrinkled linen pieces were glued together.[27] Aristophanic comedy gives a good example of the shift of meaning from *rhakos* to *prosopon*. Aristophanes observes that old women apply a heavy coat of lead or of a pink-red unguent on their faces, looking for a 'youthful bath'. This thick make-up fails: instead of virginal peachlike skin, they resemble funeral lekythoi or "a vampire belched from hell and clothed with blood and festering blisters" (Ar. *Ec*. 1056–1057; Konstan & Dillon 1981, 371–94; Said 1979, 33–69; Henderson 1987, 105–29). These comic masks resemble the tragic ones which Aristophanes designates *mormolukeion* because they provoke nightmares. Calling attention to the masks moistened with white lead, colored sometimes with pink, in which wrinkles are painted with dark colors (thus comparable with the white funeral lekythoi) Aristophanes is also showing these ladies as rags: wrinkled masks perfectly match wrinkled faces (*Ec*. 884, 925; Taillardat 1965, 53). In *Plutus*, the association between *prosopon* and *rhakos* is clearer. A young pimp, looking at his old mistress affirms: "What countless wrinkles (*rhutidôn*) does her face (*prosopôi*) contain!" And Chremylus: "But if her white-lead paint were washed away, too plain, you'd see the tatters [or rags] on her face" (1051). Since linen, wrinkles and mask match perfectly, the old hag does not need a mask, she has her face. This tasty metaphor later becomes a *topos* and even a proverb (*AP* 9.242; Zen. 6.42; Diogenian 8.70).

So Ino's *rhakea* can be associated with her tattered cloak, perhaps with her ritual lament (*rhakea* takes this meaning in theatre, Posidipp. 27.11; Plu. 2.789d) but most of all with her mask in Euripidean tragedy. As Aristophanes loves having fun, *Ach*. 474

may also be a wink to *Ino*'s final scene: the pale heroine becomes the White Goddess, Leucothea, 'the runner of the white foam', receiving a veil, a *geras*, a saviour *rhakea* for seamen in danger.

RHAKOS: THEATRICAL TERM OR THEATRICAL SLANG

This is a meta-theatrical joke: *rhakos* can be understood as a technical term encompassing all the paraphernalia needed to make a good show. As Aristophanes is playing with words, it might be possible that *rhakos* stands for text, metonymically a scroll of ancient tragedy: Telephos' rags become Euripides' *Telephos*; *rhakos* can be understood as a fragment of this drama. Such a literary joke could provoke laughter, but these lines are the most comic scene before the *parabasis*. Then, the climax of laughter comes with the confrontation between the happy farmer Dikaiopolis and the unhappy warrior Lamakos, returning from war, all wounded, newly lame, an almost beggary general. The play on theatrical costumes is indispensable. In fact, in this reunion scene, laughter is provoked by the collision between tragedy and comedy. Aristophanes provokes a great comic moment, making Dikaiopolis wear over his shabby cloak, padding and comic phallus, the tragic rags – garments and mask (Poll. 4.136; Pickard-Cambridge 1988, 194) – of Telephos or another beggar-king.

This is an opportunity for Aristophanes to introduce his ideas about theatrical *mimesis* summarised by Agathon in the *Thesmophoriazusae* (148–52): "I choose my dress to suit my poesy".[28] Euripides is in rags, being by nature a *ptochos*, thanks to his mother.[29] Composing legs akimbo, he creates raggedy characters and raggedy poetry whose reflections are these very lines. Aristophanes is not only interested in poetic scrolls or in tragic garments, however: he wants to show the important role of accessories in Euripidean drama and theatre in general. He presents Euripides as a *skeuopoios* from whom Dikaiopolis begs "what pertains to these (rags)": the Mysian cap (*pilidion Musion*, 439), beggar's staff (*ptochikou bakteriou*, 448), little basket (*spuridion*, 453), little tankard (*kotuliskion*, 459) with a broken rim, a little pitcher plugged with sponge (*chutridion*, 463), some withered leaves (*phulleia*, 469), all in bad shape. These items, while not precisely necessary, are supposed to increase the *pathos* provoked in Athenian spectators (Sousa e Silvia 1987, 120–1). Thus Euripides affirms: 'you are taking the whole tragedy' and 'my plays are disappearing'. These rags unveil Euripides' tragedy: "take away the rags and other props, and you have, quite literally, taken away his tragedies" (Reckford 1987, 176, 194). Yet Dikaiopolis also impersonates an actor: borrowing garments, accessories, the mask of Telephos and "having drunk all Euripides" (*Ach.* 484), he is able to win over his reluctant audience. Having spoiled the tragic Telephos, he can play the comic hero with joy.

If *rhakos* was not a technical theatrical term for *skeuarion*, it was certainly a theatrical slang for it. Rags or raggedy garments harked back to ancient times when dramatic shows were improvised, when poets, mostly comic, went from town to town showing their art, being *didaskaloi, skeuopoioi, prosopopoioi* (Poll. 4.115). Comic poets allude to the easiness of ancient times when costumes were improvised, when actors and chorus wore what was at hand, bedding or curtains. Later, *choregoi* would imitate this by dressing chorus and actors the same way, but such costumes were only 'trademarks' of stinginess. In the last quarter of the fifth century, costumes were magnificent: *choregoi* competed in lavishness to win the dramatic *agôn* and after the Dionysia were covered in *rhakos*. Bright, ornate or shabby, cloaks, accessories or masks, Aristophanes jokes with rags because they are the quintessence of theatre, a means to enter in the marvelous land of the mind, the Dionysiac land of otherness.

THEATRICAL RAGS AND THE RAGGEDY CITY

We must go further than parody and meta-theatrical reflection with Aristophanes' rags. Dikaiopolis/Telephos shows Athenian politics understood from the perspective of dramatic representation, as only a show (*V.* 560, 578). Decisions are not the result of popular deliberation because there is no longer deliberation in an Ekklesia dominated by demagogues: dreaming of the Great King's wealth instead of the salvation of the city-state. If decisions are the result of a masquerade, why not try the theatrical *katharsis*?[30] To deliver a speech condemning Athenian citizens, Dikaiopolis becomes a beggar, an outcast, more foreign than a foreigner, denouncing the disorder in the city, the tearing of the citizen body. Wearing Telephos' rags (*Ach.* 429), Dikaiopolis presents himself as the city's saviour, as Telephos saved the Achean army. As a ragged man, he apparently renounces his city in order to reconstruct it.

Like Euripides, Aristophanes created a many raggedy characters. They cannot all be explained as literary parodies, lampoons on Euripides, or a well-developed comic *topos* (*Pax.* 739–40). Ehrenberg argues that the small number of beggars in Athens was explained by the lack of charity (1961, 245): why then are they so important in Aristophanes' last plays? Aristophanes makes a distinction between beggars and wretches: wretches work hard and put something aside for bad days; beggars are completely dispossessed (*Pl.* 552–4). At Athens, the so-called poor were reduced to a beggary state, having nowhere to live, no *himation* but rags (*Pl.* 535–47): a good portrait of the Athenian situation around 388 BC.

In fact, after defeat in the Peloponnesian War and loss of the Empire, Athens was at pains to have an international role and to find a way of life, bouncing between incompetent politicians, sycophants and citizens lacking interest in community life. The gap between rich and poor was enlarged, and the tension between them high (David 1984, 14). In the early fourth century, pauperization and necessity were constantly in the mouths of Athenians: it is unsurprising that *rhakos* becomes the metaphor of the poverty that touches every aspect of life in the city. Only sycophants and politicians can afford *himatia*: the raggedy citizen body is as shabby and dirty as Penia and Plutus. But this reality was only the radicalisation of a situation that had existed since the Peloponnesian War, or at least, a comic radicalisation that suited Aristophanes well.

Depicting his Athens, Aristophanes dresses his people in rags: his poets, philosophers, slaves and *thetai*, wear shabby garments. Geddes regards changing clothes in the fifth century as related to changing social structure, life style and values (1987, 307–331). Men put away the long Ionian *chitôn* for a large woolen cloak, the *himation*, worn over a short *chitôn*. Although, this change mostly concerned the upper-classes, clothes are a form of rhetoric (Geddes 1987, 323; Harlow, this volume). And this Athenian discourse does not precisely tell the truth. Although the elite chose democratic standardisation in garments, they could still afford long garments. Ordinary people dressed as they always had, in *tribones* or *exomides*, because long garments were useless for hard work and too expensive (Ar. *V.* 444; *Lys.* 662).

Feigning to imitate their compatriots, wealthy people really mimic the austerity of the Spartan way of life, confirming their aristocratic ideology.[31] Philosophers also choose this path, to show themselves above the baseness of the world, self-disciplined, immune to temptations or luxury.[32] But Aristophanes spoils their mimesis, transforming Socrates into a *lopodutès*, a robber of clothes.[33] The wealthy are only giving themselves a democratic disguise: avoiding liturgies or taxes, giving up their responsibilities as citizens, the raggedy garments they wear stress the decay of the civic body. Aristophanes criticises their lack of patriotism, not only as a new *mise en scene* of the proverb 'clothes maketh the man', but also showing citizens acting, but not living, politically. Euripides is to blame.[34]

But choregy and trierarchy are not the same. Aristophanes regrets cheap choruses, but Dionysos can stand rags provided that poets are brilliant, able to impassion and educate their fellow citizens. Choruses were accustomed to dress in rags, sometimes rags were just right: initiates, or the dead, do not wear brilliant clothes but the raggedy garments of the festival or the decay of death.[35] The real difficulty is the city unable to restore herself, wealthy people acting as demagogues, stealing from the people and giving in exchange only poor *perizoma* to cover their bodies (Ar. *Pax.* 686–87). Sad is precisely when the 'coquette' "Athens wreathed with violets" becomes a pale and filthy Erinys.[36]

Using rags, firstly as a realistic expression of poverty, Aristophanes transforms Athens, or *Demos*, into a shabby, raggedy, politically destitute city. There is no difference between the Athens of *Ecclesiazusae* and *Plutus*, and the Athens of the first comedies, because Athens' problem is always politics. People are ragged because they abandon their authority: giving up their *dynamis*, their hegemony, their *kurion*, the Athenian people destroy themselves step by step. Their economic situation, their beggary position is only the result of this. Aristophanes does not pity poverty or rags, because for him they are results of a perversion of the citizens' ability to make their own decisions. Thus *Ecclesiazusae* and *Plutus* are not examples of Middle or New comedies. By his rags, Aristophanes pledges for a new conception of political life in which blindness, selfishness and surface appearance give place to real participation. In *Ecclesiazusae*, women steal their husband's garments in order to do good politics. In *Plutus*, every good citizen will receive a new garment, through the *homonoia* of the consciousness of the real place everyone has in the city: not linked with wealth but with disposition of mind. Aristophanes proposes in *Lysistrata* (574–586) to transform the political and social life of Athens by weaving her a new garment that must be fashioned from the lives, minds and strength of every Athenian, every metic, every ally. Being at the same time fabric, garment and weavers, Athenians become *demiourgoi* of a new thread, their word.

If Aristophanic theatre is full of rags, the poet does not use them only as an easy joke to make unthinking people laugh. Using rags, *rhakos* as costumes or masks, Aristophanes affirms his belief in poetry: that comedy can transform the raggedy fabric of reality into a shimmering *mimesis* that invites the whole the city to act as a unified body, perhaps because laughter is the most marvelous rag of the mind.

ACKNOWLEDGEMENTS

I am indebted to Lloyd Llewellyn Jones and Mary Harlow for inviting me to the excellent *Clothed Body* Conference. I also thank Lloyd Llewellyn-Jones for his generous advice, criticism and encouragement.

NOTES

1 Hom. *Od*. 6.178; 13.434; 14.342, 349, 512; 18.67, 74; 19.507. See also, *laiphos*, *Od*. 13.399; 20.206; *rhogaleos*: *Il*. 2.417; *Od*. 13.435; 17.198.
2 Also *berberion* for shabby garment, Anacr. 21.3.
3 Fr. 697 N 2; Enn. 341: *Regnum reliqui saeptus mendici stola.*
4 *Rhakos*: Hdt. 7.76; S. *Phil*. 39, 247; *truchos*: S. Fr. 777 N2; *lakis*: Alc. 18.8; A. *Pers*. 125, 834–35; *Supp*. 131, 905.
5 This term is a neologism that Aristophanes coined on *rhakos*: it is a joke on *peploma,* a tragic variant of *peplos*. Aristophanes is ridiculing Euripides' love for nouns in -*ma*. See Sousa Silva 1987, 122.
6 Taplin 1995, 13–14. These rags are even more astonishing if Euripides – as Geddes suggests (1987, 314) – "brought more honour to his performance" (by being even more conspicuously wasteful than his rivals).
7 Menelaus (Eur. *Hel*. 415–7; 421) victim of a shipwreck wears rags on stage. King (1932, 61–2) considers that Oedipus Coloneus is also an "imitation" of Euripides' raggedy kings.
8 Cratinos understood perfectly when he describes Aristophanes parodying Euripides as *euripidaristophanizon* (Fr. 342 K.–A. = Schol. Areth. [B] Plat. *Apol*. p. 19, p. 421 Gr.).
9 Suidas: *Inous achê.*
10 Eur. *Tr*. 496–97. In fact, servants or slaves could wear animal skins: Ar. *Lys*.1155–6, alludes to the *katonakê*. Pollux affirms that the *oiketikon graidion,* the old slave woman in tragedy, wears a lamb's-wool cap, and that the young one was called *diphtheritis,* leather-clad.
11 Eur. *El*. 501 (on Electra, 185); *Hec*. 240, 416; *Tr*. 97; A. *Supp*. 131, 903; *Ch*. 28. Pollux (4.117) is referring to a reality of the fifth century BC that he knew only from ancient books on dramaturgy. Hellenistic theatre perhaps associated rags only with Philoctetes and Telephos.
12 A. *Pers*. 607ff; E. *Hel*. 1186–92. Commenting on tragic costumes, Pollux affirms that women wear mostly royal garments of purple (4.118, A. *Pers*. 607–8) unless in mourning when they wear dark robes and coverlets of blue or green (A. *Ch*. 10–11).
13 See Eur. *El*. 184–5; *h.Cer*. 40–50. On the wrath of Electra and her forever lamenting, see Loraux 1999, 53–57. Euripides makes time stop: Electra seems to wear the same outfit she wore when her father died, Orestes is wearing the garment she wove when he was only a little baby. For a parody, Ar. *Nu*. 534–536.
14 Linders 1972, 59: 1524.130, 140 add *rhakos* to 1525.5, 13. See also 1524.132, 134, 141–3, 148 etc. Cleland, this volume; Guarducci 1969, 248.
15 *Batrachomyomachia* 179–86.
16 Eur. *IT*. 1466–7; See also Tanagra (Reinach 1899) line 24–5, in which Hiaron consecrates a jewel in Damo's name.
17 *Anepigraphos*: IG II² 1514.38–39; 1517.132; 1518.83; *agraphos*: IG II² 1514.39, 58–59; 1429.14. On these questions see Linders 1972, 11–5, 61 and Brulé 1987, 226.
18 1523.8: trierarch's wife 334/33 BC; 1524.202–204: general's daughter 325 BC; 1523.19: famous fourth

century politician's wife: Brulé 1987, 237; Guiarducci 1969, 250–55.
19 s.v. Liddel, Scott & Jones. (LSJ) Athenaeus 622b. See also Suidas, s.v. *tarantinidion*
20 Scholia *ad Ranae*, 406 : *rhakos de, hoi men to tribonion* [...] and Suidas, s.v. *rhakos, to tribonion*.
21 Robson, this volume. *Il.* 6.228–96; *Od.* 13.217–8, 15.99–105, 125–9; E. *Andr.* 147–53; *Med.* 784–6.
22 On 'new' see Cleland, this volume. If we accept, following Plu. *Sol.* 20.4, that Athenian women received a maximum of three garments as dowry, their offerings were in a way a great sacrifice. For other Solonian regulations related to garments, see Plu. *Sol.* 21.4 and Mills' commentaries on these topics (1984, 263).
23 Burkert's consideration of 'anxiety of success' and trickery aspects: "what shall be saved is so much more valuable than what is given away or destroyed. At the same time giving, in this paradigm of distribution, of handing on to partners, implies forms of mutual acquaintance" (1987, 47, 43–50).
24 We could say also, made one with the goddess as the offerings are put around the statue: 1514.22–3 = 1515.14–15, 1516.2; *AP.* 6.133; 6270 (to Eileithyia) and Linders 1972, 11–12, 14–15, 62–63; on the wall, 1514.23–24 Linders 1972, 12, *AP.* 6. 202, and Bald Romano 1988, 131.
25 Hecuba (*Tr.* 239–41 see also *Rh.* 710) recalls Odysseus' bloodied, pitiful *prosopon* when as a beggar-spy, covered in rags, he had come to Troy. Frontisi-Ducroux, 1987, 83–92.
26 Poll.4, 140; Benabo Bréa 1998, 71. In Ar. *Pl* .422–423, Poverty is presented as *ochra*; looking like a Erinys, a parody of the tragic masks – probably the *katakomos ochra*.
27 Scholia *ad Ranae*, 406 and Suidas, s.v. *rhakos. rhakos de, hoi men to tribonion, hoi de to prosopeiion hoti rhakesi katekollato*.
28 In a scene that is an auto-parody echoing again Euripides' *Telephos*. See Robson, this volume.
29 Vegetable seller: *Ach.* 479; *Th.* 387; *Ra.* 840; Scholia *ad Ach.* 426.
30 *Ach.* 117–22: Dikaiopolis recognises his fellows citizens Clisthenes and Straton in the Kings' eunuchs that they impersonate.
31 Pl.Com. Fr.124 (Kock); Plu. *Ag.* 14.2; *Phoc.* 4.2; Ael.*VH.* 9.34.
32 Pl. *Smp.* 219b, *Prt.* 335d, X. *Mem.* 1.6.2.
33 In fact, Aristophanes suggests that Socrates will keep Strepisiades himation for himself or one of his students (*Nu.* 497 ff.). Aristophanes evokes also Orestes, a famous *lopodutès* in Athens, see Ar. *Ach.*1166, *Av.* 497, 712, 1491. For thieves, see Arist. *Ath.* 52.1 and Harrisson 1968, II, 17 ff.; Gernet 1968, 303–4; Cantarella 1991, 41–6.
34 The success of a *choregos* was associated to his expenses, see Plu. *Nic.* 3.2–3; Arist. *Eth.Nic.* 1123a20. In *Ra.* 842, Aristophanes criticises again the Euripidean poetry concerned with *ptochoi*, and raggedy kings against which he opposes Aeschylus' poetry founded in dignified characters wearing dignified *himatia*.
35 See Dover 1994, 55–69.
36 Ar. *Lys.* 574–586

Chapter 8

The Semiosis of Description: Some reflections on fabric and colour in the Brauron Inventories

Liza Cleland

This paper was originally delivered as a technical outline of a methodological approach to the inventories of Artemis at Brauron as evidence for clothing.[1] At the time, this research was in progress, and incomplete: my original aim was to obtain reactions to my methodology, and feedback about its wider utility in clothing research, beyond its importance for investigating colour in Greek clothing. The size and scope of this chapter are such that it would be inappropriate to go into technical or theoretical detail (and I thank my fellow conference members for their forbearance with my youthful enthusiasm in originally doing so).[2] Instead, what I want to do is to discuss some of the specific and limited information I have obtained from this methodological approach, suggesting future directions for expansion.

The clothing sections of the Brauron Inventories are undoubtedly among the central texts for the study of Greek clothing, because of their sheer size, breadth, and unusual exclusivity.[3] They are almost universally familiar to scholars of Greek dress, gender and religion, and ubiquitously referenced. However, they are, in many ways, problematic: in their list format, and certainly in their proportion of *hapax legomena*. They are also epigraphically complex.[4] These factors are surely the major contributors to the continued lack of a complete translation, which limits their accessibility.[5] In short, this body of evidence is almost irresistibly tempting, since it details the actual garments of fourth century Athenians (so fully, yet obliquely, referenced in literature and art) but, at the same time, is overwhelming in its complexity, and its abbreviated and unusual Greek.

As such, *IG* II² 1514–30 are often mentioned, or used to support conclusions derived from other sources, rather than exclusively studied in depth as evidence for clothing. Yet there is no better source for the late Classical period. Certainly, they were unavoidably integral to my research, which required comparative evidence to substantiate the unusually detailed perspectives on colour in clothing provided by Attic drama and polychrome lekythoi.

A novice approaching the Brauron Inventories faces two major hurdles. In the list form, the absence of even the most basic grammatical or syntactical, never mind literary, context, makes meanings – even of terms which are relatively common in wider literature – questionable. Also, there are clearly areas of extensive, but not exact, duplication, increasing the volume of text, and making even the most basic statistical analysis impossible. Linders' definitive study notes duplication only incidentally, concentrating on the epigraphical context of the fragments, and being concerned with reconstructing the original stelae. It nevertheless makes clear in passing that these are the remains of successive iterations of a catalogue.

The original status of these inscriptions as a catalogue of dedications is, of course, an integral and accepted part of their significance. A number of studies have regarded them as a transparent, though incomplete, window into the material reality of Greek clothing and dedication habits (Millar 1997; Foxhall & Stears 1999). However, it is from this perspective that the ubiquity of questionable or unique terms is most problematic. Viewing the catalogue as a simple record of items, we are unavoidably hampered by having no physical (and few literary) referents for its terms. Yet a catalogue is, by its nature, not simply a record of items: it also describes a collection.

Crucially, the function of describing items within a catalogue is generally not simply to record their physical existence, but rather to distinguish them *from one another*, and to order their significance. Almost all these dedications are accompanied by their dedicant's name, yet the complexity of the descriptions varies widely from item to item. There is no practical reason why each item's physical existence could not simply have been recorded by combining a single garment type term, the dedicant's name, and the year of dedication.[6] Indeed, forty of one hundred and eighty-five complete descriptions are single term.[7] However, of these, twenty-six focus on garment type, while seven detail pattern, six mark colour, and one indicates fabric, showing that even the simplest descriptions rely on ascription of significance and considerations of distinctiveness.[8] This is much more apparent given that the remaining descriptions use between two and six terms: superfluous in asserting the items' simple existence, but clearly regarded as necessary in distinguishing their relative significance.

While these inscriptions, as remnants of a catalogue, clearly served practical and administrative functions, they surely also had a social function; the external context of their significance. I have argued that these inscriptions are essentially the female analogue of inscribed lists of office-holders (Cleland 2003, 100). They record not only the completion of the "full cycle of rituals to produce an adult woman" (Cole 1998, 39) – in which Athenian women's service to the state took the form of bearing and raising children – but also their names, their possessions, and by implication their skills and status.[9] It is in this external context that the nature of the garments, as delineated by their complex descriptions, possesses meaning.

Regardless of the social meaning of describing garments in such detail, we are still confronted by the opacity of the texts, created by their (apparently very specific and technical) vocabulary, distinct from literary descriptions of clothing. However, the very complexity of this corpus means that it has the potential (unlike most other inscriptional evidence, which tends towards sparse clothing references; Cleland 2003, 232–76) to provide its own internal context. The use of internal context to illuminate texts has its own problems, not least the dangers of falling into circular reasoning, or of imposing anachronistic patterns during analysis. Nevertheless, close reading of the texts suggests that the descriptive terms can (without recourse to exact translation) be divided into a relatively small number of categories of exclusion. All the terms used in all the descriptions can be categorised as either: garment-type terms; specifications of person (child's, man's, woman's); pattern terms; colour terms; fabric terms; coloured pattern terms; or terms for other decorative features (*pasmatia*, decorative folds, etc.: Cleland 2003, 101–19, 123–32). These categories arise naturally from a combination of the internal taxonomy of the descriptions, and the wider taxonomy of Greek clothing: it is relatively simple to establish the general reference of terms, even when their precise meaning is obscure (Cleland 2003, 134–38).

Even such simple division (accomplished through tabulation) clarifies the relationships between the descriptions immensely, allowing them to be viewed both as individual entities, and as members of various groups. Given the absence of syntactical context in the texts as a whole, abstracting the descriptions in this way reduces confusion without altering semantic content. However, it also allows the descriptions to be analysed, overall and individually, as examples of a 'vestimentary code' (Barthes 1990, 4). Each of the simple categories of exclusion outlined above can also be seen as separate areas of meaningful descriptive variation: the meanings of individual terms contributed to by their membership of descriptive sets. In many cases, the impact of this is simple common sense, but it is also useful to consider Barthes' detailed study of variants, which outlines the practical operation of particular aspects of variation.[10]

A crucial aspect of such consideration is that "variants do not present themselves as simple objects of a nomenclature, even when sorted into classes of exclusions, but rather as *oppositions* having several terms" (Barthes 1990, 111). Even more fundamentally:

> it must be kept in mind that meaning is not born of a simple qualification (*long blouses*) but from an opposition between what is noted and what is not; even if the synchrony being studied mentions only one term, the implicit term upon which its own distinction depends must always be reestablished …: thus, though blouses are never short, their length is sometimes noted (*long* blouses), so it is necessary to reconstitute a significant opposition between *long* and [normal], even if this term is not explicitly stated" (Barthes 1990, 113).

In short, "the linguistic term for the actual apparel or material is action, equivalent to speech and therefore relatively devoid of meaning, …written apparel …is institution, equivalent to language, fully symbolized, culturally bound, and, therefore, laden with meaning" (Harris 1992).

In the limited space afforded by this chapter, I think it is more useful to present results, rather than delve into theories or mechanisms in the abstract. Therefore, I want to discuss two specific categories in detail: fabric and colour. These are good to work with, because clearly all garments have both fabric and colour, and we may therefore consider why these are, or are not, described, certain that in each case a choice was made.

Garments in the catalogue are described in terms of various aspects of fabric: its composition and quality; completion; finish; and age.[11] Fabric composition appears only once as the sole defining characteristic of a garment (1524B.131–2=1525.6, *sindonites* 'a garment made of fine cloth, linen' s.v. LSJ). Otherwise, *amorginon* (lit. linen from Amorgos[12]) is by far the most common description: applied to twenty-three garments out of the twenty-six whose composition is directly specified. From a statistical perspective, it might therefore be tempting to say that most of the dedicated garments were made of *amorgos* (discussed further below).[13] This is not actually the implication however: rather, garments should have been so described because their composition was distinctive (not ordinary linen). Thus, *amorgos* was not a standard fabric for garments, although the catalogue indicates that it was relatively common amongst these dedicated garments.

Amorginon as a descriptive term can be usefully compared to *erion*, which does not appear as a qualifying term, although it is generally assumed that most Greek garments were made of wool (see van Wees, this volume). This assumption is confirmed by these descriptions – precisely because 'woollen' is never used, and there are more qualifying terms to indicate alternative composition. Although it is not used as a descriptive term, wool does appear in the catalogue, both as a dedicated item in its own right, and as part of the description of some half-woven items.[14] (It would be overstating the case to argue that all those garments not described with a fabric qualification were woollen. Probably the basic distinction between vegetable fibres and wool did not need to be drawn in every case, because the difference was immediately apparent to the Greek eye, or since some garments were accepted as almost always made of one or other.) The usual term for linen appears only once, applied to a *kandys* (sleeved fitted tunic, probably of Persian design, certainly not a standard Greek garment).[15] The other garment description (1524B. 176–79) with a direct composition specification is *trichapton*, literally 'woven of hair.'[16] Despite the modern implications of 'hair shirts', it seems to have been luxurious: smooth, embroidered, with spangles on its border.

The next most common fabric description after *amorginon* is *stuppinon*.[17] It is not entirely clear whether this term relates to composition or quality: it is defined as meaning 'of, or like, the coarse fibre of flax, hemp, tow.'[18] The distinction may not be operative: despite the clear literal meaning of *amorginon*, it is often used with connotations of fineness, while *stuppinon*, whether 'of' or 'like', clearly refers to coarseness.[19] It seems likely that the functional descriptive opposition is between *amorginon* (fine) – [ordinary] – *stuppinon* (coarse). Both these terms relate to vegetable fibres, suggesting the existence of an additional opposition, such as (vegetable fibre of high quality) – [unremarkable composition for garment] – (vegetable fibre of low quality). No such indications of composition or quality are given for woollen garments, which perhaps suggests that their relative quality was more visually emphatic. I have argued elsewhere that the ease of dyeing and wide range of colours achievable on woollen fabrics led to a more fixed association between fabric value/quality, and dye-colour value/quality, than existed for linen (2003, 208–13, 223–28)

The variant of completion seems less complicated. Some garments are designated half-woven, as in unfinished (some being accompanied by their wool) and the opposition – [finished] – is obvious.[20] However, there is a term, *polytelestatas* 'completely finished' (used in contemporary literary description of dedicated garments, *Peri Parthenion* 5–6) which is never used, possibly because it was incompatible with the garment having been worn, after which it would need to be refinished by cleaning or fulling (Cleland 2003, 126, 227–8). The complex term *rhakos* is a potential third term for this variant, but since it is added in successive iterations of this catalogue, I consider it indicative of the state of the dedications, rather than their nature (see Milanezi, this volume; Linders 1972, 11, 58, 61, 67; Gunther 1988, 215–37). The single description of a garment as *kainon* 'new' (1514.31=1515.23=1516.10) supports the idea that these garments were generally dedicated after use.[21]

Before moving on from fabric, it is worth considering the relationships of such descriptions to those of garment type. Woollen composition is only revealed by accompanying dedication of un-woven material, for 1514.53 (*chitoniskon*) and 1518B.67–68 (*himation*). Two *chitoniskoi* and a *tarantinon* are described as half-woven, but without wool (1514.59 and 1524B.213, 1522.26). Of the twelve *chitones* whose fabric is described, nine are *amorginon*, three *stuppinon*, and of the fifteen *chitonia*, nine are *amorginon*, six *stuppinon*. Of five *chitoniskoi*, one is *amorginon*, one *stuppinon*, two half-woven (one with wool) and one *karton* 'shorn smooth.' One of the two *kandys* is linen, and both have colour descriptions, while the single examples of the *diptergon* and *tryphema* are *amorginon*.[22] Only four outer garments have their fabric described: the woman's *himation* mentioned above, a *chlanis* and *chlaniskion*, both *karton*, and the *epiblema*, 'new'. It is notable that none of the outer garments are described in terms of composition.

Fifty-two of the one hundred and eighty-five complete descriptions in the catalogue mention some aspect of fabric. However, since this category encompasses a variety of different types of descriptive variant, this statistic of little import. This contrasts with the colour category, which is simple in its overall opposition: marked colour is opposed to unmarked colour (Barthes 1990:118). The particular thing to note is that one side of this opposition is, by definition, un-stated: it exists even though there is no term for 'unremarkably coloured'. Forty-eight of the complete descriptions include a 'base hue': meaning not that forty-eight garments were 'coloured', and the rest 'colourless', but that at least forty-eight were emphatically coloured, and by implication, that a description which omitted this would be inaccurate, and hinder recognition.[23]

Looking at the descriptions of colour in this way allows the unequivocal conclusion that 'white' and 'colourless' were not synonymous for Greek clothing. This is worth emphasising, given the common conception of Greek dress, and means that it is impossible to assume, when the colour of a garment or textile goes undescribed (in any context) that it was white.[24] This can be stated because white *appears as a mark* in these descriptions. Certainly, it is the most common specified colour, but this very fact precludes it being either the standard, or a neutral, colour of dress.

The opposition between marked and neutral colour in these descriptions is of greatest significance for an overall picture of the place of colour in Greek clothing.[25] However, there is a great deal of more specific information. Eighteen items are described as *leukos* 'white', thirteen as *krokotos* 'saffron', six as *batracheioun* 'frog-colour', five as *halourgos* 'sea-purple', three as *glaukeion* 'blue-grey' and one each as *thapsinon* 'broom yellow' and *melinon* 'quince colour'.[26] Overall, of one hundred and eighty-five complete descriptions, one hundred and fifteen involve either or both base colour and decorative patterns, making colour, either base or decorative, the second most significant feature of the descriptions after garment type. (Apart from one instance of *phoinikeos* all decoration of specified colour is *halourgos*.) The only base colour specified for *himatia* is white, while most, but not all, of the other items whose colour is specified are *chitoniskoi*. In short, there are three groups of colour in these catalogues: a) *halourgos* (and possibly *phoinikeos*)[27] whose presence, either as base colour, or in decoration, is always marked; b) the other six marked colours, including white; c) an indeterminate group of unmarked colours. On the basis of colour as a variant of mark in description, we should classify the latter as conceptually neutral.

A further distinction can be drawn within colour types a) and b), since three of their terms (*halourgis, batrachis,* and *krokotos*) appear as substantives for garments.[28] The use of specific forms of colour terms to carry the primary description of garments, particularly alongside other descriptions using adjectival terms, emphasises the importance of these colours for clothing. This is especially noticeable for *krokotos*: of thirteen descriptions using this colour term, three rely on it alone, and six use it in conjunction with terms describing only decoration or decorative form. Only four use it in conjunction with a garment type term. *krokotos* is distinctive in this respect, possibly because the colour was definitively linked to a specific garment type, or more likely because the significance of colour subsumed that of type.[29] At any rate, its frequent use as both a substantive and single descriptive term emphasises the conceptual importance of the colour.

Colour can also be considered in relation to different garment types. There are complete descriptions for thirty-six outer garments, by type: *himation* (sixteen), *ampechonon* (five), *chlanis* (five), *enkyklon* (four), *epiblema* (three), *tribon* (two) and *pharos* (one). Of the *himatia*, fourteen are described in terms of colour or decoration: seven are white (one described as a woman's garment, two with purple borders, one with 'sacred writing').[30] Four of the other seven, base colour unspecified, have purple borders[31] while two have purple 'in the middle' (1522.11) and one has 'gold lettering' (1529.14). Only one *ampechonon* has described decoration ('sacred writing', 1514.34–5=1515.26–7=1516.13), and two of the *chlanis* type (a border, 1514.39=1515.31=1516.17=1517B.143–4; a crimson border and 'sacred writing', 1514.40=1515.32–3=1516.18–9=1517B.145–6). All four *enkyklon* type garments are coloured or decorated (two white, 1524B.165, 223; two patterned, 1514.48=1516.25=1517B.154–5, 1529.6–7), and all three of the *epiblema* type are decorated (designs, 1514.33–4=1515.25=1516.12; pattern and image of Dionysus, 1514.31–2=1515.23–4=1516.10–11; patterned, 1529.19). The remaining three outer garments have no described colour or decoration.

The only marked base colour for outer garments is white. This does not necessarily imply that other examples were of 'neutral' colour, as the word is used in English, (indeed, other evidence suggests that Athenian outer garments usually had added colour[32]) but rather that the only actually remarkable colour was white. The only form of decoration described for *himatia* is the purple border (lettering should, I feel, be linked to the garment as a dedicated object). That some examples of the *chlanis* type have described decoration would seem to imply that the others did not, rather than that its presence was assumed.[33] In comparison, it is notable that all the examples of the other main types of outer garment have their colour and/or decoration described – except for the *ampechonon, pharos* and *tribon*, which seem to be distinguished by solely by shape/design, size, and quality, respectively.[34]

There are ninety-four complete descriptions of inner garments, forty-four with described colour or decoration. A high proportion are *chitoniskoi* (fifty-two of ninety-four; thirty-four of forty-four) and their base colours encompass the whole range used by the catalogue: five white (three also decorated); three frog-colour (two also patterned) two blue-grey; two saffron (one a child's); two purple (both patterned) and one quince-coloured.[35] Of those nineteen whose base colour is not specified, ten have purple borders, five borders of unspecified colour, and four are patterned.[36] This garment can be equated to that frequently depicted (as coloured and decorated) on white-ground lekythoi, worn over the long *chiton*.[37]

Only four of the twenty-three complete descriptions of *chitonia* have colour: yellow with purple border (1522.24); saffron (1529.17); white (1524B.133–4); patterned (1529.5). Four of the seven *tryphema* type garments have colour or decoration: saffron (1517B.162); embroidered (1518B.68–9, 1525.3); embroidered with border (1514.70–1=1516.44–5=1517B.89–90). One of the *ledion* type has a border (1529.12) but none of the *tarantinon* type have described colour or decoration (appearing only in single term descriptions, except one half-woven, 1522.26). Of the twelve *chitones* only one has decoration: purple in the middle (1529.7–8). In terms of base colour, it should be noted that white appears as a mark for the *chitoniskos* and *chitonion*, but not for the *chiton*. In fact, of the garment types overall, the *chiton* has the lowest proportion of described pattern decoration, and is never described in terms of base colour. I might argue that this implies that this garment type typically had the natural colour of its fibres, and that this was one of its distinguishing features in the wider taxonomy of Greek clothing, in contrast to the apparently otherwise similar type of the *chitonion*.

There are obviously very many more conclusions that might be drawn from the evidence presented here: what I have tried to show is that this approach, founded on an edition annotated for duplication rather than reproducing it, and on tabulation, makes such conclusions available. However, I have also attempted to indicate that such conclusions need to be drawn in detail for each specific variable and its inter-relationships, and only then extrapolated towards a more general picture. To do so is beyond the scope of this chapter. I have presented some results to suggest the level of detail which can be obtained; to emphasise that there are ways to render complexity advantageous in appreciating how different variables of clothing – type, colour, patterns and structural decoration, fabric and gender ascription – combined to produce an intelligible garment. This evidence cannot be viewed in isolation: full appreciation of its terms as descriptive variants depends on attention to their external import and contexts. Nevertheless, recognition of the nature and operation of descriptive variation within these catalogues allows a much more precise study of such external contexts, and assessment of their implications. The content of 'dress' as a symbolic statement resides not only in the direct "signifying act of wearing clothing or using materials to construct clothing" but also in indirectly "referring to dress and the materials that constitute that dress" (Harris 1992). The Brauron catalogues reveal not only such direct signifying acts of clothing the body: they also contain symbolic statements, in the form of written garments, which are "fully symbolized, culturally bound, and therefore, laden with meaning" (Harris 1992). These meanings can inform our understanding of the clothed body in the ancient world.

NOTES

1 *IG* II² 1514 etc. See e.g. Linders 1972; Foxhall & Stears 1999; Millar 1997.
2 Comprehensively discussed by Cleland 2003, 67–132, and forthcoming, which revises and expands the conclusions presented here.
3 Compare Tanagra (Casevitz 1993, 3–10); Miletus (Gunther 1988, 215–37); Asklepion (Aleshire 1989) and the Attic Stelae (Pritchett 1956) in which clothing, though recorded, is incidental. See also Milanezi, this volume.
4 13 extant fragments record dedications made in the years 349/8 to 336/5 on six separate stelae inscribed between 353/2 and 336/5: Linders 1972:67–8; Cole 1998, 37; Cleland 2003, 97–8. The fragments frequently recognisably overlap, but rarely without variation: Cleland 2003:75 and forthcoming, Milanezi, this volume.
5 Cole (1998, 37) translates a short section of 1514. See Cleland, forthcoming.
6 The catalogue is ordered by year of dedication, although not all the extant fragments now contain such a date. All but 27 of the complete descriptions include the dedicant's name, and the incidence of duplication is not high (Cleland 2003, 97).
7 Such statements depend on an edition which annotates, rather than reiterating, areas of the catalogue which happen to survive from two or more of the six stelae of origin (Linders 1972, 67–70). The creation of such an edition, and an accompanying concordance, was integral to my study (Cleland 2003: 74–96 and forthcoming). All references to the catalogue in the discussion below are to *Inscriptiones Graecae* line number or numbers.
8 All garments, being made things, have a 'type': if it is not mentioned, this implies that it is not their distinguishing feature.
9 Clothing as an important indicator of female social and economic status, Cleland 2004b, and 2003, 171–2, 256–65, 269–76 (with references); Cole 1998, 39, 41–2; Dakoronia & Gounarounopoulou 1992, 219–13.
10 1990, 115–123. I have discussed the application of derivations of Barthes' theories of the written garment, vestimentary coding, and descriptive variants at length elsewhere (2003, 120–132; forthcoming). These are 'written garments' since (at least originally) "the described object is actualized, given separately in its plastic form"– cf. literary description, in which "description is brought to bear on a hidden object (whether real or imaginary): it must make that object exist" (Barthes 1990, 12). Critically, in this type of description, purely physical variation exists in, and is apparent from, the actual garment, whereas meaningful variation is emphasised, and indeed created, by the accompanying written description. These inscriptions present an established code, since their vocabulary remains stable over repeated iterations (i.e. not innovated from the total lexical field at each composition). Its 'vestimentary' nature is indicated by subject matter, and technical nature. Apart from providing theoretical support for the commonsense implications of the categories, Barthes presents apposite and pertinent formulations of the nature and implications of different types of variation.
11 Although they could be divided into more precise categories, the size, nature, and lexical context of the Inventories as a text sample would make this less, rather than more, useful as an analytical method, cf. Barthes (1990, 115–123), and discussion of composition below.
12 A specific type of linen: s.v. LSJ; Richter 1929, 27–33; Linders 1972: 20, 45.
13 1514.10, 22 = 1515.4–5, 14–15; 1514.61 = 1516.137 = 1518B.78; 1517B.120 = 1524B.135 = 1525.9; 1518B. 65, 66, 69–70; 1523. 20–21, 21 = 1524B.194, 195; 1524B.214, 216; 1528.19; 1529.2; 1530.4. 1514. 51 =1516.28 =1517B.158; 1514.63, 64 = 1516.39, 40 = 1518B.81, 82 ; 1522.238; 1524B. 132, 211, 217; 1529. 7–8, 18.
14 Alone: 1514.57; 1518B.57 =1524.166; 1528.17; 1518B.59 = 1524.168; 1522.27. With half-woven garments: 1514.53; 1518B.67–68.
15 1524B.219; Millar (1997, 155, 165–70 (full references); Bieber 1928, 20; Pekridou-Goreki 1989, 73.
16 Pherecr. 108.28; *IG* 11(2).287A53 (Delos iiiBC); Lxx.*Ez.* 16.10, 13 cf., Poll. 2.24, 10.32.
17 Two term: 1517B.125, 127 = 1524.140, 142 = 1525.13, 15; 1518B. 66; 1523.12, 17 = 1524B.184, 190; 1528.15; 1529.15. Three-term: 1523. 27 = 1524B.202; 1529.17.
18 s.v. LSJ; *IG* 2² 1414.26; 1527.34; *PcairZen.* 755.6 (iiiBC); Ph. *Bel.* 102.15; D. *S.* 1.35: for the noun: Hdt. 8.52; X. *Cyr.* 7.5.23; D. 47.20; Aen. *Tact.* 33, 35; Plb. 1.45.12; Plu. *Cic.* 18, etc.
19 s.v. LSJ; i.e. Ar. *Lys.* 150 etc. and Labarre & Le Dinahet (1996: 49, n.3).

20 With wool: 1514.53–54 = 1516.30–31 = 1517B.161–62; 1518B.67–68. Otherwise: 1514.59 = 1516.25; 1522.26; 1524B.213.
21 The import of statistical features is not defined by volume, but rather by proportion and opposition: even the single occurrence of a term such as *kainon* is sufficient to suggest the unstated oppositional term in all the other descriptions.
22 Although, in other contexts, there is justification for regarding *amorginon* as a substantitive garment term relating to fabric, see n.18 and 25 and cf. *tarantinon*, unlike this term, *amorginon* never appears as a sole designation in these catalogues.
23 I do not discuss the much wider group of descriptions which include colour in the form of decoration, of both specified and unspecified colours separately here. However, it is in opposition to these groups that colour is considered 'base' and 'hue', see Cleland 2003:esp. 103, n.72 and 127–32, 148–51.
24 I have argued this from clothing regulations (2004b) and practical considerations (2003, 270–6) but this is the clincher (cf. second white on lekythoi, Cleland 2003, 193.
25 See Cleland 2004: 139–45.
26 Colour definitions are complex: I have discussed the limitations of these translations elsewhere (2003). White: 1514.20=1515.12; 1517B.124=1524.139=1525.12, 1517B.138=1524.153; 1523.14, 16=1524B.186, 189; 1524B.205, 206, 210, 223; 1514.16=1515.8, 1514.27=1515.19=1516.6; 1517B.135=1524.151; 1522.21; 1524B.129; 1514.40=1515.32=1516.18=1517B.145, 1514.46=1516.23=1517B.152, 1514.69=1516.42; 1524B.133=1525.7. Saffron; 1524B.213; 1529.8, 18; 1514.60, 62=1516.36, 38=1518B.78, 79; 1517B.162; 1522.9, 12, 25; 1528.23; 1514.58=1516.34; 1529.17; 1522.28. Frog-colour; 1514.16=1515.9, 1514.48=1516.25=1517B.154; 1523.14=1524B.187; 1517B.137=1524.152; 1523.24=1524B.198; 1524B.220. Purple: 1522.20; 1514.49=1516.26=1517B155, 1514.56=1516.33, 1514.12=1515.6, 1514.14. Blue-gray: 1518B.52 = 1524.161; 1518B.71; 1523.18=1524B.191. Broom yellow;1522.24. Quince colour; 1524B.132 (Linders 1972:59).
27 Probably 'crimson'. The absence of this, and *melas* 'black/dark', as base colours is explicable in light of their clothing associations (military and funereal dress) in other contexts: Cleland 2003, 47, 154–72, 266–76, with full references; Fountoulakis 2004, 110–16; Stratiki 2004, 106–9.
28 *Halourgis* 1514.56=1516.33 (complete) 1522.20 (single term, *halourges*) 1517B.166; 1518B.50 (fragmentary). *Batrachis* 1514.16=1515.9, 1514.48=1516.25=1517B (single term). *Krokotos* 1524B.213; 1529.8, 18; 1514.60, 62; 1522.9, 12, 251514.60, 62=1516.36, 38=1518B.78, 79; 1522.28; 1516.52; 1524B.235; 1528.13 (fragmentary).
29 See Ar. *Lys.* 44–51, 645 etc. Cleland 2003, 157, 159–61, 167 for dramatic references and discussion.
30 White: 1514.16=1515.8 (woman's), 1514.19–20=1515.12, 1514.27=1515.19=1516.6 (purple border) 1514.69=1516.42–3 (purple border, 'sacred writing'), 1517B.138=1524B.153, 1524B.205, 210.
31 1514.17–8=1515.9–10, 1517B.124–5=1524B.139–40=1525.12–3, 1517B.60=1524B.169, 1529.16. (None: 1514.47=1516.24=1517B.153, man's; 1518B.67 half-woven woman's).
32 Cleland 2003, 187–201, colour in clothing on white-ground lekythoi.
33 As variant of assertion of existence, Barthes 1990, 115.
34 *ampechonon*, single term except as above: 1514.36=1515.28=1516.14–5=1517B.140, 1522.17, 1524B.218, *tribon*: 1514.22=1515.14=1516.2, *pharos*: 1530.5.
35 White: 1517B.123–4=1524B.139=1525.11–12; 1517B.136=1524B.151; 1523.14=1524B.186; and patterned, 1514.45–6=1516.23–4=1517B.152–3; 1522.21. Frog-coloured: 1523.14=1524B.187 and patterned, 1517B.137=1524B.152; 1523.24=1524B.198–9. Blue-gray: 1518B.52=1524B.161; 1523.18=1524B.191. Saffron: 1525.23; 1514.58=1516.34–5. Purple: 1514.12–13=1515.6–7; 1514.14 Quince: 1524B.132=1525.6–7.
36 Purple borders: 1514.21=1515.13; 1514.54–5=1516.31; 1517B.126=1524B.141=1525.14; 1517B.132=1524B.147; 1518B.61=1524B.170; 1518B.62=1524B.171; 1523.17=1524B.189–90; 1523.18–9=1524B.191–2; 1529.9, 11. Borders: 1514.26=1515.17–8=1516.5; 1514.43, 52=1516.21, 29=1517B.148–9, 159; 1524B.208, 215. Patterned: 1514.7=1515.2; 1514.41–2=1516.20=1517B.147; 1517B.122–3=1524B.137=1525.11; 1517B.131=1524B.146.
37 Cleland 2003, 202–3 cf. Cole 1998, 37. Occasional specifications as 'child's' indicate that this aspect of the diminutive is not appropriate to these garments in general.

Chapter 9

Viewing and Obscuring the Female Breast: Glimpses of the ancient bra

Emma J. Stafford

The historian must regard it as unfortunate that underclothes are so generally associated with eroticism, often to a pathological extent; and it may well be that writers have hesitated to expand on a topic which might suggest that their interest is of that nature (Willett & Cunnington 1992 [1951], 11).

Fifty years on, we are less easily embarrassed by underwear, but there is no denying the 'association with eroticism' of the modern bra.[1] This garment has been closely bound up with women's position in society, acting, in retrospect, almost as a barometer of changing roles and perceptions.[2] Various 'bust-supporters' of the 1870s and 80s were espoused as a healthy alternative to corsets, supporting the reformed styles of dress that contributed to the crusade for women's rights. The fortunes of early bra manufacturers were closely linked to increases in women's financial independence and work outside the home. During the Second World War, purchase of a bra could even be encouraged as a patriotic act: "active women need support".[3] 1940s and 50s bra advertising tapped into a more general opening up of attitudes towards female sexuality, linking the garment to the glamour of the silver screen (see Llewellyn-Jones, this volume). Reacting against perceived sexual exploitation, the 'bra-burnings' of the late 1960s demonstrate the garment's symbolic potency. Notwithstanding the feminist movement, the image of the bra-clad cover-girl continues to be a staple of men's magazines, although more recently the bra's erotic connotations have been reclaimed in the service of 'girl power' (shown by the success of the 'Hello boys' marketing campaign, now copied by advertising the rival Ultrabra as 'Your deadliest weapon yet!').

Since the modern bra reflects broader social trends, it ought to be worthwhile to consider what Greek and Roman women wore on their breasts. However, although the existence of a basic form of breast-band is generally acknowledged, the garment has inspired very little debate: the scarcity of its appearances in our literary and visual sources has led to the assumption that it was not widely worn. However, there is enough evidence to merit considerably more discussion.[4] The most detailed, if dry, account remains Bieber's 1931 entry in Pauly-Wissowa (s.v. 'strophium') providing a definition ('Busenband, Büstenhalter der Frauen') and a basic survey of Greek and Roman terms and sources.[5] More recent works on Greek and Roman dress at least mention the breast-band, but none gives it more than a couple of paragraphs.[6] Some sense of its significance is offered by Ewing, crediting the Greeks with "introducing, or at least presaging, the most significant items of female under-clothing, the corset and the brassière".[7] While a comprehensive catalogue of the breast-band's appearances in ancient art and literature is beyond the scope of this chapter, I shall discuss the more significant evidence for its use and investigate its erotic potential.

LOOKING FOR THE GREEK AND ROMAN BRA

One might think that Greek and Roman women wore nothing at all beneath their outer clothing. The female figures on the Parthenon's east pediment are certainly not wearing anything with shoulder-straps, nor are their breasts at all constrained; even clearer cases are those late fifth-century statue-types, where one breast is bare and the other clearly visible through diaphanous drapery.[8] Likewise Lapith women at Olympia and Bassae have their chitons ripped off by centaurs to reveal a complete absence of any kind of underwear.[9] Early Attic red-figure vase-painting provides many examples of 'transparent drapery' where unconfined breasts are clearly visible beneath the *chiton*, as in the tondo of Onesimos' cup, where a fully-clad woman is about to untie her belt, to strip for a middle-aged man.[10] Later fifth-century vase-painters follow sculptors in using the folds of drapery to delineate full and clearly unrestrained breasts (Llewellyn-Jones 2002, 181–90). Most of the women engaged in sexual activity in symposium contexts on Attic pots are either fully clothed or completely naked but for jewellery or head-dresses.[11] Complete nudity seems to be the ideal favoured by Roman writers. Propertius praises female nakedness (2.15) making specific mention of bare nipples (l.5) and still-firm breasts (l.21). Martial upbraids his wife for wearing too many clothes in bed – "a girl can't be naked enough" (11.104.7–8). Juvenal talks of a prostitute "standing naked under a stinking archway" (11.171–2), and Messalina on display in the brothel "naked, with gilded nipples" (6.122–3). However, the sightings we *do* have of breast-coverings suggest that all this is poetic exaggeration and artistic convention, like the much-discussed absence of pubic hair on female nudes, and the many other facets of women's lives 'missing' from the visual repertoire.[12]

Three striking examples of the breast-band worn as part of a bikini-style costume are offered by representations of the female athlete, clearly a problematic category as far as dress is concerned. Some degree of undress is displayed by the girls competing in the Heraia contests at Olympia, who ran in a *chiton* "a little above the knee, … the right shoulder bared as far as the breast" (Paus. 5.16.3), as in a sixth-century Lakonian statuette from Albania.[13] Plutarch attributes the custom of exercising completely nude to Spartan girls (*Lyc.* 14.7); Plato perhaps offers earlier evidence (*Rep.* 452a–d, 457; David 1989, 5, n.20). Earlier still are the archaic Lakonian bronze mirror- and patera-handles, in the form of nude or nearly-nude girls, from sanctuaries and graves; there is no specific indication that they are athletes, but their nakedness inevitably calls to mind the later evidence. In Stewart's catalogue of 'girls going Dorian', fourteen out of a total thirty-nine wear the *diazoma*, a loin-cloth tucked up to make a pair of briefs, although none has an upper garment to match.[14]

Figure 9.1. Atalanta in full bikini-style outfit, with 'sports bra'. Cup by the Euaion Painter, c.470–60 BC, Louvre CA 2259. (Photo: courtesy of RMN, Chuzeville).

A similar range of dress is seen in representations of Atalanta, the mythological prototype for female athletes, whose energetic exploits include the Caledonian Boar Hunt, wrestling Peleus, and challenging would-be suitors to a running-race.[15] Atalanta generally wears a short *chiton* for the hunt, and frequently for the wrestling match, but in several Attic versions of the latter she wears just a diazoma, occasionally complemented by the cap associated with the *pankration*.[16] The single unambiguous Attic representation of the running-race, on a krater of around 420 BC by the Dinos Painter, shows Atalanta completely naked, like her suitor Hippomenes.[17] So far this parallels historical athletes; two more appearances finally bring us to the bra. In **Figure 9.1**, Atalanta appears alone, her cap immediately suggesting the wrestling match, the stele perhaps the record of her victory.[18] In addition to the *diazoma* and cap, she wears an upper garment which resembles a modern sports bra, with integral shoulder-straps to prevent it slipping down. The painter has taken pains to show the flattening effect on her breasts, and indicate embroidered decoration on both top and *diazoma*. The wrestling and running episodes seem to be conflated in **Figure 9.2**: the young man is

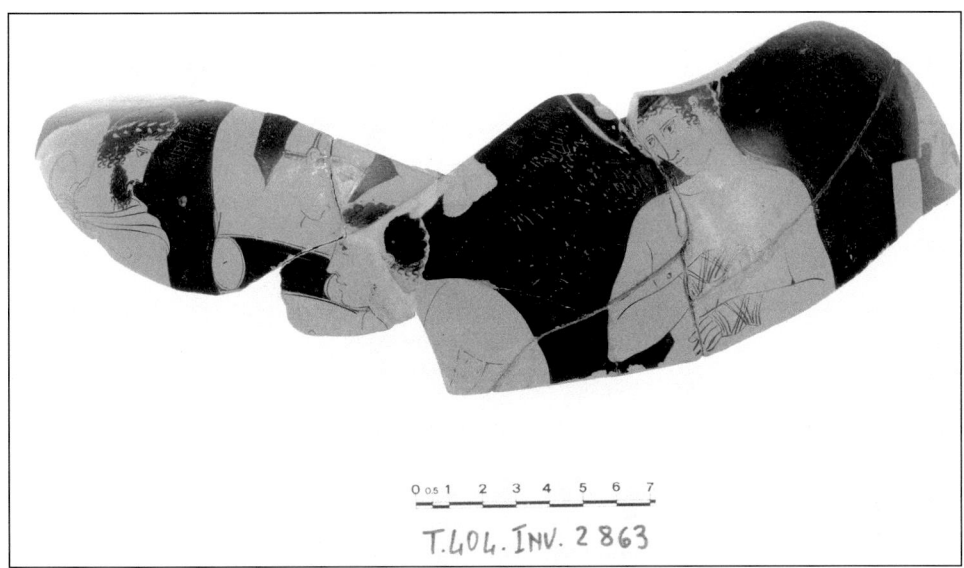

Figure 9.2. Atalanta in unusual breast-band, with Hippomenes. Fragment of krater by the Peleus Painter, c.440–30 BC, Ferrara T.404. (Photo: courtesy of Museo Archaeologico Nazionale di Ferrara).

labelled 'Hippomenes', but Atalanta wears the wrestling cap.[19] Beazley describes the garment on her upper body as "a brassière, in which the stiffer band is distinguished from the thinner and softer cups covering the breasts themselves" (1960, 223, pl.53), but it looks equally likely that her breasts are naked. Such a design might offer some control, the breast-holes helping to prevent the band, without shoulder-straps, from slipping down. Straps are again absent from the breast-bands worn by the athletic 'bikini girls' of the well known Piazza Armerina mosaic, c. 300 AD.[20] These are far removed in time and place from fifth-century Attica, but the bra-and-briefs outfit again suggests that female athletes, unlike men, require some minimal dress, whether purely for 'decency' or for the practical purpose of reducing 'bounce'.

Another category of active woman, related to the female athlete in terms of dress requirements, is the professional dancer. We may have a rare glimpse of such a woman in bikini-style costume in **Figure 9.3**, from the sanctuary of Artemis at Brauron.[21] Its specific find-spot, in the *heroon* of Iphigeneia, links it to the female dedications of richly decorated garments made in connection with childbirth, which are of such interest to the clothes historian.[22] Two women stand facing each other, the one to the right fully clad but raising her arms as if to remove her *himation* like the woman to the left, whose outer clothes are already piled on top of a chest behind her. Her upper garment is not just a straightforward band around the breasts, but has a cross-strap over each shoulder to prevent slippage; both this and the briefs are richly decorated

Figure 9.3. Dancer in bikini-style outfit with shoulder-straps, holding castanets. Plate from the sanctuary of Artemis at Brauron, c.430–20 BC, Brauron 721. (Photo: courtesy of the Archaeological Society at Athens).

with embroidered patterns, like **Figure 9.1**, and she holds castenets. These are women rather than the girls usually associated with rituals at Brauron, depicted on *krateriskoi* fragments as being between the ages of about five and ten, either completely naked or wearing short *chitons*.[23] Both the *castanets* and decorative costume are easier to read as belonging to professional dancers, either ritual performers or simply dancing as a 'side-show' to the festival proper.[24] While female dancers and musicians need not always have combined their skills with sexual services, they are often associated with the symposium (X. *Symp.* 2.1). We have just one Attic example of a breast-band worn in this context (**Figure 9.4**).[25] Three more or less naked heterosexual couples can be distinguished: it is not clear what stage the central couple have reached, but the woman is wearing a decorated breast-band with cross-straps similar to **Figure 9.3**, the one novel feature being a disc over her left breast, which the man is fondling. The most plausible explanation for this elaborate design is that it was meant to be seen on a regular basis, rather than being underwear 'accidentally' revealed. This is our earliest sight of the breast-band being so explicitly exploited for erotic effect.

From these examples, it would seem that even exceptionally active women are only

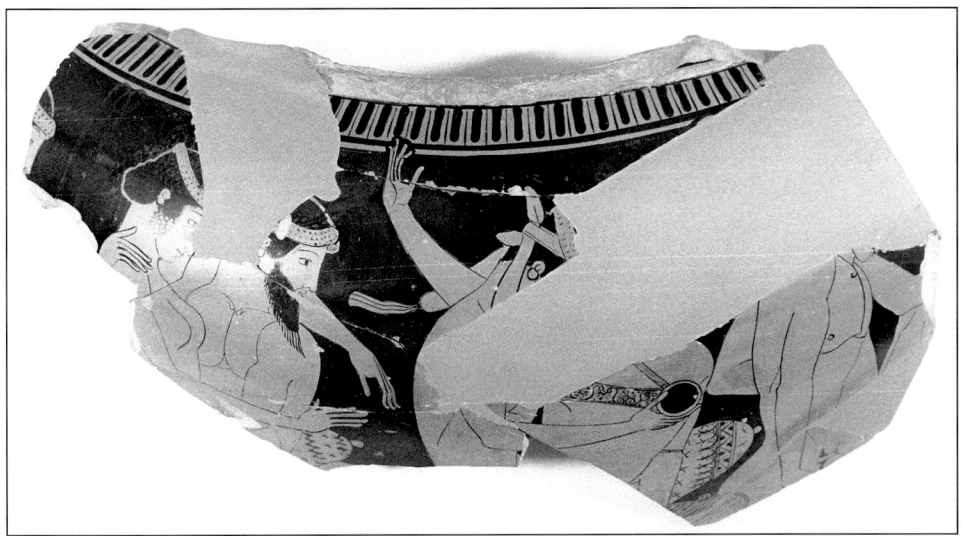

Figure 9.4. Woman in symposium scene, wearing breast-band with shoulder-straps. Fragmentary dinos by the Pan Painter, c.470 BC, Athens, Vlastos-Serpieri Collection 480. (Photo: courtesy of Vlastos-Serpieri Collection).

occasionally conceived as wearing anything to constrain their breasts. We do, however, have quite compelling evidence for more widespread undergarment use from Aristophanes. In later literature the meaning of strophion, literally 'something turned' or 'twisted', varies – sometimes it clearly means 'head-band' being explicitly linked with head or hair,[26] and it could even indicate a boxer's hand-binding [27] – but Aristophanes' use of the word is consistently suggestive of the breast-band. The *strophion* appears in the scene in the *Lysistrata* where Myrrhine performs a prolonged prick-tease on her husband (931–2):

> Myr.: I'm just undoing my *strophion*. Remember, now: don't let me down over the peace talks.

A reference to underwear would certainly be appropriate here, although as Myrrhine does not take us systematically through the rest of her undressing, this does not in itself provide a definite identification of the garment. The *Thesmophoriazusae* is more helpful, first in a speech by the Kinsman, contrasting typically feminine and 'masculine' objects: the strophion is as foreign to the oil-flask (*lekythos*, 139) as the saffron dress (*krokotos*) is to the lute (*barbitos*) (etc. see Robson, this volume). Later the Kinsman's dressing-up process is detailed (249–56):

> Euripides: Agathon, since you refuse to help me in person, at least lend us a cloak (*himation*) and a *strophion* for this man here; you can't say you haven't got such things.

Agathon:	Take and use them. I don't mind.
Kinsman:	Which one should I take?
Euripides:	Which? Take the saffron dress (*krokotos*) first and put it on.
Kinsman:	By Aphrodite, this has a nice smell of willy! Hurry and belt it. Now pass me a *strophion*.
Euripides:	Here you are.
Kinsman:	Come on now, sort me out around the legs (*katasteilon me ta peri tô skelei*).

The sequence of dressing is slightly confusing: the dress seems to be put on before the strophion. Sommerstein takes these passages as evidence that women usually belted their *chiton* or *peplos* round the waist, before drawing up the top half to be pinned at the shoulders, making this a sensible point at which to put on the breast-band.[28] I would suggest, however, that the scene is funnier if the incompetent men were trying to put the *strophion* on on top of the dress: **Figure 9.5** shows a different (un)dressing sequence, with the *chiton* clearly pulled off rather than unpinned. A later passage gives conclusive identification of the *strophion* as worn around the breasts (638–40):

Kleisthenes:	Loosen that *strophion* immediately, you shameless wretch!
First Woman:	How sturdy and strong they look. And by Zeus, her breasts aren't a bit like ours!

The removal of the *strophion* reveals the kinsman to have the wrong sort of breasts, which he tries, unsuccessfully, to attribute to never having had a child. Finally, a fragment (Fr. 664 Kassell-Austin) quoted by Pollux (*Onomastikon* 7.67.7–8) says: "But when the *strophion* was undone, my *karua* fell out"; *karua* (literally 'nuts') seem to be a euphemism for firm young breasts (cf. *mêla*, 'apples', 'fruit').[29] Altogether, Aristophanes' usage not only identifies the *strophion* as a breast-band, but also suggests it was something one would expect a woman to be wearing – a necessary part of the transvestite's costume.[30]

Literary evidence presents a great variety of Greek and Latin terms used to designate the breast-band. Pollux offers some definition of the promising term *stêthodesmos*, 'breast-binding' (*Onomastikon* 7.66.6–10 on Aristophanes Fr. 338 Kassell-Austin):

> Instead of what women now called a *stêthodesmos*, in Aristophanes' Thesmophoriazusae you would find something called an *apodesmos*:
> '... having undone the flap of your under-tunic (*chitonion*)
> and of your *apodesmoi*, which your tits (*titthidia*) were in.'

Pollux's description of the *stêthodesmos* as so-called by present-day women suggests that the word belongs to a distinctively female vocabulary, usually only being spoken of by women.[31] There are a few instances of related words (*stêthodesmê*, *stêthodesmis*, *stêthodesmia*, *stêthodesmion*), but none that offer a clear identification of the breast-band. *Mitra* is more common, and again varied in meaning, often indicating a woman's hair-

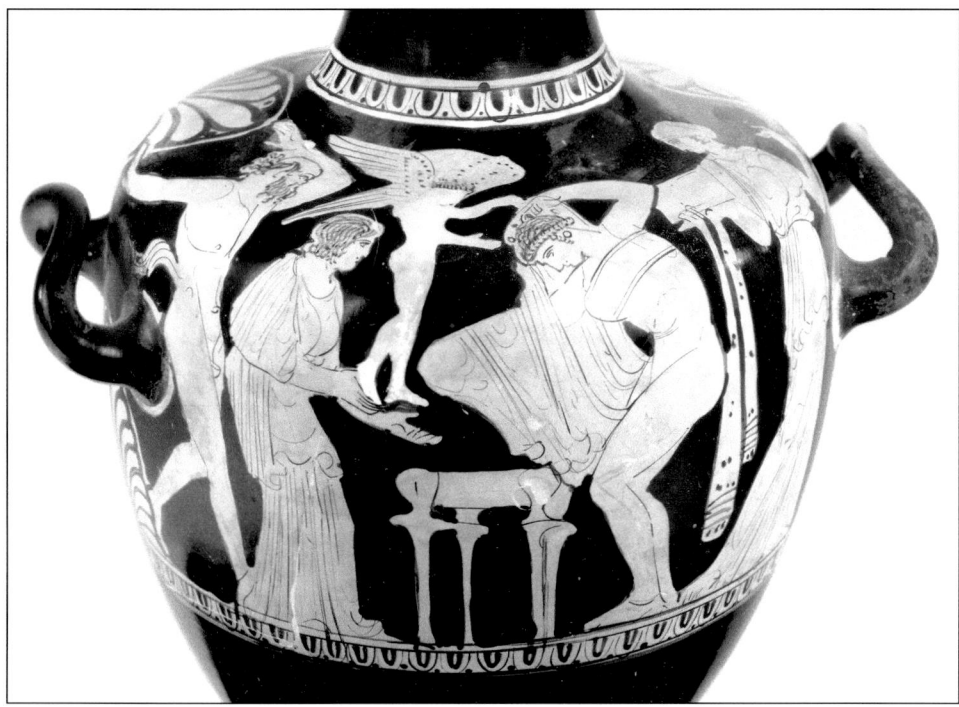

Figure 9.5. Aphrodite/woman undressing. Attic Hydria from Cyrenaica, Group of London E230 (name vase), 370–50 BC. (Photo: © British Museum).

band or snood, various forms of oriental headdresses, or metal waist-armour, a man's or woman's belt, but there are several clear instances as 'breast-band' in Hellenistic literature.[32] In an epigram by the third-century Hedylos (*AP* 5.199) the garment is included in lists of female accoutrements dedicated to Aphrodite after an erotic encounter brought on by wine and sleep:

> these moist spoils of maidenly desires, still all oozing with perfume, her sandals and yielding *mitrai*, garment of the breasts (*mastôn endumata*), as witnesses of her sleep and what has been taken from her.

In an epigram by Callimachus (*AP* 13.24) a *bacchante* similarly dedicates to Aphrodite her torch and thyrsos, and "the *mitra* which had kissed her breasts" (3–4). Leonidas of Tarentum's Kallikleia gives Aphrodite even more (*AP* 6.211):

> the silver Eros and ankle bracelet, the purple Lesbian hair band, the alabaster-coloured *melouchos*, the bronze mirror and the wide box-wood hair-trawling comb.

The term *melouchos*, 'apple-holder', must be the breast-band again, although it is a *hapax legomenon*. Pirenne-Delforge takes *AP* 5.199 and 6.211 as reasonable evidence for actual religious practice (1994, 378–80). Such dedications to Aphrodite are certainly consonant with women's clothes dedications to Brauronian Artemis (n.22 above; Cleland, this volume). Two more epigrams list female garments being dedicated to Artemis specifically in thanks for safe childbirth: Perses (*AP* 6.272) has Timaessa dedicate the mitra "bound tight around her breasts" (l.2), while Marcus Argentarius introduces another one-off term into the list of Euphrante's gifts (*AP* 6.201):

> Sandals and a very beautiful *mitra* (hair-band?), and a perfume-breathing twisted curl from her pretty locks, and a belt (*zone*), and this fine under-chiton and bright *mastodeta* from round her chest…

In Latin we find both *strophium* and *mitra* again, and the even vaguer *fascia*, indicating any kind of wrapping, although occasionally context allows identification of the breast-band.[33] All three appear in Cicero's list of garments worn by Clodius during his infiltration of the Bona Dea festival of 62 BC, a context reminiscent of the *Thesmophoriazusai* plot (*De Haruspicum Responso* 44):

> Publius Clodius, leaving behind his saffron dress (*crocata*), his head-band (*mitra*), his womanish sandals and little purple leggings (*purpureisque fasceolis*), his *strophium*, his lute, his shameful act and his disgrace, unexpectedly became a man of the people.[34]

What is important here too is the garments' distinctively feminine nature, even if the context offers no clear definition. One clear example of fascia as 'breast-band' comes in Martial's *Epigrams* Book 14, a collection of two-liners supposedly accompanying items given as gifts at the Saturnalia (Leary 1996, 1–9, and ad loc.). No. *134* is headed *fascia pectoralis*, 'a breast-band':

> *Fascia*, confine my mistress' growing tits,
> so my hand may cover what it grasps.[35]

Elsewhere Martial supplies our only attestation of yet another term for the same garment, with the heading *mamillare* (14.66):

> You could have bound your breast with bull's hide:
> other leather can't hold your breasts.

Both couplets conjure up particularly large-breasted women, emphasising the breast-band's constrictive quality, the second suggesting that soft leather was the common material for the garment Martial knows (cf. **Figure 9.2**) rather than the embroidered fabric of **Figures 9.1, 9.3** and **9.4**.

EROTICISING THE BRA

So far the breast-band emerges as a practical garment worn by female athletes and dancers, and probably more widely by ordinary women; it is common enough to be mentioned as a standard item of female dress by writers as diverse as Aristophanes, Hellenistic epigramatists, Cicero and Martial. At a basic level, its erotic potential arises from its association with the female breast, an area which both Greek and Roman men obviously found erotic (Gerber 1978; Kilmer 1993, 26–7; Llewellyn-Jones 2002, 181–3).

All our evidence, however, suggests that it constrains and flattens the breasts, rather than fulfilling the 'lift and separate' function required for the full-breasted look which much sculpture and vase-painting present as the ideal. From his survey of erotic literature, Gerber (1978) likewise concludes that the ideal breast is small and firm, as suggested by the equation of breasts with *mêla*. The question of size is difficult to judge, being so relative, but firmness is certainly a good thing in Philodemos' praise of the sixty-year-old Charito (*AP* 5.13.3–4): her hair is still dark, "and those marble-white cones of her breasts still stand firm on her chest, bare of any encircling *mitra*". This seems to suggest that the breast-band is associated with less-than-perfect breasts, sagging after childbirth or with advancing age. Ovid recommends the absence of a fascia from big breasts as a cure for love (*Remedia Amoris* 338), though at the other end of the scale he advises wearing "a *fascia* around a narrow chest" (*Ars Amatoria* 3.274), presumably to give the impression of fuller breasts to the flat-chested.

There is some evidence for a garment enhancing the curve of the breasts worn externally rather than being an undergarment: the cross-band, generally worn by Artemis, Athena or young girls, over the *chiton* or *peplos*, passing over each shoulder and diagonally across the chest, crossing both front and back to form an X or saltire. Villing notes the garment's breast-emphasising quality, suggesting a reference to the *parthenos*' reproductive potential (2000, 368). The few mortal girls wearing the cross-band (on grave stelai) do not have much bust to emphasise, but some more fully developed divine wearers have more obvious erotic appeal.[36] The much discussed *kestos himas* of Aphrodite should probably be understood as a similar garment (*Iliad* 14.214–17):

> She spoke, and from her breast loosed the elaborately decorated strap (*keston himanta poikilon*); there on it are love, and desire, and the persuasive discourse that craftily steals away the mind even of the wise.

The goddess removes this 'decorated strap' from her breast, but it does not seem to be an undergarment; other uses of *himas* suggest a narrow leather thong rather than the broad band of cloth or leather used for the breast-band. In later literature (e.g. *AP* 2.99–101), the *kestos* can even be described as 'flowing' and 'hanging from the neck', hardly suggesting a garment drawn tight around the breasts. The most convincing candidate remains that suggested by Bonner, who argues that *himas kestos* means the 'decorated strap' worn by statuettes of (otherwise nude) Near Eastern love goddesses.[37]

Whatever its exact nature, the ancient *kestos* is invariably worn by Aphrodite, never by ordinary women, who make do with the more prosaic breast-band. Despite its flattening effect, there are suggestions of eroticism in the evidence we have already surveyed. Symposium ware (**Figures 9.1–2**) presupposes a mildly erotic gaze for Atalanta's outfit, while (**Figure 9.4**) includes the breast-band in an explicitly erotic scene. The dedicatory epigrams link the breast-band directly with Aphrodite, the erotic element heavily emphasised in Hedylos' description of Aglaonike's *mitrai* "all oozing with perfume" (*AP* 5.199). Another "sweet-smelling" *mitra* is worn by Apollonius' Medea around her "ambrosial breasts", and she carries in it the pharmakon which will give Jason superhuman strength (*Argonautika* 3.867–8 and l.1013–14). Aglaonike and

Medea are clearly not to be imagined as having anything less than perfect, desirable, youthful breasts, nor is the Ariadne of Catullus 64 (63–5):

> ... neither keeping the fine band (*mitram*) on her golden head, nor with her veiled breast covered by the light garment (*levi... amictu*), nor with her milk-white breasts constrained by the tightly-twisted *strophium*...

Here the *strophium* is obviously a breast-band, the *mitra* a headband, and some kind of under-tunic must be indicated by *levis amictus*. The description of her disarray contributes to the pathos of Ariadne's immediate situation, but the broader context is certainly erotic – having just spent the night with one lover, she will soon attract Bacchus' amorous attentions.[38] Quite explicitly erotic is the scene in Apuleius' *Metamorphoses* (10.21) where Lucius, in his ass' incarnation, is compelled to service a beautiful but sexually voracious noblewoman, who prepares by removing all her clothes, 'even the band which bound her pretty nipples (*taenia quoque, qua decoras deuinxerat papillas*)'.

The strongest evidence for the breast-band's eroticism, however, is its appearance in visual art of the Roman period. Women wearing nothing but a breast-band appear in a whole series of erotic representations amongst the Fourth Style wall-paintings of Pompeii (62–79 AD). A number of images from private houses depict pairs of lovers where the woman wears just a breast-band: its colour varies (blue, red, yellow, mauve), as does the sexual position, the woman sometimes on top, sometimes on all fours.[39] Only one example departs in favour of a vest-top type, similar to Atalanta's 'sports bra'; the scene, from a private house, is accompanied by an inscription presumably aimed at imitators – *lente impelle*, 'penetrate gently'.[40] The status of these women is impossible to establish – mythological nymphs, real-life wives or ideal mistresses – but there are several examples from the brothel, where the women are certainly prostitutes.[41] Here one might surmise that removal of the breast-band was an extra, or that the garment compensated for less-than-perfect breasts; but such pragmatic explanations do not account for the idealised private images. Perhaps the strophium in these scenes "illustrates the erotic charge unleashed even then by lingerie, which helped women to look their best for their lovers" (Varone 2000, 83). Lingerie's exotic connotations are a little difficult to reconcile with this plain, constrictive breast-band, but perhaps concealment alone makes it alluring, playing with the apparent preference for full nudity.

Figure 9.5 links the elaborate breast-bands of fifth-century vase-painting and the plainer undergarment of the Pompeii wall-paintings: a woman is depicted in the act of taking her *chiton* off over her head, revealing nothing but a breast-band and a pair of shoes beneath (London E230; Boardman 1989, fig. 386). The breast-band is of the simple wrap-around variety, with no shoulder-straps and no visible embroidered decoration. The scene is sometimes labelled 'Aphrodite at her toilet', the identification suggested by the Eros and especially the satyr, out of place in a non-mythological scene (Walters 1931, pl. 97.2). Whether or not the woman is meant to be Aphrodite herself, the satyr's reaction illustrates the response expected of the male viewer on seeing a female in her underwear, placing the scene in a whole tradition of erotic discoveries, of sleeping nymphs by satyrs or bathing goddesses by men.[42] This *topos* is

Figure 9.6. Aphrodite (un)tying her strophium. Terracotta statuette, mid-3rd century BC, Staatliche Antikensammlungen und Glyptothek München 8516. (Photo: courtesy of Staatliche Antikensammlungen und Glyptothek).

often adduced in connection with the sculptural development (more or less contemporary with the London hydria) of the nude Aphrodite of Knidos.[43] There are hundreds of variations on the theme by the late Hellenistic period, many types playing with the conceit of undressing, showing clutched or discarded drapery. One particular variation seems to take **Figure 9.5** a step further: in half a dozen extant examples the otherwise nude Aphrodite is shown untying (or tying) her strophion (**Figure 9.6**).[44] Here the breast-band plays very much the part of modern lingerie, adding that extra touch of the erotic to the naked body. The motif later recurs on a Roman lamp from Carthage, a medium especially given to erotic scenes.[45] A final bathing female with breast-band can be seen in a mosaic of c. 200 AD from a house in Palaeopaphos, Cyprus: she is depicted from behind as she steps into a river, the bathing motif emphasised by a *louterion* and a mirror in the foreground; a swan pulls at the drapery she holds around her legs, but otherwise the breast-band is her only costume.[46]

CONCLUSION

To sum up, then, the absence of any kind of bra from so much ancient art is probably a convention of representation rather than a reflection of historical reality. Ancient Greek and Roman women would have varied in their breast-size and practical need for the garment, but fifth-century sources suggest that basic breast-bands were available, and widely enough worn to be recognised by Aristophanes' audience; more elaborate types could be worn alone by the occasional female athlete or dancer. The undergarment's potential for eroticism begins to be exploited in art from the mid-fourth century, and is elaborated in Hellenistic literature. By the first century AD the breast-band has become a commonplace of erotic imagery. This increasing visibility suggests two possible conclusions. Firstly, breast-bands might in fact have become more widely worn over the Hellenistic period, perhaps because of women's increasing freedom of activity outside the home. Alternatively, male artists simply became more interested in depicting women's underwear, as a result of the growing popularity of the female nude. The breast-band provided a variation on the theme of teasingly-distributed drapery, as well as placing a firmly heterosexual emphasis on the female breast as a focus of erotic attention. In either case, the few examples we *do* have of the garment should make us at least question its absence from so many of our sources, and perhaps even wonder how familiar some Greek and Roman men were with their wives' more intimate layers of clothing.

ACKNOWLEDGEMENTS

I would like to thank all those who contributed to a lively debate at the conference, as well as Rebecca Flemming and Eleanor OKell, who supplied useful ideas and references afterwards. I owe apologies to Robin Osborne for my title.

NOTES

1. The abbreviation is common enough to appear in the OED. See Farrell-Beck & Gau 2001, 18, 72–3, fig. 7.
2. Farrell-Beck & Gau (2001) for a history of the bra in twentieth-century American society. On the garment itself, and its antecedents, see Ewing 1978 (1350 AD to the late 1970s), or Willett & Cunnington 1992 (medieval period to 1939).
3. Advert from Women's Home Companion, May 1943: Farrell-Beck & Gau 2001, fig. 23.
4. Surveying the circumstances in which breasts are revealed in Greek art, Cohen (1997, 68) remarks that "as undergarments were not customary, a loosened or opened dress would readily have laid bare the female breast". Informed by her experience as an archaeologist, Granger-Taylor (1996, 497) takes a more generous view: "Underclothes, like tunics, were probably worn more widely than ancient art or literature suggests".
5. Mau (1909) includes a section on the fascia pectoralis. Evans (1893) does not include the *strophion*, even in a chapter devoted to 'under-garments of the women'. Abrahams regards *strophion* "sometimes worn by women under the breasts, to serve the purpose of modern corsets" (1908 in Johnson 1964, 70) but cites London E230, where the garment is clearly worn over the breasts. Also Wilson 1938 (below n. 33).
6. Olson 2003, 203–5; Croom 2000, 93–4, figs 43 & 44.1, col. pl. 18; Losfeld 1991, 222–3; Symons 1987a, 28; 1987b, 23.

7   Ewing 1978, 15; the opening chapter covers 3000 BC to 1350 AD in ten pages.
8   Parthenon: London, figures K, L, M; Boardman 1985, fig. 80.3. Paionios' Nike: Olympia; Boardman 1985, fig. 139; Stewart 1997, fig. 30. Venus Genetrix: Paris, Louvre 525; Boardman 1985, fig. 197; Stewart 1997, fig. 62. Barberini Suppliant: Paris, Louvre MA 3433; Boardman 1985, fig. 221; Cohen 1997, fig. 3. Leda: Boston 04.14; Boardman 1985, fig. 140; Cohen 1997, fig. 4.
9   Olympia: west pediment, figures H and R; Boardman 1985, figs 21.4 and 21.8; Cohen 1997, fig. 5; Stewart 1997, fig. 9. Bassae: west frieze, London 524; Boardman 1995, fig. 5.5.
10 London E44, c.500 BC; Boardman 1975, fig. 222; Kilmer 1993, R445. See Blundell 2002, 156–8 fig. 7.
11 See Lewis 2002, 101–29 on the status of women in erotic scenes.
12 In general see Lewis 2002; cf. Llewellyn-Jones 2003 on veiling, and Kilmer 1993, 133–59 on pubic hair.
13 London 208; Stewart 1997, fig. 19. Serwint (1993) discusses the its possible initiatory significance and distinctive dress.
14 Stewart 1997, 108–18, 231–4 (catalogue); col. pl. VI and fig. 66 wearing the diazoma.
15 On Atalanta's outfits, and possible relationship to historical female hunters and athletes, see Parisinou 2002, 55–72; Scanlon 2002, 189; Stewart 1997, 120–4 figs 70–2; Seltman 1956, 121–2 pls 8–9 and 24.
16 LIMC s.v. Atalanta nos. 62–80. Diazoma and cap: Bologna 361 (Oltos); Boardman 1975, fig. 62; Ferrara T.991 (Aberdeen Painter); Stewart 1997, fig. 71; Boston 03.820 (Aberdeen Painter); Boardman 1989, fig. 88.
17 Bologna 300; LIMC s.v. Atalante no. 81*; Boardman 1989, fig. 179.
18 Louvre CA 2259; LIMC s.v. Atalante no. 60*; Boardman 1975, fig. 369.
19 Ferrara T.404; LIMC s.v. Atalante no. 73*; Boardman 1989, fig. 143.
20 Piazza Armerina, Room 34a (second service room to the dominus' apartment); Carandini et al. 1982, 150–6 figs 73–5 and 77, pl. 17. Details are much cited by clothes historians, e.g. Goldman 1994, fig. 13.26. Croom 2000, 93, col. pl. 18: practical experiments demonstrate that a cloth had to be c.5m long, wrapped around the breasts 6–7 times, in order not to slip down.
21 Brauron 721; Kahil 1963, 20–1 no. 43 pl. 12; Kahil 1983, 240 fig. 15.14.
22 Euripides, *Iphigeneia at Tauris* 1464–7; Linders 1972.
23 Lonsdale 1993, 171–93; cf. Stewart (1997, 122–4) on the girls' nudity. Keuls' discussion of **Figure 9.3** (1985, 312–16 fig. 280) ignores this age difference.
24 Female dancers with castanets: woman naked except for a leopard-skin, cup by Epiktetos (London E38; Boardman 1975, fig. 75.2); woman in 'transparent' chiton, cup near the Brygos Painter (London E61; Llewellyn-Jones 2002, 187 fig. 10); naked woman, cup by the Foundry Painter (London 95.5–13.1; Kilmer 1993, R527.2; Stewart 1997, fig. 37); girl wearing a short chiton, phiale by the Phiale Painter (Boston 97.371; Boardman 1989, fig. 128; on her status Lewis 2002, 29–33 fig. 1.17). Possible use of castanets in Artemis' ritual: *krateriskoi* fragments from Mounichia (Piraeus Museum Kk21 and 57; Palaiokrassa 1991, 153 and 162, pls. 40b and 41; on the *krateriskoi* and ritual, see Hamilton 1989).
25 Athens, Vlastos-Serpieri Collection 480; Boardman 1975, fig. 346; Kilmer 1993, R697.
26 E.g. Plutarch, *Aristides* 5.7, Athenaios 12.62.25.
27 Philostratos *De Gymnastica* 10. The ancient lexicon entries are of little help, since they define it as 'the round belt' (Hesychios and Photios, s.v. *strophion*) with no indication of where it was worn.
28 Sommerstein 1990, ad Lys. 931–2.
29 Henderson 1991, 149; cf. Gerber 1978, 204–5. Henderson (1991, 126) notes instances of *karua* as slang for male genitalia; cross-dressing or even a *double entendre* could be intended here
30 Cf. Hawley (1998, 92–3) different levels of 'feminisation' through costume by Agathon and the Kinsman, also Robson this volume.
31 Pollux (7.95–96) also quotes a longer passage from the second Thesmophoriazusae (fr. 332 Kassel-Austin), where the words *strophon* [sic], *mitra*, and *apodesmoi* all feature in a list of luxuries and women's belongings. Other instances of *apodesmos* seem not to mean breast-band: Hesychios (s.v.) clearly indicates a head-band.
32 At length, Bezantakos 1987, esp. 182–90.
33 Wilson (1938, 164) notes that *fascia* and *strophium* "served the same purpose as the modern brassières or bust supporters", though both could also indicate other garments; Varro once uses *capitium* (LL 5.131), usually meaning a head-covering or head-hole in a tunic. Goldman (1994, 223–5) gives practical experiments in reconstructing the *strophium* and other undergarments.

34 Cf. *In P. Clodium et C. Curionem* frs 22 and 24 Schoell.
35 Cf. Tacitus, *Annals* 15.57. The title of Richlin's article 'Pliny's brassiere' (1997) arises from her understanding of Pliny (NH 28.76): "headaches are relieved by tying a woman's brassiere on the head". Richlin's overall argument (that the garment's supposed curative powers belong to a tradition of medicinal properties associated with women's bodies) remains valid, but the delightful image of Pliny sitting with a bra on his head is unjustified: the Latin is simply *fascia mulieris*, which could indicate a variety of female 'wrappings'. The standard translations in Loeb (Jones, 1963) and Budé (Ernout, 1962) likewise render the term 'woman's breast-band' and 'soutien-gorge', the latter adducing Martial 14.134 as support for the unwarranted comment that it was worn to halt the development of women's breasts. Bostock & Riley (1856), pre-dating the invention of the modern bra, give a probably more accurate rendering: 'woman's fillet', glossed 'either a stomacher, or a fillet for the head'.
36 E.g. Athens NM 1305 (grave stele); Villing 2000, fig. 6; Parthenon east pediment figure N (goddess), London; Boardman 1985, fig. 80.4. A related garment is the figure-of-eight shoulder-strap (crossing only the back) securing the *chiton* of (male) charioteers and some active females; Harrison's (1977) identification with the *strophion* is not convincing. Some kind of over-garment must be indicated by the *strophion* in some early fourth-century inventories from the Athenian Akropolis, one cited in LSJ s.v. *strophion* = 'breast-band' (*IG* II^2 1388.9; cf. *IG* II^2 1383.8, 1400.9–10, 1407.9, 1428col.1.30). The word appears alongside a *thôrax* (breastplate, cuirass) in each case, and the context indicates that both are component parts of a gold statue of Nike (Harris 1995, 131–2).
37 Bonner 1949. Janko (1992, ad 214–17) cites Bonner with approval, but then refers to "this sexy brassière", obfuscating the distinction between undergarment and ornament. See Faraone 1990, 220–3 for previous scholarship, and Alden 1998 on 'Kestos' as trade-name for an early modern bra.
38 Earlier abandoned Ariadnes generally remain fully clad, but she has lost her top on Boston 00.349; *LIMC* s.v. Ariadne no. 54*.
39 E.g. House of the Centenary, cubiculum (IX.8.6); Naples Inv. No. 27686 and 110569 (from the House of Caecilius Jucundus). See Varone 2000, figs. 49, 62 and 70; Clarke 1998, pls. 7–8 and 49 (Third Style).
40 From the House of the King of Prussia (VII.9.33); Naples Inv. No. 27690; inscription = *CIL* IV 794; Varone 2000, fig. 48.
41 South wall of brothel (VII.12.18), east and west sections; Varone 2000, figs. 84 and 57. Probably also in this category is the scene from the apodyterium of the Suburban baths complex, where two men cavort 'doggie-style' with a woman in a breast-band; Varone 2000, fig. 32; Clarke 1998, pl. 14. On the paintings' contexts, see Clarke 1998, 145–240.
42 Satyrs discovering sleeping maenads, Osborne 1992, 72–6. Women undressing/washing as erotic theme, Sutton 1992, 22–4, cf. Lewis 2002, 142–9.
43 Critical review, Havelock 1995, 19–37; also Stewart 1997, 97–106.
44 LIMC s.v Aphrodite nos. 505–13 (**Figure 9.6** = no. 511*, Munich Antikensammlungen 8516). LIMC adopts the traditional dating (earliest example of the type – terracotta – in the early fourth century, others mid-third to late first century BC); Havelock's (1995) down-dating of the Aphrodite of Knidos' influence suggests a starting date no earlier than mid second century BC; the issue remains contentious. A related type of Aphrodite holding a folded breastband is popular from the late first century BC in the east (LIMC s.v. 'Aphrodite [in peripheria orientalis]' nos. 132–53 (nude) and 154–9 (dressed)).
45 Goldman 1994, fig. 13.27. Croom (2000) has two breast-band-tying images: a bronze Aphrodite statuette from the Museum Burg Linn, Germany (fig. 43), and a nymph, detail of a mosaic from Hippo Regius, Algeria (fig. 44.1).
46 Nikosia, Cyprus Museum no. 234; Karageorghis 1998, fig. 234. Identified as Aphrodite or Leda, because of the swan: the image is clearly erotic.

PART III
THE CLOTHED BODY IN ROME AND LATE ANTIQUITY

Chapter 10

The *toga praetexta* of Roman Children and Praetextate Garments

Judith Sebesta

The oldest Roman garment, according to the antiquarian Varro, was the plain white toga, which in earliest times was worn by men and women both day and night.[1] Its purple-bordered variant, called the *toga praetexta*, was also considered a garment of great antiquity. Pliny the Elder states that Rome's third king, Tullus Hostilius, adopted this garment for himself and Roman magistrates from Etruscan magisterial insignia.[2] Both Roman boys and girls, however, wore the *toga praetexta*. This chapter explores why Roman children wore a *toga praetexta* by examining certain Roman concepts of sexuality and locating the child's toga within the category of praetextate garments.

Many of the textual references to the *toga praetexta* refer simply to "the wearers of the (*toga*) *praetexta*" (*praetextati*) in which the Latin term denotes boys who had not yet formally entered adulthood.[3] For instance, Cicero states that Archias was the teacher of Lucullus while Lucullus was a *praetextatus* (Cicero *Pro Archia* 5) A number of references, however, occur in contexts that give some indication of the restrictions on the behavior of adults in the presence of a child clothed in a *toga praetexta*.

These textual references indicate clearly that a praetextate child was not to be sexualized explicitly or implicitly. This prohibition underlies the incidents Cicero cites in his speeches against Verres, in which he rebukes Verres for bringing his son to Sicily to share his life of vice. For example, Cicero explains that Verres held picnics at which he and his praetextate son were the only males present among women of high rank but questionable repute. Cicero does not say that there was any overt sexual behavior at such picnics. What was improper was the presence of women who did not conform to standards of matronal modesty: shown by their presence unattended by their husbands. Cicero configures this as a statement of the sexual accessibility of the matrons' bodies. The situation was one at least of latent, if not overt sexuality, and therefore inappropriate for a praetextate youth. Cicero upbraids Verres, saying,

> You stationed your son, clad in his *toga praetexta*, among women of this sort, so that at his age, which is most particularly hazardous and dangerous, the life of his father should offer examples of vicious living.[4]

What made the son's age 'most particularly hazardous and dangerous' is that he was at the age that was attractive not only to Roman women, but to Roman men as well.

Craig Williams comments that:

> the ideal male partner, the *youth* or *boy* of our sources, belonged to the age-group roughly equivalent to what is now called adolescence. For Romans, this period's beginning was marked by the onset of puberty (generally held to occur between the twelfth and fourteenth years…) …and its end was marked by what they saw as the completion of the process of maturation… (…around the twentieth year). In between those two extremes lay the golden years, the "flower of youth" (*flos aetatis*), when boys were no longer prepubescent children, but not yet men; when they were at the peak of desirability and thus of vulnerability (1999, 16).

Such vulnerability makes another situation even more inappropriate for Verres' praetextate son. One of Verres' chief minions, Apronius, was a man as foul in body odor and appearance as he was in character. Verres was, nevertheless, so enamored of the man, Cicero tells us, that he permitted Apronius all sorts of liberties, to the extent of letting him dance at a dinner party in his loincloth (if *nudus* does not here mean completely naked) even though Verres' son was reclining on one of the dining couches, clad in his *toga praetexta*.[5] While Apronius made no overt sexual overtures to the praetextate son, his conduct was at best lascivious, at worst, an implicit assault upon the boy's *pudicitia*.

The concept of *pudicitia* reinforced the nonsexual status of a Roman child by governing the range of licit expressions of sexuality, which were radically different for adult Roman males and females. A Roman *matrona* could properly employ her body sexually only with one man, her husband, and was ideally to remain his widow for the rest of her life, as the honorific funerary epithet *univira* ('wife of one man') indicates. A Roman man, however, could licitly engage in sex not only with his wife, but also with anyone who was not a Roman citizen regardless of that person's sex or age. While to us both of these two spheres of licit sexual relations – sexuality engaged in only with one's husband vs. practically unbounded sexual activity – are distinctly different, the Romans linked them conceptually under the term *pudicitia*. Often translated as 'modesty' or 'chastity', *pudicitia* is better paraphrased as the proper sexual employment of one's body. In the case of a Roman man, the proper employment was nuanced. While he could – and was even expected to – engage in sex with his wife, with a prostitute, or even with a male or female slave of any age, he was not to do so with another Roman citizen, male or female, of any age. If he did so, as for example in the rape of a *matrona* or adult Roman male, he violated that citizen's *pudicitia* and committed *stuprum*.

Stuprum was both a crime and a disgraceful act that could be committed only on free-born Romans. It did not relate to the use of prostitutes, or debauched living in general, or the sexual use of adult slaves, male or female. Nor did *stuprum* result from the sexual use of boys or girls provided they were not Romans. Slave children were licit sexual partners for adult Roman men, whose sexual activity was governed by two protocols:[6]

> a self-respecting Roman man must always give the appearance of playing the insertive role in penetrative acts, and not the receptive role… [The second protocol] concerned the status of their partners, and here too the rule applied regardless of their partners' sex:

apart from his wife, freeborn Romans both male and female were officially off-limits sexual partners for a Roman man.[7]

While a Roman man did not incur *stuprum* through engaging in sex with a slave child, girl or boy, he did incur *stuprum* through engaging in sex with a Roman child, girl or boy, for whom the only proper sexual employment of the body was a strict and absolute chastity. A praetorian edict of the second century BC addressed the perpetration of *stuprum* upon a praetextate child, stating that the perpetrator shall be liable for punishment if he

> shall be said to have abducted the attendant of a matron or of a boy or girl wearing the *praetexta*, or to have accosted or pursued him or her contrary to decent ways.[8]

The Digest makes explicit what is meant by 'accost' and 'pursue':

> It is one thing to accost, another to pursue: for he accosts, who makes trial of someone's chastity by speech, he pursues who follows someone constantly and silently.[9]

There are two significant aspects here. The first aspect is that the law addresses the intent of committing *stuprum* as well as the actual accomplishment of it. In recognizing the distinction, the Digest assigns different punishment to the intent in contrast to the perpetration of *stuprum*:

> Whoever shall persuade a boy wearing the toga praetexta to commit *stuprum* or any other offense... if the offense is actually perpetrated he is punished capitally; if not, he is deported to an island.[10]

That the *toga praetexta* clearly identified a child as 'Roman and off-limits' is clear from Propertius' recall of his assumption of the adult male's plain white toga:

> When for me the modesty of the *praetexta* mantle was lifted away, and freedom to know the path of love was given me...[11]

The second aspect is that any impingement of sexuality on the Roman child is absolutely forbidden. Not only is it forbidden to touch or assault a Roman child physically, but it is forbidden to 'touch or assault' the child verbally. Forbidden also is the physical non-touching of the child through 'silent following'. In short, it is forbidden to create or set up a situation that sexualized the Roman child through any action or speech. The *toga praetexta* functioned as an insignia of free-birth and free condition (*insignia ingenuitatis et libertatis*) to advise adults to avoid any expression of sexuality of any kind toward or around the child (Gabelmann 1985, 513).

Stuprum, however, concerned only expressions of sexuality that were directed toward a Roman child by an adult male. The non-sexual status of a Roman child encompassed more than that: it included an injunction on the praetextate child that he or she should not create or participate in a sexualized situation. A passage from Juvenal illustrates that the maintenance of a Roman child's nonsexual status did not involve only an external sexual assault on a child's body, but also involved the praetextate child keeping himself/herself out of the sexual sphere. Juvenal includes praetextate adulterers in a list of those who have engaged in sexual activity inappropriate to their status:

> Who is able to sleep when confronted with a daughter-in-law seduced by love of money, or a bride who has lost her virginity, or a praetextate adulterer? (77–78).

Juvenal's list castigates the daughter-in-law who engages in illicit sex after marriage, the bride who does so before her marriage, and, as the climax of his tricolon – and so, presumably, the most reprehensible – the praetextate youth who engages in sex prohibited to one of nonsexual status.

Two entries in the antiquarian dictionary of Paulus and Festus evince how fundamental in the Roman mind was the necessity to separate Roman children and sexuality. Paulus defines the term "praetextate speech" (*praetextus sermo*) as speech that is devoid of obscenity. He explains that such chaste speech is called "praetextate" because it is contrary to divine law (*nefas*) for *praetextati* to use obscene words. Festus also offers a second reason, connected with those boys of praetextate age that attended a bride. During her journey to her husband's home these boys shouted lewd words, but, Festus notes, they first put aside their *togae praetextae* (Festus 282 L; Paulus 283 L) Once divested of their *togae praetextae*, the boys, in effect, removed themselves temporarily from the class of nonsexual *praetextati* and could now engage in ritual sexual language.

Underlying this insistence on separating *praetextati* and sexuality is their ambiguous status as non-gendered beings, a status reflected in the fact that both boys and girls wore the *toga praetexta*. Mary Beard has pointed out that:

> ...creatures or things that are interstitial, which somehow fall between those categories we generally use to structure our environment or partake of more than one category are looked upon in traditional societies as particularly powerful, sacred, or dangerous – or a combination of the three (1980, 20).

That the *praetexta* indicated a special social category is shown by its etymological meaning 'woven first/woven before'.[12] This etymology derives from the weaving technique required by the warp-weighted loom originally used by the Romans.[13] Weaving on such a loom required the weaver to begin by making a heading band.[14] While for regular garments, the weaver used white wool for weft and warp, to create a *praetexta* the weaver used purple and white yarn (Sebesta 1994b, 66). As the verb *praetexere* is used in the sense of protecting and defending (*TLL* 1045), so the *praetexta* denoted the weaving of a religious garment, as well as protecting the act of its weaving from religious pollution by warning by-standers to refrain from sacrilegious words, gestures, or activity.

At this point it is necessary to examine the other praetextate garments in order to put the child's *toga praetexta* in a wider social context. The *toga praetexta* was also worn by: the Roman kings (and, in the imperial period, the emperor); and magistrates, among whose duties were the conduct of state religious rites, including the various *Ludi*.[15] It was also worn by those performing or participating in rites on behalf of the state, such as generals celebrating an *ovatio*[16]; those committing *devotio*[17]; and the male populace when celebrating the *Ludi*[18]. Others wearers include augurs, the pontifex maximus and flamens[19]; matrons sacrificing to Mutinus Titinus[20]; and freedwomen and female slaves engaged in the rites of Juno Caprotina and the Ludi Apollinares.[21] *Popae* and *servi publici* assisting in public sacrifices wore around their waists the *limus*, a long, rectangular 'skirt' with a praetexate lower border.[22] Vestal virgins wore a praetextate head covering (*suffibulum*).[23] Mourning women wore a praetextate mantle over their heads (*recinium*)[24] while the adult male who actually performed the funeral rites wore a praetextate dark-coloured mourning toga (Festus, 272 L, 273 L). As they were in perpetual mourning, widows also wore the praetextate *ricinium*. Lastly statues of deities were dressed in *togae praetextae*.[25]

All of these adult wearers of praetextate garments are united either by their contact with the numinous world or, in the case of statues of deities, are representations of that numinous world. During this time they are segregated into a 'holy' societal category marked both by ritual rules (taboos) and their praetextate garments. Sources give details about several ritual rules for those engaged in religious rites, public and private. Some of these pertain only to a specific priest or celebrant. One ritual rule forbade Vestal Virgins to engage in sex during their term of office: transgressors were buried alive. This ritual rule springs from the connection between their virginity and their holy purity. Mary Beard has observed that:

> ...It is well known that the popular belief that sexual activity was polluting and thus disqualified a person from close contact with the deity found expression in many sets of cult regulations. (1980, 12)

This connection between sex and pollution, however, was also expressed in a general ritual rule that forbade anyone who had sexual relations from participating in religious rites. In his poem on the Ambivarilia, Tibullus writes:

> Let him depart from the altars to whom Venus brought "evening joys" last night; chaste things please the gods. Come with pure garment and take up the waters of the fountain with pure hands (2.1.11–14).

Cicero comments in his treatise on the laws that,

> the law bids us come chastely to the gods, in mind of course, in which there is everything; it (chastity of mind) does not remove the requirement for the chastity of body, for that is removed by the sprinkling of water or by a certain number of days (*de Leg.* 2.1024).

This general ritual rule, requiring anyone who was to engage in a religious rite of any kind to refrain from sex, or celebrants to purify themselves if they had engaged in sex, points to why children were ideal participants for religious rituals. Columella explains that children were ideal intermediaries between the gods of the food store-room, the Penates, and other family members because:

> Only children, or at least someone that has been continent, should handle the equipment for preparing food. Anyone, male or female, that has engaged in sex should wash in a river or in flowing water before handling the stores of food. It was for this reason that my sources believed that it was necessary that only a boy or girl should really distribute the daily food rations.[26]

The *praetexta* on the child's toga advertised that its wearer was to be kept inviolable from any sexual action, speech, or even suggestion that would transfer the child from its non-gendered, nonsexual category into a gendered, sexual category and so incur the child's religious pollution. As Mary Douglas has pointed out,

> Holiness requires that individuals shall conform to the class to which they belong... Holiness means keeping distinct the categories of creation. It therefore involves correct definition, discrimination and order. Under this head all the rules of sexual morality exemplify the holy (1966, 54).

Roman children, therefore, were extremely appropriate attendants (*camilli, camillae*) for the Flamen and Flaminica Dialis whose ritual purity would otherwise have been imperiled if they were served, instead, by adults who, *ipso facto*, were gendered, sexual beings. To guard against the children coming into contact with sexuality in any form, even 'passively' in the form of speech, their nonsexual status was signaled and protected by the *toga praetexta*.[27]

Just as the *praetexta* on the clothing of priests and priestesses advised all beholders that, in the words of Seneca, they should refrain from things *obscaena*,[28] so the *praetexta* on the child's toga advised all beholders of the child's inviolable state. The words of the emperor Julian, in his role as Pontifex Maximus, are as appropriate for the *pueri praetextati* as for the priests he was addressing:

> ...when we wear in public the sacred dress [we] make it a public property ...for whenever this happens, many who are not purified come near us, and by this means the symbols of the gods are polluted.[29]

For children, who, like priests and Vestals, possessed a ritual purity, the *praetexta* signaled their holy status and, through warning others of that status, protected it from profanation. The *praetexta* bestowed honor (*maiestas*) on children and guarded their weakness.[30] It was, in the words of one Roman,

> that sacred *praetexta* by which we make sacred
> and venerable the weakness of childhood.[31]

NOTES

1. Varro in Nonius 541 M.
2. Pliny the Elder, *Natural History* 9.63. See also Macrobius, *Saturnalia* 1.6.7. While the Romans did adapt the toga from the curved Etruscan *tebenna* and borders did typically adorn Etruscan garments, there is no evidence, however, that these borders had any symbolic meaning for the Etruscans, for whom clothing decoration was "purely ornamental." See Bonfante 1975, 15, 48.
3. Because Roman texts privilege the male, most of the textual references refer to boys, rather than girls.
4. Cicero, *In Verrem* 2.3.159; 2.5.81 and 2.5.137.
5. Cicero, *In Verrem* 3.23. On the connotations of *nudus*, see Heskel 1994, 136–139.
6. This term was first used by Winkler (1990). Valerius Maximus (Book 6.1) gives a number of historical examples of *stuprum* committed, or attempted, against unmarried Roman girls, youths, wives, and even adult men.
7. Williams 1999, 18–19. Williams points out that a Roman male could use his freedmen and freedwomen sexually without committing *stuprum*, such use falling within his rights as patron (1999, 100).
8. Williams 1999, 121 and 315 n. 106.
9. Digest 47.10.15. 22: *aliud est appellare, aliud adsectari: appellat enim, qui sermone pudicitiam adtemptat, adsectatur, qui tacitus frequenter sequitur.*
10. Williams 1999, 120–121. Digest 47.11.1.2. See also Gaius, *Institutiones* 3.220.
11. Propertius, 3.15.3–4: *ut mihi praetexti pudor est relevatus amictus / et data libertas noscere amoris iter.* Valerius Maximus (preface Book 6) also describes the *toga praetexta* as the protector of boyhood *pudicitia*:

"by your [=Pudicitia] protection the insignia of boyhood are defended, by your guardianship the flower of youth remains pure, and through your keeping the stola of the matron is valued." (*tuo praesidio puerilis aetatis insignia munita sunt, tui numinis respectu sincerus iuventae flos permanet, te custode matronalis stola censetur.*)

12 That the *praetexta* was indeed woven first underlies the proverb quoted by Quintilian: "I cannot expect a *toga praetexta* when I see that the beginning is dark-grey." (*Institutio Oratoria* 5.10.81: *non possum togam praetextam sperare cum exordium pullum videam.*)
13 Sometime in the first century AD a second upright loom came into use in which the vertical warp threads are tied to a lower beam and the weaver begins weaving at the bottom of the loom. See Wilson 1938, 17, 21, and Barber 1991, 125.
14 Granger-Taylor (1982, 5) identifies such a "starting border" or transverse selvedge on the tunic of the Arringatore.
15 In this the Roman kings imitated Etruscan kings who wore the *toga praetexta*. See Festus 430 L; Livy 1.8.3; and Pliny the Elder, *Natural History* 8.195 and 9.136. These magistrates were tribunes, aediles, praetors, consuls, consul designates (CIL I[2] 582), censors, the *triumviri*, *vicomagistri* (at the Compitalia) and *magistri* of *collegia*, and magistrates of *coloniae*. (The *decemviri* of the early Republic also wore *togae praetextae*.) All of these could conduct religious rites on behalf of the state.
16 Velleius Paterculus states (2.40.4) that T. Ampius and T. Labienus, tribunes, passed a law that Caesar could wear at the Ludi Circenses the golden crown and all the paraphernalia of a triumphator, and at the Ludi Scaenici he could wear a *toga praetexta* and golden crown.
17 As the *devotio* is a religious action, that of self-sacrifice, a magistrate would, of course, wear a *toga praetexta*. Historical examples of *devotio* are limited to magistrates with *imperium*. As in a sense they were committing *devotio*, the *senes* in Rome awaiting the Gauls in 390 BC also wore *togae praetextae*. See Versnel 1970, 358, 383; and Livy 8.95, 10.7.5.
18 According to Festus (428–430 L) these include the *vicimagistri* celebrating the *Ludi Compitalicii*; see, Palmer 1974, 13. Cicero (*Second Philippic* 110) upbraids Antony for not wearing a *toga praetexta* even though the citizens are *feriati* due to their celebrating the *Ludi Circenses*.
19 The *Fratres Arvales* wore *togae praetextae* at their sacrifices. Others include the *epulones* and the *quindecemviri*.
20 Paul. ex. Festus 143 L. Boels-Janssen (1993, 102) suggests that women sacrificed to Mutinus Titinus in a *toga praetexta* because he was the god to whom they had offered their virginity on the marriage bed; hence it was proper that they should wear the *toga praetexta* of the *virgo nubens*. She also notes that according to Festus (4 L s.v. *armita*), Vestals sacrificed in a toga, though Festus does not specifically state that it was a *praetexta*.
21 According to Varro, L.L. 6.18, after Rome had been weakened by the Gallic invasion of 390 BC, the Fidenae, Ficuli and other Italians demanded that the Romans hand over their wives and daughters. The Romans persuaded freedwomen and female slaves to dress as their (former) mistresses and go to the enemy. The women got the enemy drunk, and when they were asleep, summoned the Romans who routed them. As a result, the Senate voted the women various gifts including the garments they had worn. Annually thereafter, on the Nonae Caprotinae (July 7), freedwomen and female slaves engaged in a mock battle with wild fig staves. These women were presented with *togae praetextae* at the Ludi Apollinares. Kent 1958, 191 note d, 192 note e, states that the connection of figs and Juno in the Nonae Caprotinae implies an original fertility rite.
22 Servius, *in Vergili Aeneadem* 12.120.
23 The *suffibulum* was a short, white veil with purple border worn by Vestals and fastened with a pin. See La Follette 1994, 58–59. Paulus ex. Fest. 474, 475 L.
24 The *ricinium* was a double-folded veil worn by widows, women mourning, and women in times of public mourning. See Festus (342 L); Sebesta 1994a, 50. Torelli (1984, 71) argues that the widow assumes the praetextate *ricinium* because she is restored to her prenuptial condition when, as an unmarried girl, she wore the *toga praetexta*.
25 Mentioned by various authors are Jupiter, Clitumnus, Fortuna (Pliny N.H. 8.197), and Asclepius. A *lararium* at Pompeii shows a Genius in a *toga praetexta* sacrificing at an altar.
26 Columella, *Res Rustica* 12.4.3. See also Fowler 1920, 42–52 and Wiedemann 1989, 181–182.
27 Boels-Janssen 1993, 20–21.

28 Seneca, *Controversiae* 1.2.7: *coram sacerdotes obscenis homines abstinent* – "in the presence of priests men abstain from things obscene".
29 Julian, *Letter to a Priest*, translated by Wright 1913–23, 1:332–35.
30 Pliny, *N.H.* 9.127 describes the purple dye as *pro maiestate pueritiae est*.
31 Pseudo-Quintilian, *Declamatio* 340: *Illud sacrum praetextatum quo infirmitatem pueritiae sacram facimus et venerabilem*.

Chapter 11

What Made the Roman Toga *virilis*?

Glenys Davies

Quintilian, writing in the late first century AD, says that the Roman orator's dress should be *splendidus et virilis*:

> With regard to dress, there is no special garb peculiar to the orator, but his dress comes more under the public eye than that of other men. It should, therefore, be distinguished and manly *(splendidus et virilis)*, as, indeed, it ought to be with all men of position (*Institutio Oratoria* 11.3.137).[1]

From what Quintilian says later it is clear that the orator wears a tunic and toga, but presumably Quintilian is not just thinking of the *toga virilis* – the plain white toga worn by Roman citizens and adopted by boys when they officially pass from boyhood to manhood.[2] So what connotations does *virilis* have in this context? The toga was not *per se* a 'manly' garment: according to Roman tradition it was originally worn by women as well as men, might be worn by girls before puberty, and was associated with prostitutes and adulteresses.[3] Indeed it was this that enabled Cicero to taunt Antony with the jibe that as soon as he put on the *toga virilis* it became a *toga muliebris* (Cicero, *Philippics* 2.44; Dyck 2001). What makes the garment *virilis* is not so much the toga itself as how it is worn, and the behaviour of the wearer.

Some idea of what Quintilian may have meant by *splendidus et virilis* is suggested by the statue (of Titus?), now in the Vatican (**Figure 11.1**).[4] Such statues, presumably, do not show the toga as it normally appeared on real people, but how ideally it ought to look. There are several features which make this a powerful and impressive image. The statue is noticeably wide, with the arms held well away from the body: the figure gesticulates with both hands, neither of which are obscured by the fabric of toga or tunic. The toga falls in a series of bold sweeping folds that form three grand U-shapes across the body: it falls to the feet, but does not cover them. The toga was not structurally a particularly complex garment: although a more complex shape than the simple rectangle of the *pallium* it has no seams or fringes.[5] In this form – typical of the first and second centuries – it is its *draping* which is complex and it must in practice have been difficult to keep in place, but on statues the wearers show immaculate control. It appears so well balanced on Titus' left shoulder that the viewer need have no anxiety that it will fail to stay in place.

'Stressing width' is a male characteristic, as Marianne Wex's photographs taken of people in Hamburg in the 1970s show (Wex 1979; see also Davies 1997). Women tend

Figure 11.1 (left). Togate statue with a portrait head of Titus, Vatican Museum. (Photo: Musei Vaticani).

Figure 11.2 (right). Togate statue of Augustus from the Via Labicana, Museo Nazionale Romano. (Photo DAIR neg. 65.1111 Koppermann).

to stand with arms held in to the body and the legs close together, and to sit with legs crossed. This use of size and width is not just a human characteristic: for many animals making oneself larger is a way of displaying power and dominance; it is generally something that the males of the species do to establish a pecking order, and is less common among females (Morris 1969, 103; Davis & Weitz 1981, 81–2). For the Romans donning the toga is perhaps the equivalent of raising the hackles and making the hair stand on end. It makes the figure look bigger and so more powerful and dominant.

Quintilian's handbook for aspiring orators shows that he is quite aware of the importance of non-verbal communication through the use of the body, and that this includes the use of dress as an accessory.

> All emotional appeals will inevitably fall flat, unless they are given the fire that voice, look, and the whole carriage of the body can give them (*totius prope habitu corporis*) (*Inst Orat.* 11.3.2).

The head should be carried naturally and erect:

> For a droop suggests humility, while if it be thrown back it seems to express arrogance, if inclined to one side it gives an impression of languor, while if it is held too stiffly and rigidly it appears to indicate a rude and savage temper. (*Inst. Orat.* 11.3.69)

Later he says:

> It is, as a rule, unbecoming to raise or contract the shoulders. For it shortens the neck and produces a mean and servile gesture, which is even suggestive of dishonesty. (*Inst. Orat.* 11.3.83)

The orator should avoid appearing too humble but he should also not appear too arrogant, as that would issue a challenge to the other males in the room, and he wishes to persuade rather than dominate. Hence the concept of 'modesty' which appears several times in Quintilian's pages.[6]

Quintilian recognises that 'stressing width' can be achieved by use of clothing.

> We should not cover the shoulder and the whole of the throat, otherwise our dress will be unduly narrowed (*angustus*) and will lose the impressive effect produced by breadth at the chest. (*Inst. Orat.* 11.3.141)

This perhaps explains Augustus' rather unnaturally wide right shoulder in the Via Labicana statue (**Figure 11.2**).[7] This statue presents us with a psychologically more complex image than the statue of 'Titus': we see not the orator persuading and dominating his audience, but a statue which is designed to convey Augustus's piety and humility before the gods as well as his dominant position as *pontifex maximus*. Thus the figure appears narrower, the arms are less widespread, and the head inclined to look down slightly; the drapery is raised over the head, but still falls in a bold pattern of deeply cut sweeping folds. These somewhat contradictory signals perhaps result in a rather false impression of modesty and humility.

The 'manly' aspects of the toga can be seen best when togate statues of men are compared with portrait statues of women (**Figure 11.3**).[8] Statue types used for women tend to adopt narrow body postures, with the arms often held into and across the body; the drapery falling in a variety of complex, even fussy folds suggesting expensive fabrics, and the dress always long enough to trail over the feet. The contrasts between the breadth of the male figure and the narrowness of the female; the broad sweeping curves of his drapery with the more complex patterns on hers; her hands covered by or occupied with the drapery, his hands free to gesture openly, can be seen not only on the two statues illustrated here (**Figures 11.2** and **11.3**) but on countless others from the Roman world.[9] The complex fold patterns of women's drapery may reflect a variety of different fabrics; in contrast, the toga was supposed to be made of wool. Another difference which we cannot see today, but which might have been

Figure 11.3 (left). Portrait statue of a woman in the "pudicitia" pose, Severan period. Capitoline Museum. (Photo: author's own).
Figure 11.4 (right). Togate statue of Hadrian, Capitoline Museum. (Photo: DAIR neg. 55.212 Sansaini).

obvious when looking at such statues in their original state was that the toga was normally white (or at least the natural colour of white wool), whereas women's clothing could be dyed a variety of colours. Emperors, especially later ones, might wear purple togas, and magistrates were entitled to the purple stripe of the *toga praetexta*, but white predominated (Sebesta, this volume).

It seems that for Romans of the early-mid empire long sleeves hanging over the hands, and long tunics falling to the feet, were feminine forms of dress, and when worn by men were a sign of effeminacy.[10] The *lacinia* of a man's toga may fall to the ground, but on statues the toga does not obscure the feet. Statues of women also frequently show another female characteristic: the tendency to fiddle with the drapery, as if it is impossible for them to keep it under control (**Figures 11.3** and **11.6**). Men are not shown hitching up their togas (though on occasion they are shown with one hand holding onto it lightly)[11] – despite the fact that we might suspect that in real life they would have needed to do this repeatedly. The impression togate statues give is one of effortless control, of a garment that miraculously stays in place leaving the wearer free to gesticulate with his hands and move comparatively freely.

Quintilian in fact intimates that this degree of control, although essential at the beginning of the orator's speech, is not expected to last throughout it: he goes on to describe how progressive – though artfully planned – dishevelment should accompany the orator's increasing involvement in the cause he is arguing. But before the orator starts speaking:

> Our attitude should be upright, our feet level and a slight distance apart, or the left may be very slightly advanced... The arms should be held slightly away from the side... (*Inst Orat.* 11.3.159)

He gives a list of irritating movements which should be avoided: looking at the ceiling, rubbing the face, craning forward, frowning, brushing the hair back from the face, twitching fingers and lips as if rehearsing what to say, clearing the throat, thrusting out one foot, grasping a fold of the toga in the left hand, standing with feet wide apart, hunching the shoulders like a wrestler about to fight (*Inst. Orat.* 11.3.160). And as for the toga:

> if the toga falls down at the beginning of our speech, or when we have only proceeded but a little way, the failure to replace it is a sign of indifference, or sloth, or sheer ignorance of the way clothes should be worn. (*Inst. Orat.* 11.3. 149)

Toga-control, then, is an important lesson for the young orator to learn, and, it seems, it was just as important in other areas of public life. Suetonius tells how Caligula rushed out of the theatre in a rage and tripped over the end of his toga – one of many instances where Caligula's dress betrays his unsuitability as an emperor.[12]

Togate portrait statues should not only be compared with statues of women: it is also instructive to compare them with male figures wearing the *pallium* (i.e. 'Greek' dress): compare **Figure 11.4** (Hadrian in a toga) with **Figure 11.5** ('Hadrian' in a *pallium*).[13] Compared to many of the statue types used for women, the *palliatus* has considerable freedom of movement, but compared to the togate figure, we can see some of the traits visible on the female statues – the more fiddly drapery patterns, one arm wrapped in the drapery, the narrower body posture. Indeed the upright stance of Hadrian in a toga contrasts with the more slumped posture adopted by the figure wearing the *pallium*: the emperor carrying out his civilian duties as opposed to the intellectual. The toga was a national dress which distinguished the Romans (the *gens togata* of Vergil) from other peoples.[14] It is significant that the *pallium* (the Greek *himation*) appears to be a form of dress less distinctly distinguished from female drapery than the toga – which thus appears to be a more 'manly' garment.[15]

The togate statues of the imperial period – especially the type in vogue in the first and second centuries AD (Goette's B types, represented here by **Figures 11.1, 11.2** and

Figure 11.5 (left). Man wearing a pallium *(wrongly restored with head of Hadrian) from Cyrene, in the British Museum. (Photo © Copyright The British Museum).*
Figure 11.6 (right). Funerary relief of a couple, from the Via Statilia, in the Palazzo dei Conservatori. (Photo: DAIR neg. 99.825 Faraglia).

11.4)[16] are designed to express masculine power and control: the pose of the figure and the drapery patterns are clearly contrasted with those used for female statues, and also with statues of men wearing other forms of dress. What is interesting is that this does not appear to be as true of *Republican* togate statues. The toga could be worn one of two basic ways in late Republican art. It could be wrapped diagonally round the body, but in a way which appears less impressive than the later imperial toga, because there is less material in the toga, and because it is worn more tightly wound round the body.[17] More commonly it is represented being worn with both shoulders covered and an 'arm-sling' (as with the male figure in **Figure 11.6**) – a style of draping which makes the toga much less visibly distinguishable from the *pallium* (indeed Goette calls it the 'pallium-toga').[18] Because one arm is bound in close to the body by the drapery, this way of draping the toga fails to provide the same opportunities for stressing width, demonstrating control, or manual gesticulation, as the other method of draping. It is also much less clearly differentiated from female statues (**Figure 11.6**, see Hales and Harlow, this volume).

The toga appears in these statues and reliefs as typically Roman dress, even as a symbol of citizen status. It continued to be used in this way into the empire: freedmen took considerable pride in advertising their new status as Roman citizens by having themselves depicted wearing the toga on their funerary monuments.[19] But the Republican toga did not emphasise the distinction between male and female dress, and did not exploit the potential for expressing the virile power which characterised the men who ruled the Roman empire.

It is not accident that the new, bulkier toga with its richer drapery patterns appears in the time of Augustus. The Ara Pacis illustrates the transition, several ways of draping the toga being illustrated on the processional friezes, including the older arm-sling and the newer imperial type of draping.[20] It is highly significant that this change occurs in the reign of an emperor who did so much to reinforce traditional social hierarchies and to emphasise the toga as the symbol of Roman citizenship. This all fits with his requirement that citizens wear the toga when engaged in any kind of public activity, with his prescriptions about who could sit where in the theatre, and with the attempt to make the *stola* the distinctive badge of matrons. Suetonius (*Augustus* 40.5) recounts that he grew angry when he saw a crowd of people at a public meeting dressed in dark clothes (if they were wearing togas they would be in white) – it was this incident which famously caused him to quote Vergil "The Romans, lords of the world, the nation clad in the toga!"

Toga-wearing in real life, it has been argued, went down hill after this.[21] Nevertheless, the toga continued to be required for Roman citizens appearing in the law courts, while its wearing was forbidden to those who were sent into exile. Hadrian is recorded as being keen to be seen wearing the toga when in Italy, and demanding the same of others (senators and equites, at least).[22] Toga-wearing, I would suggest, *did* remain on the agenda for Rome's ruling classes: hence Quintilian's concern that young orators should be impressed with the need to learn to wear the toga properly, and Suetonius' picture of good toga-wearing emperors (while bad emperors wear all sorts of other unsuitable costumes, see Hales and Harlow, this volume). Hence also the large numbers of togate statues from the imperial period, many of them of men who were not emperors. The imperial toga was large and expensive: wearing it well was an art which had to be learned (and which also presumably required trained servants): it was an art too which must have reinforced the distinction between them and us – wearing a scruffy garment which just about qualified for the name of toga was one thing, but wearing the full imperial toga effortlessly must have been much like being able to tie an impeccable bow tie in more modern times. It singled out those who belonged to the class fit to rule the Roman world. Broad, confident, toga-wearing statues present this idea in permanent form: it is the ultimate in power-dressing, and articulated the Roman elite's rightful control of the government of Rome. Paradoxically perhaps emperors did not always feel the same need to be seen in the toga: Suetonius' *12 Caesars* has many instances of emperors who resist the toga for more gaudy and interesting (and often more comfortable) garments.[23] Suetonius, as I have already suggested, does not approve: the emperor for him should be a *civilis princeps* who dresses and behaves as a senator ought.[24] So, whatever they might wear in reality, emperors did continue to be presented in art wearing the toga, as a way of indicating their devotion to their civil duties: such representations appear alongside the other more dramatic images available for emperors (such as the heroic nude or a statue in armour, see Hales, this volume).

But if the toga signified male power and control, how do we explain the tradition that it was worn by little girls as well as boys, and also by prostitutes and adulteresses? It could be argued that this was just a hang-over from earlier traditions. It is uncertain to what extent either girls or prostitutes really wore the toga, and if so, what form it took (did prostitutes, for example, wear mannish white woollen togas – or did they have versions made up in brighter colours and fancier fabrics?). There are two little girls on the Ara Pacis who are thought to be wearing togas: the more certain of the two is on the fragment in the Louvre.[25] The other is the older girl usually identified as Domitia: it has been disputed whether the garment she is wearing is a toga or a *palla*.[26] Since she wears it draped in such a way as to form an arm-sling the identification depends on whether the lower edge of the garment is curved or not. The point is that the differentiation is not as clear as one might expect if this really mattered. There are a handful of other representations of girls or women in togas cited by Goette, but, perhaps not surprisingly, none of women who might be prostitutes or adulteresses.[27]

The essential point is that the toga in the imperial period could not be worn by respectable women, and particularly not by matrons, whose dress was carefully distinguished from that of men both by Augustus' encouragement of the *stola* and by the new conventions for representing the toga in art. As Vout has said, forcing a woman to wear the toga "openly denied her the status of Roman matron. It was to deny her her femininity by denying her the dress which in Roman rhetoric defined her as female" (1996, 215). Making the toga the form of dress that was abandoned by a girl when she became a woman, only to be taken up again if she became a prostitute or an adulteress, served to ensure that it could not be worn by mature women with aspiration to power. Augustus' wife could be a *Ulysses stolatus* but she could never aspire to be *Livia togata*.[28]

NOTES

1   The Loeb translation is used for all quotations.
2   On the toga in general see: Wilson 1924; 1938, Ch. 4; Stone 1994. For the adoption of the *toga virilis* by boys on reaching manhood, Stone 1994, 13 and n.14.
3   Toga originally worn by women as well as men: Nonius (citing Varro) 540, 31. Toga worn by girls: Propertius 4.11.33; Arnobius *Adversae Nationes* 2.67; Gabelmann 1985, 517–22. Toga worn by prostitutes and adulteresses: Stone 1994, 13 and n.7; Goette 1990, 6 n.42; Wilson 1938, 137; Sebesta 1994, 50–51; Cicero *Philippics* 2.44; Horace *Satires* 1.2.63; Martial 2.39, 10.52; Juvenal 2.68.

4   Vatican Museums, Braccio Nuovo 26 Inv. 2282: Goette 1990, 127, cat. Ba 290, pl. 12,1; Stone 1994, 21 fig. 1.10. Goette maintains that the head of Titus was not the original head of the statue, cf. Stone (1994, 42, n. 50) for the head being the original.
5   The precise shape of the toga, and particular the location of the purple stripe on the *toga praetexta* is a matter on which there are differing views: compare the diagrams produced by Lillian Wilson (1924, fig. 27a & b, reproduced in Stone 1994 fig. 1.5a & b) with Goette 1990, 3–4, figs. 1 & 3. For the shape and other technical details of the early toga worn by the Arringatore see Granger-Taylor 1982.
6   For recent studies of oratorical body language see Graf 1991, Aldrete 1999; Corbeill 2004, 107–139; for deportment more generally, Gleason 1995, esp. Ch. 3. Christ (1997, 28–9) comments specifically on the emphasis on 'modesty'.
7   Museo Nazionale Romano Inv. 56230, currently on display in the Palazzo Massimo. Goette 1990, 115, Cat. Ba32, pl. 6,3; Stone 1994 fig. 1.8.
8   Portrait statue of a woman in the so-called 'Pudicitia' pose, Capitoline Museum, Inv. 636. Early Severan. Fittschen & Zanker 1983, 97, no.141, pl. 168.
9   The contrast can be seen particularly well in the togate male and female statues displayed on the fountain of Herodes Atticus at Olympia (Bol 1984; Davies 2002).
10 Aulus Gellius *Attic Nights* 6.12.1–5. See also Suetonius *Julius Caesar* 45. Heskel 1994, 134, 140.
11 As M. Nonius Balbus does in his statue from Herculaneum (now in the Naples National Museum; Stone 1994, 21–2, fig. 1.7) but other examples (Goette 1990 pls. 4 & 5) are few in number compared to those illustrated with arms held away from the body.
12 Suetonius *Caligula* 35.3. In portrait statues of Caligula his toga does tend to appear more crumpled than usual – but this may just be a result of the sculptural style of the time.
13 Hadrian in toga: Capitoline Museum, Fittschen & Zanker 1985, 53–4, no.51, pl. 57; male figure in pallium restored with head of Hadrian: statue from Cyrene in the British Museum Inv. 1381. Recent investigation by Neil Adams has shown that the head of Hadrian does not belong to this statue: the correct head is that of another individual of late Antonine date. This discovery means there is no known example of a statue of an emperor in a *pallium*. Comparison of these two statues perhaps shows why. Compare also the togate statues with the *palliate* statues from the Fountain of Herodes Atticus at Olympia (Bol 1984, pl. 25, 26, 65 & 31, 57; Smith 1998, 75–77).
14 *Aeneid* 1.282; famously quoted by Augustus (Suetonius *Augustus* 40). Vout 1996, 213–4.
15 This argument is more fully explored and developed in Christ 1997.
16 Goette 1990: type Ba and Bb with U-shaped *umbo*.
17 As on the Arringatore (Goette 1990 pl. 1,1) and the sacrificing figure on the relief from the 'altar of Domitius Ahenobarbus' in the Louvre (Goette 1990 pl. 1, 3). See Goette's type Aa.
18 Funerary relief of a couple from the Via Statilia in the Museo del Palazzo dei Conservatori, Rome Inv. 2142: Goette 1990 Ab16; Kleiner 1992 fig. 21 (where it is dated 75–50 BC). See Goette 1990 types Ab and Ac. This is the type of draping identified by the Richardsons as the *ad cohibendum bracchium* mentioned by Cicero in *Pro Caelio* 5.11 and discussed in Richardson & Richardson 1966.
19 For freedmen on funerary monuments see Kleiner 1977 & 1987; D'Ambra 1998, 39–50 & 99–100; (in Northern Italy) Dexheimer 2000.
20 Stone 1994, 17–21; Richardson & Richardson 1966, 255; the processional friezes of the Ara Pacis are conveniently illustrated in Kleiner 1992, 94–5, figs. 74–7.
21 Stone 1994, 21–24; Vout 1996, 216. However, the sources most quoted for this are perhaps not the most reliable or unbiased commentators – Martial 4.66 (it was worn only on holidays), Juvenal 3.171–2 (it was worn only by the dead when buried) and Tertullian, *De pallio*.
22 Suetonius *Claudius* 15.2 (law courts); Pliny *Letters* 4.11 (forbidden to exiles – Licinianus was not only no longer allowed to wear his toga, he had also been demoted from an orator to a teacher of rhetoric); SHA *Hadrian* 22.
23 Suetonius *Julius Caesar* 45.3 (long fringed sleeves, loose belt); *Tiberius* 13.1 (*pallium* and slippers when on Rhodes); *Caligula* 11(in disguise at night); 19.2 (golden cloak; charioteer's dress); 32.3 (the dress of a *popa*); 52 (various kinds of fancy dress); *Claudius* 2.2 (Greek cloak to games – but elsewhere Claudius is a good toga-wearing emperor); *Nero* 25.1 (extravagant dress on entry into Rome); 48.1 and 51 (casual dress when appearing in public); *Domitian* 1.2 (disguise as follower of Isis); 4 (presided over contests in Greek shoes, purple toga *Graecanica* and a fancy gold crown).

24 For the concept of the *civilis princeps* see Wallace-Hadrill 1982.
25 Gabelmann 1985, 517, fig. 7; Goette, 80 and 158, no. N2a, pl. 70,2.
26 Gabelmann (1985, 523) thinks she is wearing a toga, but Stone (1994, 20) that she is wearing a *palla*. Goette (1990, 80 & 158, no. N2b pl 70, 3) also accepts this as a toga.
27 Goette 1990, 80–82 and 158–9, nos. N1–14.
28 Suetonius *Caligula* 23.2: according to Suetonius, Caligula often called his grandmother Livia this as a way of belittling her.

Chapter 12

Men are Mars, Women are Venus: Divine Costumes in Imperial Rome

Shelley Hales

Furthermore, he used to perform the story of Paris in his house, taking the role of Venus himself, in such a way that his clothes would suddenly drop to his feet and he would kneel, naked, with one hand placed on his breast and another on his private parts, with his buttocks projecting and thrust back on front of his debaucher. Moreover he used to make up his face to look like a painting of Venus, and was depilated all over his body – thinking that it was the principal enjoyment of life to appear worthy and suited for the lusts of the greatest number.
(SHA *Elagabalus* 5 [trans. Birley])

It is easy to identify Elagabalus' dressing up as the work of a 'bad' emperor.[1] Where Caligula had dressed up as Venus (Suet. *Gaius* 52; Dio 59.26), Elagabalus removes all his clothes for the ultimate recreation of the goddess of lust. At first sight, it is easy to identify the counts on which Elagabalus' 'badness' is summed up in this act of cross-(un)dressing at its most ludicrous and unconvincing: he transgresses boundaries between actor and emperor, man and woman, human and divine, flesh and art. This chapter will survey some aspects of the importance of dress in emperors' self-construction and representation in art and literature, focusing on the evolving ideology and adoption of costumes of divinity.

Elagabalus' biography shows him in many costumes (SHA *Elag.* 23, 26, 28). Although biographers might be attacked for dwelling on useless information, specifically details of emperors' dress (SHA *Macrinus* 1, see Harlow, this volume), this emphasis on imperial clothing is replicated throughout the *Historia Augusta* and Suetonius' *Lives*. Inspecting their clothes (or lack of) was clearly a crucial part of figuring responses to emperors. Both Caligula (Tacitus *Ann.* 1.41; Suet. *Gaius* 9) and Caracalla (SHA *Caracalla* 21) were even named after their clothes. Costume would be crucial for imperial families whose claim to power lay, in not inconsiderable measure, in their very visibility. Emperors and their entourage were everywhere: in person around Rome, and in the thousands of images set up around the empire. Whilst portrait heads changed, imperial outfits remained largely constant: as priest in a veiled toga, as warrior in full armour, togate to preside over civic ceremonies, or naked in Olympian splendour (**Figure 12.1**). It was precisely through acquaintance with these

Figure 12.1. Augustus as Mars and Livia as Venus, Ravenna Relief. (Photo: DAIR 38.1407).

constants that the empire's population learnt how to recognise emperors and their roles in society. As a result, power could be negotiated by the wearing, shedding and swapping of clothes (Tacitus *Hist.* 1.35, 1.81, 2.29, 2.59, 3.67, Suet. *Galba* 11).

The way in which an emperor dressed was an obvious starting point for determining whether he was a 'good' or 'bad' emperor. Constructed retrospectively as the antithesis of every bad emperor, Augustus, as *primus inter pares*, looked the perfect Roman – his toga was outstanding in precisely its ordinariness, its stripes neither too broad or too narrow (Suet. *Aug.* 73). He learned to hide both his strengths and weaknesses under the costume of Roman manliness and statesmanship.[2] In winter, rather than admit to bad health, layers of underpants and vests protected his puny body (Suet. *Aug.* 82). At times of uncertainty, he strapped on a 'bullet-proof vest' under his tunic (Suet. *Aug.* 35). All Augustus' costumes were convincing and appropriate: he knew how to dress for every occasion, carrying spare outfits to cover all eventualities (Suet. *Aug.* 73).

Bad emperors wore inappropriate clothes (Suet. *Nero* 38), or had the costume right but the performance disastrously wrong. Claudius advertised his weaknesses to one and all, bundled up in a cloak (Suet. *Claudius* 2). Caligula looked every inch the pious emperor as he prepared to sacrifice the victim, but rather spoilt the performance by taking a swing at an audience member instead (Suet. *Gaius* 32). The rise of would-be emperors is marked by a sequence of telling costume changes as they change from usurpers into emperors (Tacitus *Hist*. 2.89). Challengers who forget to make the change, or who fail to assume the right clothes, lose (Tacitus *Hist*. 2.20). Even if they make the costume, failure to live up to the actions prescribed for that outfit marks impostors (Tacitus *Hist*. 4.59; Dio 73.6; Suet. *Aug*. 10 cf. *Caesar* 64). It is at these moments that such men show their clothes to be nothing but costume and disguise.

Bad emperors were also obsessed with dressing up and pretence.[3] Nero is dismissed as merely a bad actor (Dio 63.22) – always recognisable even in what he thinks must be his deepest disguise. In fact, his most shabby clothes reveal him for exactly the man he is.[4] Elagabalus' real notoriety did not stem from his attempts to (un)dress like a woman, but rather his real (bad) acting whenever he had to be a man (Dio 80.14). His mother demonstrated his claim by dressing him in Caracalla's old clothes and parading him with Caracalla's statues (Dio 79.33). Dio presses home his conviction that Elagabalus is simply an impostor in disguise by constantly referring to him as Pseudo Antoninus.

Good emperors were able to distinguish between themselves and their images. Elagabalus' imitation of images of Venus was not simply an attempt to aestheticise his body, but also an explicit act of self-divinisation. Such acts were played out around cult statues. Caligula made a statue of himself as a god, insisting that it receive cult and wear the same clothes as him every day (Suet. *Gaius* 22; Dio 59.28; Dio 59.30).[5] Octavian, on the other hand, never repeated the mistake of dressing up as Apollo (Suet. *Aug*. 70).

The elite writers' condemnation of an emperor's indistinguishability from his statues was, of course, somewhat disingenuous, since this was a condition peculiar to all emperors.[6] One of the most crucial verifications of power was the omnipresence of imperial statues. Marcus Aurelius' ascension was marked by a dream in which he literally begins to turn into a statue (SHA *Marcus Antoninus* 5; Dio 72.36).[7] Statues also extended the imperial wardrobe, not only by reminding the audience of different outfits but also allowing a step up to divinity and nudity (Bonfante 1989). The statue was a permanent presence that transcended mortality and mortal costume and action. It 'proved' the emperor's status, as a reminder that, for him, at least, divine costume was more than allegory. What would be dressing up for anybody else was a natural step on the way to becoming *divus*.

In order to present Augustus as a 'good' (most palatable to the elite) emperor, writers deliberately made few references to his statues, even presenting him as melting them down (Dio 53.22; Suet. *Aug*. 52).[8] Instead, he is shown building a favourable, lasting image in the minds of his subjects, thus living on in memory, every man his statue (Dio 52.35). This reveals something of the tension between different media of imperial representation: the literary elite clearly expected to preserve and shape such memory with their words, glossing over the implications of imperial sculpture.[9]

That literary elite also preferred to cast the emperor in the role and costume of the ideal senator – a true reflection of themselves.[10] But just as the Senate's dress regulated that of the emperor, the emperor was in a position to manipulate the dress of the Senate. Augustus' careful specifications of who could wear what and where in Rome did not simply control the people of Rome, but circumscribed his own wardrobe (Suet. *Aug.* 40, 44; Dio 53.13; Spencer 2002, 191–2). In order to be reflected in a wider social context, Augustus allowed the *Augustales*, often freedmen, to wear his toga (Beard, North & Price 1998, 358; Zanker 1988, 126–35). Similarly, the senate seem to have been eager to give the *toga praetexta* to people near the emperor (Dio 58.11–12; SHA *Alexander Severus* 21; Suet. *Aug.* 60). Of course, the emperor can be defied – Silo sells his senatorial outfit (Dio 60.24), Tiberius swaps a toga for a tunic until his return from Rhodes (Suet. *Aug.* 13) – and resistance demonstrated by rejecting the façade of clothes: tunics were ripped off to expose battle scars, the real marks of relationship to the emperor (Dio 54.14, Macrobius *Sat.* 4.27).

Meanwhile, bad emperors upset dress codes, demeaning their subjects by dressing their horses in human clothes and forcing others to wear what their whims dictated.[11] On the other hand, in trying to recreate the people as reflections of themselves, they also extended the right to wear what you like (Dio 61.33). As Caligula indulged in the most ridiculous costumes, so he allowed his retinue to show up in their own fantastic outfits: to swap the restrictions of Roman norms for those of the imagination (Dio 59.17). The result was visual mayhem.

By controlling the honours and statues dedicated to Rome's heroes, past and present, emperors also controlled the memory of costume. The Fora of Augustus and Trajan were filled with triumphal and military statues of leading men.[12] Access to the Forum of Augustus was restricted to those who were dressed, and comporting themselves properly, in the toga (Suet. *Aug.* 40). There they might contrast themselves with the ideal of Mars Ultor, reflected in the images of Augustus and the principate's leading generals.

These military and triumphal costumes reflected an ideal of the all-Roman hero. As the emperors began to restrict opportunities for others to wear such costumes in life (the actual act of triumph being quickly reserved for the royal family; Augustus still awarded his friends the regalia, rendered somewhat impotent when divorced from convincing action) they themselves assumed these outfits more and more (Versnel 1970, 56–93). Even Galba, though clearly too old to fight, makes a gallant effort to buckle on his cuirass before being murdered in the forum (Tacitus *Ann.* 1.35). Caracalla, too weak, even in his prime, to wear a heavy breastplate wore a 'falsie' (constructed from reinforced linen, Dio 79.3) being so pleased with the military look that he insisted on wearing it constantly, thereby emphasising the obvious deception. Triumphal garb was preferred for important festivals, and compulsory for the emperor at his funeral, where he hovered in a vacuum between mortal and divine power, between flesh and image.[13]

MARS

The costume of triumph, of course, already moved its wearer closer to the divine. The robes were famously copies of those of Jupiter Optimus Maximus (Pliny *N.H.* 33.36.111; Beard 2003, 39–43).[14] The military cuirass was related to the costume of Mars.[15] Statues of emperors show them as Mars and Jupiter, full-blooded Olympian males who know how to fight, rule and love like men.[16] This virility was often flaunted in the guise of divine nudity, a powerful display that further disgraces Elagabalus' own effeminate, bared physique.

In managing to mismanage heroic nudity to the extent that it is exposed as simple undressing, Elagabalus was not alone. Augustus' nemesis Antony had also been derided as appearing naked in the forum (Dio 45.31 Tanner 2000, 30ff). In fact, the model for the bad emperor can be traced back to Antony, lounging around in eastern costume; the loose robes and lopsided ivy crown of Dionysus. Antony had always been easily swayed by the lure of exotica, returning from Gaul in Gallic shoes before going east to play Alexander and Dionysus (Cicero *Phil*. 2.30).[17] Back home, Romans scoffed at his unconvincing costumes whilst also fearing them (Dio 50.5, 25). His role models, Dionysus and Alexander, continued to provide the anti-model of imperial behaviour throughout antiquity (Spencer 2002). In fact, nearly all 'bad' emperors wanted to be Hellenistic kings – fopping around in fringed silk, loose clothes and slippers (Suet. *Gaius* 52, *Nero* 51; Dio 73.17) – without any of the good qualities of their bad paradigm. Caligula, triumphal and military, shared many of Alexander's vices but looks faintly ridiculous in his breastplate (Suet. *Gaius* 52).

Antony, however, was not the first Roman to borrow Dionysus' *thyrsus* or Alexander's wig. All the great generals came back from the east somehow influenced by the model of Alexander and his Dionysiac posing: Marius drank from Bacchic cups after his triumph (Pliny *N.H.* 33.53.150; Val.Max. 3.6.6) and even Pompey adopted the *anastole* (Plutarch *Pompey* 2; Smith 1988, 136). However, this eastern preening was not simply an exotic affectation. With the exception of Pompey, accusations of eastern dress were almost always levelled at *populares*, and it would seem that it was not so much the orientalising but the emasculation of the costumes that fuelled outrage.

Corbeill's excellent interpretation of late Republican accusations of effeminacy shows that this was not just a convenient slur employed against *populares* but also a strategy deliberately employed by them.[18] The dodgy sexuality of an eastern god like Dionysus, of course, provided an excellent divine role model for these men. Furthermore, Dionysus' Roman counterpart, Liber Pater, was an explicitly plebeian god (Bruhl 1953, 30–45). Dionysian accoutrements, then, had a twin appeal to these politicians, combining dressing-up (exotic divinity) and dressing down (the common touch). In this model, the refusal to dress Augustus in Antony's costumes is not just a rejection of the east but also an attempt to claim Augustus for the aristocratic status quo, literally and metaphorically restrained by his toga.[19] All subsequent emperors who wear eastern clothes are also accused of both populist gestures and deviant masculinity (Tacitus *Ann*. 15.37). Not simply a trope of madness, this signifies their attempts to shift the mirror of their rule to a wider audience. This might be as extreme as Caligula hearing trials while dressed as Dionysus (Ath. *Deip.* 4.148d) but is also indicated by the significant, plebeian manner in which Claudius' hand protrudes from his toga (Suet. *Claudius* 21). Awareness of the effect of this realignment might be demonstrated by Nero not wanting Corbulo, the active military man, to see him dressed as an eastern queen (Dio 63.17).

The Mars look constructed by and for Augustus was thus the antithesis of the costumes of the effeminate rulers of the east. It was a divine costume that the Senate were prepared to stomach, so that, by the time of Claudius, such costumes were available for statues of emperors during their lifetimes, further blurring the line between inactive image and proactive emperor. Meanwhile any potentially bad costumes were edited out of the life of Augustus and relocated in the lives of bad emperors. Yet, Augustus, as the first emperor, also had the potential to be very bad indeed. There were vested interests in squeezing him into Dionysus' buskins. An altar of Dionysus in Thrace, having foretold Alexander's destiny, did the same for Augustus (Suet. *Aug.* 94). Cleopatra sent him a DIY Hellenistic king outfit as a symbol of her acceptance of his victory (Dio 51.6). Back home, coins struck in 18 BC by Petronius Turpilianus put Augustus and Liber on the same coin (*BMCRE* I.2).

Augustus himself flirted with Dionysian imagery, covering the Ara Pacis in vines (Zanker 1988, 179–82; Castriota 1995, 87–123) and with the model of Alexander. The man who knocked the nose off Alexander's crumbling corpse (Dio 51.16) also began his career with an image of Alexander on his seal before replacing it with himself (Suet. *Aug.* 50), and paraded Alexander's images and architecture in his Forum (Pliny *N.H.* 34.18.48, 35.36.93–4). The Prima Porta Augustus, a product of his lifetime, still preserves these elements, which are played down in literary sources. The even features and Polycleitan stance flirt with Alexander's look through a Roman filter (Zanker 1988, 188–92; Elsner 1995, 161–72; Smith 1988, 137–9). Divine nudity is implied despite the heavy cuirass on which Augustus literally bears the cosmos. But if the cuirass implies that that divinity comes from Mars, the presence of Cupid at his feet is the attribute of only one deity. This butch emperor here indulges in the most subtle crossdressing, assimilating himself with Venus and providing a sculptural hint for Caligula and Elagabalus to literalise in the flesh.

VENUS

When Augustus came of age, the toga he was wearing split at the seams: the man who wore stack heels and an extra vest was literally too big for his boots – senatorial costume could not contain a man of such power and destiny (Suet. *Aug.* 94). Nor, the Prima Porta Augustus implies, could other boundaries. The emperor is simultaneously Roman and Greek, mortal and divine, virile and womanly. The result is a rather uncomfortable, overloaded image, which does not easily fit the literary paradigm of a good emperor: a man comfortable in his toga. But could it be possible that the one thing worse than an emperor playing Venus would be an empress doing so?

Assimilating the accessories of Venus was imperative for Augustus (Schilling 1982, 325–40). Julius Caesar had made his ancestry evident on his own body, saying that he got a bloom of youth from Venus herself and wearing her armoured image on his ring (Dio 43.43). But although Caesar facilitated this divine connection for Augustus, his relationship with Cleopatra also made it highly problematic. Cleopatra, as Aphrodite, had made the perfect Hellenistic pairing with Antony's Dionysus (Wyke 1992 100–3; Roy 1998, 120). But the look came rather closer to Rome when she produced Caesar's son and began to appear on coins with him playing Cupid to her Venus. Back in Rome, Julius Caesar put a golden image of Cleopatra in his new temple of Venus

Genetrix (Dio 51.22; Appian *B.C.* 2.102; Schilling 1982, 301–319). Augustus would have to sever these connotations before a Roman woman could be Venus.[20]

Virgil helped by deliberately separating Cleopatra from Venus (Virgil *Aen.* 8.698–700). Venus was removed from any possible connection to Hellenistic Dionysus by marrying her off to Mars. Once smutty lovers in Homer (*Od.* 8.266–367), the couple were now transformed into the proud parents of Rome (Ovid *Fasti* 4.57–60; Schilling 1982 331–41). They were featured together in the Temple of Mars Ultor and the interior of the Pantheon (Dio 53.27). By taking Cleopatra's necklace and putting it on his own Venus in the Pantheon, Augustus clearly symbolised the queen's defeat by the Roman goddess (Schilling 1982, 330). The family link was made slightly more explicit when a statue of a recently deceased imperial grandchild was dedicated as Cupid in the temple of Capitoline Venus (Suet. *Gaius* 7). However, no imperial woman of Augustus' court got to play Venus in Rome: Augustus maintained an element of distance from his father's Venus temple and its seductive lodger.

In fact, the return to the temple was left to Caligula. Apparently distraught at the death of his sister Drusilla, Caligula deified her and insisted on her worship in the form of a statue set beside the image of Venus in Caesar's temple (Dio 59.11; Wood 1995, 457–82). This was an explicit emulation of Hellenistic kingship, a sister-brother partnership based on divinisation in the guise of Dionysus and Aphrodite. Caligula also dressed his women in the *stephane* or diadem worn by Hellenistic queens. Whilst the Dionysus outfit went straight back into storage after Caligula's murder, the diadem and the Venus outfit stuck firmly to images of imperial women.

The success of this scheme might be attributed to the fact Augustus had begun the trend for elevating imperial women by voting public statues for both Livia and his sister Octavia (Rose 1997, 8). The move would become tremendously significant. Although women had become tools in the increasingly dynastic power struggles of the late Republic, they still remained almost invisible in public life, particularly in terms of civic sculpture. An emperor who professed himself to dress as other men, showed his difference by the extent to which he put his wife on show throughout the empire, not just as decoration but as an effective political sign. Although Livia was distanced from Cleopatra in Rome, and never appeared on coins there in her lifetime, she was emphasised in Egypt, apparently substituting for Cleopatra (Kleiner 2000). Livia also appeared on various cameos with her children, her dress slipping off her shoulder in imitation of Julius Caesar's Venus Genetrix (Rose 1997, 100–2; Bartman 1999, 134–8; Matheson 1996). When she was eventually deified by Claudius, Livia finally appeared dressed as Venus alongside Augustus as Mars (**Figure 12.1**). Another imperial matriarch, Antonia, appears as Venus at the grotto at Baiae (Rose 1997, 82–3; Zevi & Andreae 1982 143–7).

This division of imperial labour might seem an obvious expression of Roman gender roles. However, the presentation of imperial women in sculptural, and particularly divine, form took them beyond their sex. The recorded struggles over their dress demonstrate the extent to which their status could not be accommodated by the traditional clothes of the Roman female. Whilst Livia stuck to heavy matronly garb (Bartman 1999, 40–6), Augustus and his daughter fought pitched battles of the 'you're not going out dressed like that' variety about what clothes were fitting for

Caesar's daughter (Macrobius *Sat.* 5.3). There being no obvious costume, imperial first ladies were able to flout conventions and invent their own looks, seemingly concentrated on jewels, to reflect status and public roles that had no mirror in Republican tradition (Tacitus *Ann.* 13.13). Presumably, toleration of this dressing up was ensured by the ideal that they should be living statues not active individuals.

The boundaries of tradition and gender transgressed by this new look and visibility are revealed by the attacks levelled at imperial women. Just as 'bad' emperors are effeminised, empresses are charged with masculinisation – from Livia as "Ulysses in a *stola*" (Suet. *Gaius* 23) to Agrippina the Younger in a *chlamys* (Dio 61.33, Pliny *N.H.* 32.63).[21] These women show their true colours, and the extent of their political ambition, by attempting to usurp not only the wardrobes, but also the roles, of their husbands and fathers. That emperors themselves realised the danger of such masculine women, in marble and in the flesh, is implied by the revealing fact that far more imperial *damnationes* were enacted against female than male imperial family members (Varner 2000, 13–17; Kleiner 2000). Whilst allowing their women to claim divinity, emperors assured their own superior godliness by retaining divine nudity for themselves. In addition, whilst their own mortal and divine images were increasingly identical, transforming Livia into a goddess entailed changes to both her portrait and dress which demonstrated her distance from her mortal self, her female relatives, and the women of Rome (Bartman 1999, 27, 41; Rose 1997, 75–6).

Whilst the Venus Genetrix look provided a clever way of emphasising the divine lineage of the Julio-Claudians, the Flavian dynasty's need to disassociate itself from Nero entailed the creation of a new Venus for a new dynasty. The Aphrodite of Paphos (Suet. *Titus* 5) – worshipped in the shape of a cone, though more widely visualised as the nude goddess – was chosen as patroness. A bare-bottomed Venus Victrix became popular on Flavian coins minted at Rome and the ladies of the Flavian household likewise disrobed (Matheson 1996, 189).[22]

The adoption of a naked Venus body associated imperial women with a body type hugely popular throughout the empire (famously derived from a notorious Hellenistic prototype, the Aphrodite of Knidos) without stirring up memories of Cleopatra, who had never gone naked in her Greek style portraits. Most importantly, divesting themselves of their clothes breached a last bastion of difference from their husbands. In this respect, the apparent exposure of their femininity again reveals the extent to which the imperial women encroached on traditionally male territory.[23] The period of the adoptive emperors saw the increasingly fair division of Mars and Venus roles (Schilling 1982, 379–80). Entire series of coins minted for the women featured Venus on the reverse, whilst she appears barely at all on their husbands' coins.[24] The popularity of the 'Venus of Capua/Ares Borghese' group as a portrait vehicle for the emperor and his wife further emphasised their respective roles.[25] Later dynasties' escape from the model of Livia's Venus Genetrix was paralleled by imperial association with the temple in Julius Caesar's forum rebuilt by Domitian and Trajan (Anderson 1984, 55–8; Dio 75.3).

Imperial women also sought reflection in the women of Rome. Elagabalus' mother set herself up as a leader of Roman women, attempting to dictate what they should wear just as Augustus had dictated to men (SHA *Elag.* 4). Women shared the imperial fashion for imitating naked Venus (in sculpture) and slavishly followed imperial hairdos. Empresses had located their mirror (Wrede 1981, 125–66; D'Ambra 1996). The 'Venus of Capua/Ares Borghese' group became popular for portraits of married couples (Kleiner 1981). Interestingly, though, it would seem that some women going Capuan preferred to protect their modesty with clothes, suggesting that not everybody felt entirely comfortable in taking the step-up of their imperial counterparts.[26]

DIONYSUS

Through these developments, the later imperial women managed to realign their femininity to become queens of the entire globe, effectively merging Roman Venus and eastern Aphrodite in their costumes. Dionysiac costume, however, long remained a threatening 'other', approached only by female members of the imperial family. Both Livia and Antonia were depicted in contexts which saw them sharing floor space with images of Dionysus (Rose 1997, 82–3; Bartman 1999, 136–7). Women proved that they could exploit such connections with dangerous consequences: in 48 AD, Claudius' wife Messalina married Silius during a Bacchic ceremony. She was dressed as a bacchant and he as Dionysus (Tacitus *Ann.* 11.32). This was a direct political challenge to Messalina's (other) husband, Claudius' rather less convincing Jupiter. Messalina had realised the potential of her costume and proved that women were capable of action.

The Dionysus costume was clearly initially reserved for usurpers and enemies (Cicero *Pro Flac.* 60; Dio 54.34). But closing a potential route to dissent was not the only reason for accommodating Dionysus. Liber Pater had a very precise role to play in Roman costume and masculinity. Roman adolescents assumed the *toga virilis* during his festival, with Ovid speculating that it was precisely his ambiguous nature that fitted him for this role (*Fasti* 3.771–790). If he played such a crucial role in shaping Roman men, then he surely ought to be reflected in the imperial household.

If emperors were wary of taking up the ivy themselves, they needed to find someone within the imperial circle who could keep the costume occupied.[27] Hadrian came up with the perfect clothes-horse – his lover, Antinous (Meyer 1991, Lambert 1997). Antinous's images dominate the art of the Hadrianic era in both public and private settings all over the empire (**Figure 12.2**). That an ex-slave from Bithynia, a literal nobody, could dominate the era remains so surprising to many that this has been dismissed as a simple expression of Hadrian's lust (Dio 69.11; SHA *Hadrian* 14). If so, its object was very politically convenient: Antinous was dressed as a whole range of gods, most popularly Osiris and Dionysus (Meyer 1991, 231–5; Beaujeu 1955, 165–75). A colossal Antinous-Dionysus from Praeneste suggests a public setting and there were images in the same guise from Rome itself (Lambert 1997, 188, 209–221).

Antinous' suitability for this flamboyant wardrobe was assured by his low status. As with early imperial women, imperial boyfriend was a new role, whose image could therefore be invented from scratch, independent of associated conventions of behaviour. Antinous was even easier to manipulate than those women, who at least had a recognisable role as wives and mothers. His mask couldn't slip because he was nothing but mask. Bland, idealised features removed him from real flesh and elevated

Figure 12.2. Antinous as Dionysus, Bust from Tivoli. (Photo © The British Museum).

him to fashion icon (Pausanias 8.9). He reflected and was reflected in the series of dedications, beginning in the Trajanic era, to youths consecrated as Dionysus (Wrede 1981, 259–63).[28] In this way, Hadrian managed to bring Dionysus back into the fold. By casting himself as bearded lover to Antinous' pretty love object, by creating Antinous as pure image, he maintained the upper hand. He may have gone Greek but he had put Dionysus in his place.[29] After Hadrian's master-stroke, the Dionysus look was brought deeper into the imperial circle (Bruhl 1953, 189–94). Antonine princes were dressed in ivy wreaths on coins (Alföldi 1935, 123, pl. 11.25) and Faustina the Younger appeared on a coin as a rider in Dionysus' triumphal, panther-drawn chariot, her male companion seen by some as Dionysus, but by others as Marcus Aurelius himself.[30] The costume took on more meaning under Septimius Severus, who built a huge temple of

Dionysus and Hercules, his home-town's patron deities, in Rome (Dio 77.16).[31]

The Antonine emperors, by delegating divine roles to other members of their households, thus managed to find a home for Mars, Venus/Aphrodite and Dionysus. It could be a slightly tricky ménâge à trois, dependent on everyone sticking to their appropriate roles. The SHA consistently present the imitation of Alexander or Dionysus by an emperor as a bad thing, perhaps because it was a look mostly associated with minor members of the household.[32] However, such divisions were more blurred in the case of boy emperors like Elagabalus. Just as he had given us his Aphrodite, the mad, bad emperor also regaled audiences with his Bacchus. Sat on his throne, he hammed it up at the expense of the senate, asking them impudent questions with a decidedly plebeian sense of humour (SHA *Elag.* 11). Like all bad emperors, he had an eye to the cheap seats.

CONCLUSION

The extent to which the imperial household came to play to a wider audience is demonstrated by the other costumes adopted by later 'bad' emperors. Whereas, in the early principate, the battle between good and bad had been played out in terms of Hellenistic and Roman models, later emperors adopted far more flamboyant costumes, with Elagabalus plundering Syria and even the western provinces for outfits (see also SHA *Pertinax* 8). Once Hadrian had got away with his beard, 'Graeculus' was no longer a valid insult.[33] Marcus Aurelius got full thumbs-up for his bearded, philosopher look (SHA *Marcus Ant.* 3), whilst Lucius Verus' bad character was intimated by the 'barbaric' trim of his beard (SHA *Lucius Verus* 11). The cloak that gave Caracalla his name was of Celtic or Germanic derivation and, tellingly, was a gift shared not with the Senate but with the people (SHA *Severus* 21, *Caracalla* 9; Dio 79.3). Whilst some of this amplification can be attributed to the need to keep a flagging literary trope alive, it is also a sign that the emperors' mirror audience had changed, and with it the role, and the costume, of the emperors themselves.

It is not enough to dismiss Elagabalus' dressing up as simply the activities of Rome's greatest walking disaster. His antics reveal some of the difficulties of dressing like an emperor. Emperors trod a fine line between reflecting their audience and differentiating themselves, between the memory of themselves shaped by the literary elite (who insisted on the humanity of the emperor and his actions) and their statues (which emphasised the iconic status and super-human potential of the emperor).

NOTES

1 SHA *Marcus Antoninus* 28 or Juvenal *Sat.* 4.37–8 for evidence of the creation of a typology of bad emperors.
2 On ideological implications of the toga: Wallace-Hadrill 1998; Vout 1996; Davies, this volume.
3 Bartsch 1994; Suet. *Gaius* 54; Dio 59.27; Tacitus *Ann.* 14.15–16; Suet. *Nero* 20–25, 39; Dio 62.9. SHA *Elagabalus* 32.
4 Tacitus *Ann.*13.25; Suet. *Nero* 21, 48; Dio 62.9. See also Suet. *Gaius* 11; SHA *Lucius Verus* 4.
5 Caligula's attempts to imitate Jupiter sometimes backfired, Dio 59.26–27.

6 Tacitus *Hist.* 1.36, 3.85; Dio 51.12; SHA *Hadrian* 6 and esp. Amm. *Mar.* 16.10. Hopkins (1978, 215–31) offers a classic discussion. Gregory (1994) and Tanner (2000) have emphasised the socio-political importance of images in figuring responses to public figures. Varner (2000) concentrates on such negative responses as Vitellius dragged off to prison along with his statues (Dio 64.20.1–2), highlighting the gulf between heroic image and naked man.
7 The complicity between emperor and image is apparent from imperial portraits on seal rings. Suet. *Tib.* 73; *Gaius* 12; SHA *Hadrian* 26.
8 Preoccupation with one's own statues as a bad thing: Suet. *Caesar* 76, *Domitian* 13; Dio 59.4.
9 Dio 68.5 and Suet. *Aug* 7 demonstrate the extent to which the elite liked to see themselves as bestowing power on, and forming the *memoria* of, each emperor. The SHA often mention people reading imperial biographies (SHA *Commodus* 10, *Severus* 2).
10 Reflection in audience: Barton 2002; Frontisi-Ducroux 1997, 53–71; Balensiefen 1990, 158–161.
11 Suet. *Gaius* 55; Dio 61.6 – the well dressed horse. Bad emperors (un)dressing people: Suet. *Gaius* 26; Dio 67.8; SHA *Commodus* 16, *Elagabalus* 29; Bartsch 1994, 1–35.
12 Tacitus. *Hist.*1.79; Dio 55.10; Suet. *Aug.* 31; Tacitus *Ann.* 15.72; SHA *Marcus Antoninus* 22. Anderson 1984, 81–5, 161–70. Alston's (1998) discussion of masculinity under autocracy may explain emphasis on heroism.
13 Dio 51.20, 53.26, 59.7, 60.6, 67.4. Imperial children also wore triumphal clothes: Tacitus *Ann.* 12.41; SHA *Marcus Antoninius* 12. Imperial funerals: Dio 56.34, 75.4; Price 1987.
14 Beard (2003) plays on the inter-relations of reality and presentation in the triumph.
15 Augustus does get to be Apollo on coins from eastern mints (*BMCRE* I.103–4).
16 Rose 1997 (Mars) 100–2, 167; (Jupiter) 91–2, 98, 100, 116–18, 131–2, 135–6, 147–9, 160, 184–185.
17 Dio 48.39,50.5; Plutarch *Ant.* 4, 24, 26, 33, 54, 60; Elder Seneca *Suasoria* 1.5–6; Bruhl 1953, 127–9. Association between Dionysus and hellenistic kings: Bruhl 1953, 53–7; Nock 1928; Chaniotis 1997. Smith (1988, 136–7) regards Antony's association with Dionysus as incidental. The idea certainly took on amongst his critics back at Rome.
18 Corbeill 2002; Edwards 1993, 63–9. Gardener (1998) discusses the masculinity or otherwise of clothing.
19 Octavian accused of effeminacy: Suet. *Aug.* 68.
20 Wyke (1992) and (2002, 195–243) investigates the Augustan reception of Cleopatra.
21 The essential masculinity of statues is implied by the statue of Cloelia (Pliny *NH* 34.13.28–9). Bartman 1999, 134–5.
22 *BMCRE* II.224, 225, 227, 247. This Venus appeared on Augustan coins from eastern mints (*BMCRE* I.100).
23 The transgressive nature of Venus' own nudity is discussed by Arscott & Scott (2000, 1–23) and Hales (2002).
24 Exceptions include 2 'hybrid' coin types. See *BMCRE* IV.610, 687 (2nd ed).
25 Vermeule (1977, 54) locates the original group in the portico of the temple of Mars Ultor. For Mars and Venus as a couple on Antonine coins, see *BMCRE* IV. 543, 544 (2nd ed.). Kleiner (1981) does not see imperial portraits in the extant versions of this group, but does accept an imperial prototype.
26 The increasing flamboyance of freedwomen memorials is, however, very evident. Kleiner 1977, 180–91; 1981.
27 In the east, the link was established. See Bruhl 1953, 185–7.
28 Meyer (1991) notes that portraits of youths tend to follow Antinous' portrait type. Henrichs (1982, 148) suggests that Dionysus and Aphrodite also become popular subjects on sarcophagi.
29 Meyer (1991, 189–211) and Beaujeu (1955, 243–57) emphasise the close association between cults of Antinous and imperial cult.
30 Bruhl (1953, 188–94) following Strack (1937, 33) who disagrees with Gnecchi (1912, 36, pl.65.77).
31 Dionysus is very popular on Severan coins (*BMCRE* V.29, 31, 34, 56, 60, 255, 419).
32 Dio 78.7; SHA *Trig. Tyr.* 14. Beaujeu (1955, 217–9) notes Hadrian's tactic of embracing the east without succumbing to Nero's reputation.
33 Zanker (1995, 198–266) and Gleason (1995, 21–54) note the central role of Hadrian and his beard in the cultural realignment of empire.

Chapter 13

Dress in the *Historia Augusta*: the role of dress in historical narrative[1]

Mary Harlow

"Written documents are just as frustrating as any other source: to avoid stress, it is better to travel hopefully than to imagine one has arrived." John Peter Wild (2000, 211)

Taking Wild's advice (together with the comment offered to the author of the *Historia Augusta*: "Write what you will. You will be safe in saying whatever you wish, since you will have as comrades in falsehood those authors whom we admire for the style of their histories" *Aur.* 2.2), it might seem foolish even to attempt a project which aims to highlight the role of dress in the particular and problematic narrative of the *Historia Augusta*.

Historians of dress in the ancient world do not, for the most part, have the luxury of artefact based research. The range of surviving articles or fragments of clothing is very limited. We rely heavily on visual representations in a range of media, and literary texts from a range of genres. This chapter will examine how written images of the clothed body, and of certain items of clothing, function within a single text. Existing studies of clothing describe the nature and make-up of garments, or offer interpretations of the multiple meanings of certain items and their roles as codes and signifiers. In other words, they attempt to explain the 'language of dress.' This is one way of expressing how dress and adornment can convey messages, but we should not assume that it is an unproblematic metaphor. It cannot serve as a universally convenient, descriptive shorthand approach to the expressive medium of dress. Text and image rarely operate in tandem in the ancient world and herein lies a problem. Dress as written, dress as illustrated, and surviving textile remains, cannot transmit similar messages; art, literature and material culture do not speak the same language. Each type of evidence is governed by rules which are specific to particular media, and to particular types of genre within such media. The medium affects the type of message that can be transmitted. Clearly, in attempting to establish and attribute meaning to a chronology of dress in the ancient world, we must exploit the remains of material culture, visual images and written texts, but each nuances the evidence in a specific way.[2]

Anthropologists and social scientists have identified dress as a mechanism that reveals both cultural categories and cultural principles (McCraken 1988, 59). Greek and Roman dress is thus categorised as a material representation of the social world. Following patterns established by these disciplines, we interpret representations of the clothed body in the ancient world as reflecting status, rank, age, gender, ethnicity, otherness etc., seeking to see the basic principles that govern society expressed in the way people dress. The period covered by the *Historia Augusta* (Hadrian to Carinus, 138–285 AD) was one of change and transformation, as was the author's late fourth century milieu. The balance of power was shifting away from Rome and into the hands of individuals with whom Romans of the classical period might have struggled to find common ground.

The *Historia Augusta* is a problematic text and I do not claim to be an expert on all, or even most, of its nuances. A series of biographies of emperors and usurpers, purporting to have been written by a series of authors, it is now generally accepted as having been produced in the late fourth century by a single author setting himself up as a whole biographical tradition (Syme 1968, 94–102; 1971; Gentili & Cerri 1988, 61–85; Meckler 1993, 364–75). It is an extremely beguiling text, once read, not easily forgotten. It cannot be regarded as a piece of serious biography or history, although the author attempts to maintain this fiction by including criticisms of fictitious authors for writing trivia and reporting gossip (*Gord.* 21.3) and by debating the role of elements such as dress in imperial biographies. He criticises the fictitious authority, Junius Cordus, for recounting absurd and trivial tales and including such details as when an emperor varied his diet, how often he changed his clothes, how many cloaks he possessed and how many slaves he had (*Macr.* 1.4 ff; *Gord.* 21). The author claims that unless light can be thrown on character (*Macr.* 1.5) "knowledge of this sort of thing does no one any good. It is the duty of historians, rather to set down in their histories such things as are to be avoided or sought after" (*Gord.* 21.4). Despite this grand claim, the text is delightfully full of references to such 'trivia': the guise of multiple identities allows carefully constructed personae to address such matters. The veracity of events and individuals reported in the text is not an issue here. In terms of the study of dress, the *Historia Augusta* offers the opportunity of examining the role of dress as a narrative and rhetorical tool; and of tracing underlying Roman attitudes to certain types of dress, styles and textiles and their ascribed values. More controversially perhaps, it allows us to see whether changes in fashion are transmitted in the text.

References to dress occur in three main, intertwined, contexts in the *Historia Augusta*: as descriptions of the garb of individual emperors (which serve to credit or discredit their characters depending on the style and its appropriateness for a given occasion); in catalogues (of gifts and privileges granted by emperors to individuals, or as donatives, or as lists of luxury items removed from the palace of the previous emperor by his successor); and as attempts at control or sumptuary legislation. Female dress is rarely mentioned in the *Historia Augusta* and, pertaining to women, only in terms of control (with the exception of two lists of betrothal and marriage gifts; *Maxim.* 27.8; *Firmus*, 15.8). This chapter does not cover every mention of dress in the *Historia*; instead it offers, by way of case studies, an overall view of the way the clothed body is portrayed within a literary rhetoric of dress.

DRESS AS AN EXTENSION OF CHARACTER

To use dress as a commentary on the character of an individual was not an innovation of the author of the *Historia Augusta*, although, given his freedom with his subject matter, he exploited this literary tradition to excess in some of his biographies.[3] Ancient biographies concentrated on the character of the individual and his moral ability to fulfil his role in society: imperial virtues and vices were considered self evident in Roman society, and, although few emperors are regarded in a wholly positive light, others are viewed entirely negatively. One signal of how to read the character, behaviour and subsequent reputation of emperors was to examine how they dressed for particular occasions. The appropriateness or otherwise of appearance was considered a direct reflection of moral suitability for rule. In this text, character is also enhanced and denigrated by contrasting one rule with the preceding one; clothing proves a particularly useful tool in creating such dramatic effects.

In visual representations emperors usually appear in one of three guises: the general/victor in military dress; as the serving first citizen in a toga; as sacrificing priest with toga pulled over the head.[4] Similar representations are also evident in the written text. While the earliest lives in the series have very little mention of clothing, both that of Hadrian (117–38 AD) and Marcus Aurelius (161–76 AD) do stress the fact that in Italy military clothing was laid aside for the quintessential Roman garment, the toga (*Hadrian* 22.2; *M.Ant.* 27.3; *Alex.Sev.* 40.8). This had long been traditional practice, recognising that the emperor was not at war in Italy and acknowledging the superior position of Italy and Rome as the mother country of the empire. It demonstrated respect for Roman traditions and associated the emperor with earlier positive precedents such as Augustus and Trajan.[5]

It has been argued that the toga was rarely worn except on ceremonial occasions by the mid-second century, but continued to be the garb of choice for visual representations for emperors and citizens (Stone 1994; Davies, this volume). Whatever the reality of its popularity as everyday clothing, it also has a long life within the *Historia Augusta*. While the style of the toga evolved, its associations with Roman citizenship, office holding, and duty and loyalty to the state remained, also linking it closely to ideas of masculinity in the Roman mind.[6] In the *Historia Augusta* it is used in its most common embodiment, signalling the moderation and moral uprightness of the wearer, and their legitimacy in holding imperial power. Emperors are described togate throughout the *Historia Augusta*. The emperor Tacitus (275–6 AD) was complimented on his moderation and frugality for continuing to wear, as emperor, the same tunics and togas he had worn as a private citizen (*Tacitus* 10.1).

Moderation and morality were part of the panoply of imperial virtues. Ideally, emperors should practice restraint in all areas of life, including dress, personal appearance and behaviour. The association of the toga with traditional Roman values was one way of expressing these virtues, but ideas of moderation and frugality could also be extended to other garments in the right context. Septimius Severus (193–8 AD), for example, was said to dress plainly with very little purple in his tunic and a shaggy cloak (*hirta chlamyde*; *Sev.* 19.7). Alexander Severus (222–35 AD), who wore a plain white robe without any gold, and ordinary cloaks (*paenula*)[7] and togas (*Alex.Sev.* 4.2), has one of the most consistently positive reputations in the *Historia Augusta*. He is said to have reintroduced the rough cloaks used by Severus, tunics without a purple stripe, long-sleeved and small purple tunics (*Alex.Sev.* 33.3–4) for his own use, and to have complained about roughness of purple dye and the stiffness of golden thread (40.10–11). The stress here is on the lack of conspicuous consumption in the minimal use of expensive purple dye and gold, and, of course, the emulation of Severus. The author declares that Alexander recognised that imperial power was based not on outward show but on valour (33.3–4).

The mention of the tunic and cloak (*chlamys*) ensemble, and the explicit description of long-sleeved tunic (*machrocheras*), at this period are interesting. By the late fourth century, long sleeved, full length tunics had become part of the standard wardrobe in which officials and emperors were portrayed in public art.[8] The ensemble had a close affiliation with military dress, and it may be that the author is both projecting current fashion into the past, and associating it with good emperors, to enhance its legitimacy in his own time. On the other hand, it may also be that as the toga was worn less in private, the wardrobe of the domestic arena was slowly encroaching into the public realm. Thus, in the period between the death of Severus and the accession of Tacitus, the toga still served its purpose as a narrative tool, conveying a message of traditional Roman virtues, while other garments made their debut in the imperial wardrobe. If the descriptions of these new items of imperial clothing occur within the context of associated positive character traits (frugal diet, handsome physical attributes, good relations with the essential power groups – army, senate and people), then they acquire, by association, positive values.

The biography of Tacitus (275–6 AD) contains the description of a single panel portrait in which he appears in five different guises: in a toga, in a military cloak (*chlamydatus*), in armour, in a *pallium*, and as a hunter (Callu, forthcoming). According to the author, writers of epigrams could not resist the temptation to satirise this by saying that they only recognised the image of Tacitus in a toga (*Tac.* 16.2–4). The tensions between an emperor's portrayal in art, and the portrayal's interpretation in words, are instructive. Only the symbolism of the togate figure is self-explanatory: the other portrayals have more ambivalent potential.

The *chlamydatus* and *armatus* figures illustrate the militaristic character of the ideal emperor: the image in full armour suggesting the emperor on active service, the *chlamydatus* (Latin: *paladamentum*) presumably showing the long, purple cloak worn when on campaign. These could both be positive images, the wearing of the *chlamys* being acceptable in visual imagery by the early fourth century, as is evidenced by the Piazza Armerina mosaics (Rinaldi 1964–5, 13–14, 200–268). However, in other lives, the *chlamys* is often used in contrast to the toga (e.g. below, *Gall.* 16.4) to indicate a rejection, or failure to recognise, traditional Roman values. Thus, even the apparently clear message of these military images can be double-edged. A similar ambiguity affects those of the emperor at leisure. The *pallium* (being much easier to wear than the toga) is a mantle associated with private leisure activities. It was a garment worn by philosophers and those who were attracted to the Greek way of life, and as such could have both positive and negative connotations. It was not thought suitable for public representations of the emperor, but this painting is said to be in the private house of the Qunitilii. Like the *chlamys*, the *pallium* could serve as a rhetorical foil for the toga. Tertullian expressed this most succinctly in a tract encouraging Christians to take up the *pallium* and reject the toga, thus rejecting the implicit values of Roman citizenship that wearing the toga implied (Tertullian *De Pallio*; Vout 1996, 204–20). Therefore, while the *pallium* might emphasise Tacitus' literary and philosophical pretensions, it could also be read as a rejection of Roman values, if an audience so chose. The hunter's dress could possess similar double meaning. Hunting was considered a noble sport for emperors (e.g. *Hadrian* 2.1; 26.3; *Ant.Pius* 11.2; *Alex.Sev.* 29.3), yet poor emperors might use it as an alternative to warfare (*Maxim.* 8.4) or hunt when warfare was required (*Verus* 6.9). The epigram thus informs our reading of this portrait: written text enhances painted image. By mentioning the epigram, the author undermines the potentially positive reading of the images of Tacitus' clothed body. Legitimacy by wardrobe appears to be a central tool in the rhetorical armoury of the author.

The assumption that the toga formed the gold standard for upright character is illustrated by the literary images of emperors who did not wear it on appropriate occasions, or dressed to excess in other ways. There are any number of examples of inappropriate dress in the *Historia*: the author seems to delight in this type of descriptive character assassination, despite attributing much of it to the fictitious Junius Cordus. As in earlier biographies, the wearing of inappropriate dress was invariably linked with excessive behaviour in other areas of life (Suetonius *Gaius* 13, 52; *Nero* 50). Commodus (176–80 AD) is charged with going to the Circus in a dalmatic rather than a toga (*Comm.* 8.8), although this sartorial sin seems small compared with the catalogue of gross behaviour that follows: ordering devotees of Bellona to cut off one of their arms; dressing lame men as serpents and then shooting them with arrows; plucking out eyes and cutting off feet (*Comm.* 9–11.13). Elagabalus (218–22 AD) is, of course, the prime example of this type of character assassination. His depictions in both the *Historia Augusta* and Herodian are full of references to his personal appearance: a tunic of cloth of gold, or a Persian tunic studded with jewels, and jewels on his shoes – "a practice which aroused the derision of all…" (*Elag.* 23.4)[9] It is said that in private he wore a jewelled diadem so that his face might look more like a woman's, was the first of all the Romans to wear clothing made wholly of silk (*holosericus*), and would never wear linen garments more than once. Elagablaus also appeared in a dalmatic (*Elag.* 23.3–6; 26.1–2). Such descriptions elide ideas of eastern decadence and effeminacy, and make covert allusions to other bad emperors (cf. Suetonius *Gaius* 52; *Nero* 51).

Gallienus (253–68 AD) is derided for appearing in a purple cloak (*chlamys*) with jewelled and golden fibulae "at Rome where emperors always wore the toga" (*Gall.* 16.4). His masculinity was also called into question by the passing remark that he called his boots 'reticulate' (*reticulum* being a hairnet worn by women, or effeminate men, cf. *Elag.* 11.7). He is charged not only with belittling imperial power and trivialising the state of the empire by associating it with the availability of particular types of clothing (he responded to revolt in Egypt with "What! We cannot do without Egyptian linen!" and of Gaul ruled by Postumus, was to said to remark "Can the state be safe without Atrebatic cloaks?" *Gall.* 6.4, 6), but also with removing senators from military posts.

Such emperors serve as foils to express the relative better qualities of either their predecessors or successors: Marcus Aurelius shines in contrast with his son, Commodus; Elagabalus is followed by the far more moderate Alexander Severus; Gallienus' successor, Claudius, was alleged to be an ancestor of Constantine Chlorus, father of Constantine the Great. The author of the *Historia Augusta* follows other ancient writers of history in maintaining the image of supporting emperors who display moderation and morality, and those who treat the Senate with due respect (Syme 1971, 44).

Certain styles, garments and textiles being considered inappropriate dress appear over and over again in the *Historia Augusta*. Silk, for instance, is invariably regarded as a luxury item. Due to the difficulty of its production, its rarity, expense and eastern origin, it had always carried connotations of excess. Early emperors had attempted to regulate its use for men (e.g. Tiberius: Tacitus *Annals* 2.33), while others set a pattern of making the wearing of such a luxury item synonymous with a lack of self control and a blatant disregard for Roman traditions. The subtext of Suetonius's comments on Caligula, who sometimes appeared in silk and in a woman's robe (*sericatus et cycladatus*; *Gaius* 52) is unambiguous: Caligula's effeminacy clearly brings into doubt his ability to wield power. The *Historia Augusta* continues this association of silk with luxury, effeminacy and over indulgence. A distinction is made between garments made wholly of silk (*holosericus*) and those made partly of silk (*subsericus*), whose rhetorical purpose is none too subtle in the narrative: good emperors have few garments of part-silk and none made wholly of silk and forbid such garments to men (e.g. *Alex.Sev.* 40.1;*Tac.* 10.4); bad emperors wear wholly silk garments excessively, devaluing both whole and part-silk garments by giving them away indiscriminately (e.g. *Elag.* 26.1).

Part-silk garments are clearly not seen to be quite as decadent as those made completely of silk as they often appear in the lists of gifts. The assessment of Aurelian's life credits him, like Alexander Severus, with neither having garments of pure silk (*holosericus*) in his own wardrobe, nor giving them to others. When his wife implored him to retain a single purple silk robe (*pallio blatteo serico*) he replied that a fabric should not be worth its weight in gold. The author claims that at that time a pound of silk was worth a pound of gold (*Aur.* 45.5). Double-dyed purple silk is one of the most expensive items in the Price Edict of Diocletian (301 AD), priced at 150,000 *denarii* a pound against gold at 72,000 *denarii* a pound (Corcoran 1996, 226).

We have seen that the dalmatic or large, decorated tunic with sleeves, was not well regarded in the *Historia Augusta*. Ideally the Roman tunic came to mid-calf (cf. Quintilian 11.3. 138–9), any arm covering being incidental, and its only decoration was the purple stripe displaying rank. Traditionally, both full length tunics and long, tight-fitting sleeves were perceived as effeminate (Aulus Gellius *Attic Nights* 6.12). The *Historia Augusta* makes a distinction between the dalmatic, a tunic with long-sleeves and a foreign name, and a long-sleeved tunic. Both visual imagery and other literary sources of the late third and fourth centuries demonstrate that the ankle length, long sleeved tunic was clearly worn and deemed suitable for public representations of Roman officials. It could be worn on its own, under the toga, or with the *chlamys*. As we have seen above, its acceptability as a garment was dependent on context. When worn under the *chlamys*, it could serve as a rhetorical foil for the toga. In other contexts it was acceptable for emperors to wear and to give to officials (e.g. *Alex.Sev.* 23.4; *Aur.*58.5). Presumably the literate, late fourth-century audience understood the subtext well enough and were unfazed by the tension between the text, images of the relevant emperor, and the clothes they wore themselves.

Like silk, jewellery was also problematic: jewels were for women and should not be given to soldiers or worn by men (*Alex.Sev.* 51.1). Alexander Severus is said to have removed jewels from the imperial footwear and garments used by Elagabalus (*Alex.Sev.* 4.2; cf. *Carinus* 17.1). Thus when the younger Maximinus is described as being more elegantly groomed than any woman (*Maxim.* 28.5–6) having his helmets and cheek pieces inset with jewels, and silver and gold swords (*Maxim.* 29.8–9), it is clear his character, and thus his right to rule, is being attacked (cf. *Gord.* 16.4). On the other hand, jewellery and jewelled items were not uncommon in the catalogues of gifts. As with silk, the association with *luxuria* and corruption was always close, and thus could be manipulated at the author's whim. An emperor who gave jewelled plate to a subject could be seen to be generous and the subject's status suitably recognised. Conversely, as in the case of Elagabalus and Maximinus, jewellery could be used as another weapon in the author's rhetoric of denigration. These examples bear little relation to the reality of emperor's lives and looks, but demonstrate the role that jewellery and dress could play in the construction of an emperor's reputation. Even if entirely fictitious they expose society's ideals and prejudices.

CATALOGUES

Clothes often appear in lists of items that represent the wealth and status of an individual. Clothing was considered part of the stored wealth and assets of a household, and was often a key element in bequests (e.g. *Digest* 34.2). There are several catalogues of clothing items in the *Historia Augusta*. They occur in two main contexts: items removed from the palace by an emperor on his accession; and privileges, rewards or donatives granted by the emperor to an individual or to the people.

The first type of catalogue is used to expand the list of unsuitable items seen in the character descriptions, thus serving as part of the message that the newly installed regime would not indulge in the excesses of the predecessor, and therefore also reflecting imperial character. Pertinax held a sale of Commodus's belongings on his accession, among which were: robes of silk foundation with gold work of remarkable workmanship; tunics, *paenulae* and cloaks; tunics with long sleeves in the manner of the Dalmations (*chiridotas Dalmatarum*) and fringed military cloaks; purple cloaks made in the Greek fashion (*chlamys*) for service in the camp; also Bardaean hooded cloaks (*cuculli Bardaici*) and a gladiator's toga and harness finished in gold and jewels (*Pertinax* 8.2–4). The association with Commodus gives all these items a negative connotation in this context, despite the fact that in other contexts they were neutral or even positively valued. The action of selling the goods of a degenerate character reflects well on the reigning emperor. The funds thus raised by Pertinax went to pay a donative to the soldiers (*Pertinax* 7.11). He is credited further with paying arrears of salaries and restoring the treasury to its normal condition (*Pertinax* 9.1). Alexander

Severus likewise removed the jewels and garments of Elagabalus from the palace (*Alex.Sev.* 4.2) and sold these and other jewels, giving the proceeds to the treasury (41.1). These actions contrast his behaviour favourably with the outrageousness of Elagabalus. The lists themselves emphasise the intrinsic monetary value of clothing and jewellery.

The catalogues of gifts and privileges should, in theory, give an insight into what was considered appropriate dress, for why would an emperor grant a citizen inappropriate items? Alexander Severus regularly gave officials entering office two garments for the forum (presumably togas), two for domestic use, and one for the baths (*Alex.Sev.* 42.4, see Callu forthcoming). However, as we have seen it is often the context of clothing articles that nuances their meaning. Many of these lists occur in fictitious letters from reigning emperors, enhancing the status of the subject and presaging his accession to imperial power. On the occasion of being granted the tribuneship, Claudius was also granted, among a long list of food supplies and money, military tunics (red) and cloaks, silver and gold armour, jewelled rings (*Claud.* 14.5); part-silk garments (*Claud*, 14.8); undergarments (white) and togas, including *togae praetextae*, and tunics (*Claud.* 14.10, interestingly, the tunics are to be returned, as are a cook and muleteer). Claudius also received gifts from Gallienus including a huge amount of bejewelled gold and silver plate, and: "two cloaks with purple borders of the true brilliance, sixteen garments of various kinds, a white part-silk tunic, a tunic with borders (*paragaudes*), three ounces in weight, three pairs of Parthian shoes from our own supply, ten simple Dalmatics, one Dardanian cloak (*chlamys mantuelem*), one Illyrian mantle (*paenula*), one hooded cloak (*bardocucullus*), two shaggy hoods (*cucutia villosa*) and four handkerchiefs" (*Claud.* 17.6–7).[10] In a (fictitious) list of goods granted to Aurelian so he could afford the consulship were ten finely woven male tunics and twenty tunics of Egyptian linen (*Aur.* 12.2; 48.5). As booty, probably also fictitious, he received: red general's tunics, proconsul's cloaks; tunics with long sleeves (*Aur.* 13.8; white, 48.5); *tunica palmata* and *toga picta* (*Aur.* 13.3).[11] Aurelian himself was said to be the first to give tunics with bands of embroidery/tapestry weave (*paragauduas*) to troops and presented soldiers with tunics of up to five such bands. The author comments that these are like linen tunics of his own day (46.6).

These catalogues demonstrate the ambiguous meaning of certain items. Dalmatics, for instance, are sold by one emperor only to be granted by another. Decorated tunics are rejected by good emperors but given as gifts by the same emperors. The relationship between clothes as actually worn and clothes as written seems to become more distant in these lists. They are primarily about status and wealth; the power of the donor to give, and the increased wealth, and thus status, of the recipient. The rhetoric here is as much about the social value of possessions as the intrinsic economic value of clothes.[12]

DRESS AND SOCIAL CONTROL

Just as the dress worn by an individual emperor and the types of clothes he gave as gifts could provide commentary on his character and ability to rule, so too could his attempts at social control through dress. Sumptuary legislation had been a regular feature of Roman life from Republican times. Its debatable efficacy did not prevent successive emperors attempting to control conspicuous consumption among the elite. The life of Alexander Severus contains an interesting section claiming that he wished to assign a particular type of clothing to each member of the imperial staff, and to slaves. This was prevented by Ulpian and Paulus, but, according to this passage, it was decided to make a distinction between equestrians and senators by the width of the purple stripe (*Alex.Sev.* 27.1–4). The same section also gives permission for old men to wear cloaks (*paenulae*) within the city as protection against the cold, a privilege previously denied them unless on a journey or in rainy weather. Women, on the other hand, were forbidden to wear *paenulae* in the city, but permitted to use them on a journey (27.4). While this distinction in the width of the purple stripe had been in existence since the Republic, commentators have not failed to notice the similarity between this passage and *C.Th.* 14.10, of 382 AD. This date is close to the date of authorship, thus neatly linking the policies of the reigning emperor, Theodosius, closely to those of Alexander Severus, one of the most highly regarded emperors in the *Historia Augusta*. The association with Ulpian is also intriguing, since an entry in the Digest attributed to him, under a section on legacies, lists different types of clothing suitable for men or women. There the *paenula* is mentioned first as female dress, and later as suitable for both sexes (*Digest* 34.2.23.2).

Aurelian forbade boots of purple, wax-colour, white, or the 'colour of ivy', to men but allowed them to women (49.7). He also intended to forbid the use of gold in ceilings, tunics and leather, allegedly put up to this by his frugal successor, Tacitus (*Aur.* 46.1; *Tac.* 11.6). It should come as no surprise that social control of this type occurs in the lives of Alexander Severus and Aurelian, the two emperors who are ascribed the most positive images. These emperors also attempted to control female dress, at least within their own households. Women were indulged somewhat in terms of dress, being allowed some silk and purple although the number of such garments was restricted (*Alex.Sev.* 40.1; *Aur.* 46.1).

Sumptuary legislation has the aim of controlling competition by limiting access to conspicuous consumption. It also allowed the emperor a monopoly on some items, such as purple silk. However, in the *Historia Augusta*, it appears to serve as another reflection of the imperial character. Good emperors are not only moderate in their own life styles, but attempt to extend such ideals to the rest of society.

CONCLUSIONS

The clothed body in the *Historia Augusta* relays a series of messages to an audience. The meaning of these messages is complex and dependent on the context of the description. Certain items of clothing have multiple meanings and the reading of such descriptions depends as much on the function of the item in the text as on the clothes described. The range of garments listed is quite wide but several items occur repeatedly: togas, *chlamys*, long-sleeved tunics; cloaks; silk and gold decorated items. There is also repetition in both the descriptions of clothed emperors and their attitudes towards certain items of clothing (e.g. positive images: Alexander Severus and Aurelian; negative images: Commodus and Elagabalus). This repetition reinforces the implicit messages about the characters of emperors, and does so in terms of dress. It highlights the fact that there is a rhetorical message here that has little to do with dress as actually worn, and also allows for anachronisms (such as the claim that Alexander Severus was the first to insist on the different width of purple stripes).

Using dress to track change over time is as complex a business as tracking changes in dress. The text does show that in the late fourth century dress could be used as a marker of status, rank and morality in ways that were very similar to its role in classical literature, but it also shows dress as only part of a much wider discourse. The literate fourth century audience would have recognised and interpreted the subtexts of the *Historia Augusta*. According to Ammianus, they were well versed in this genre, reading Juvenal and Marius Maximus avidly (Ammianus 28.4.14; Syme 1968; 1971, 47).[13] This audience would also recognise discrepancies between clothed emperors as portrayed in statues, emperors as described in texts, and the clothes that they themselves wore. The lack of attention to women in the text also reflects late fourth century attitudes to gender. In the end, the *Historia Augusta* tells us much more about late fourth century assumptions concerning imperial standards, than it does about the history of dress. However, it also imparts a body of data, and a panoply of symbolic meanings for the clothed body, that we can process together with surviving visual material. It is an example of *a language* of dress in action, but not of dress in action.

NOTES

1. I have to thank Dr Leslie Brubaker for commenting on earlier drafts of this paper. Unfortunately, I had finished this paper before I discovered: http://www.intratext.com/X/LAT0229.htm, with the text of the *Historia Augusta*. This will form an invaluable tool for further research. I have also been unable to obtain a copy of Molinier-Arbo's paper presented at Nanterre, 2001, but have had the benefit of Callu's forthcoming article. The three volume Loeb edition, translated by Magie (2000), is used here.
2. Brubaker fully articulates this argument in the case of Byzantine manuscripts in her forthcoming article, which I thank her for allowing me to read in advance of publication.
3. See, for example, Hales, this volume; Heskel 1994, 133–45; Bender 1994, 146–152; Edwards 1994, 153–9; Dyck 2001, 119–30.
4. See Kleiner 1992 and Goette 1990 for images.
5. For Augustus, Trajan and Marcus Aurelius (sometimes elided with Antoninus Pius) as prime role models for emperors in the *Historia Augusta* see *Claud.* 2.3; Syme 1971, 89–112.
6. Davies, this volume. Development of the toga: Goette 1990; Stone 1994, 13–45; Wilson 1924.
7. The *paenula* has a chequered history in the *Historia Augusta*, sometimes acceptable and other times not. According to the life of Hadrian, emperors never wore a *paenula*, and do not appear in public wearing them (*Hadrian* 3.4). However this fact is offered as part proof of an omen predicting Hadrian's imperial power. For a detailed study see Kolb 1974, 81–101.
8. See Goette 1990 and Stone 1994 for images, and Harlow, forthcoming.
9. For Herodian as source for the *Historia Augusta* see Syme 1971, 51, 58.
10. *Paragauda* is translated in the Loeb edition as 'embroidered' and by Lewis and Short (1966, 1301) as 'border' or 'a laced garment'. Both may be misleading. Embroidery in the modern sense is not known from ancient surviving textiles, but tapestry weave decoration is. See Wild (2000, 210) for a similar problem with *plumarius*, translated as 'embroiderer' but more likely to mean 'tapestry weaver.' Magie's commentary on the HA informs us that the *paragaudes/paragauda* is identified by John Lydus (*de*

Magistratibus, 1.7; 2.4) as a tunic of eastern origin, having sleeves and a purple border with designs of gold (Loeb *SHA* Vol. 3, 188). See also James & Tougher, this volume.

11 The *tunica palmata and toga picta* were garments specifically for triumphs, and a single set was kept in the Temple of Jupiter. Gordian I was said to be the first ever to own his own, thus demonstrating his excessive wealth (*Gord.* 4.4). It is unclear at what stage consuls began to wear this outfit on accession to office, but it was a custom well established by the late fourth century. See Goette (1989) for development.

12 The penultimate paragraph of the Historia Augusta stresses the role of clothing as stored wealth. A certain Junius Messalla is directly accused of cutting off his heirs by giving away his ancestral fortune to actors and actresses. The fortune consists of purple and gold clothing (Carus 20.4–6).

13 Ammianus, it must be said, viewed both these authors with disdain but was not above his own rhetorical use of dress (e.g. 28.4.18ff). See also MacMullen 1964, 435–55.

Chapter 14

Get Your Kit On! Some issues in the depiction of clothing in Byzantium[1]

Liz James and Shaun Tougher

This mosaic panel (**Figure 14.1**) from the apse of the sixth-century church of San Vitale in Ravenna depicts the empress Theodora with her court of women and men. Opposite it is an image of the emperor Justinian with his court, soldiers, courtiers and clergy. These images are both perennial favourites with historians of dress, used to suggest that Byzantine clothing was spectacular in its use of colours, embroideries and elaborate textiles.[2]

Figure 14.1. *Theodora and her court, mosaic panel, Church of San Vitale, Ravenna, sixth century AD. (Photo © E. James).*

This chapter considers the question of the display of status through dress in a specifically Byzantine context, but also through the perspective of the 'distorting mirror' that all images offer. There is a double concern here: the consideration of these images as pictures, or illustrations, of clothes; and the consideration of the garments themselves as images. How far do images of clothed Byzantines represent the clothes actual Byzantines wore? Do these images instead depict an idealisation of Byzantine dress that carries with it an additional iconographic significance? At least one of the patterns shown on the garments of the waiting women in the Theodora panel, the motif of spades, is replicated in surviving Byzantine silks, but whether Theodora ever owned a robe like the one she is shown wearing here is a moot point.[3] Is this dress merely a way of identifying an empress as such? Theodora's garb is essentially male costume (James 2001, 26–49). She wears a longer version of the male cloak and tunic worn by Justinian, and the cloak is pinned with a man's brooch. Should we therefore deduce from this that Byzantine imperial costume was a case of cross-dressing? Clearly this pushes the issue of images as illustrations of clothes to its limit, but it does raise the important question of what it might mean to show an empress in male dress.

Similar questions about the function of clothing can be asked of any Byzantine image. A miniature in an eleventh-century manuscript, a copy of the *Homilies* of John Chrysostom, depicts the emperor with his courtiers and personifications of Truth and Justice.[4] Emperor and courtiers wear colourful and elaborately patterned robes; the personifications wear simpler, classicising tunics. Which of these garments are 'real' and which 'imaginary'? A fourteenth-century mosaic from the church of Christ in Chora (the Kariye Camii) in Constantinople depicts the donor of the church, Theodore Metochites, offering his building to Christ.[5] Theodore is dressed in a lavish blue-green robe decorated with gold spades and leaves, and with gold and red embroidery at collar, cuffs, hem and front. He wears a seemingly fantastical hat, almost a billowing turban decorated with broad vertical red and gold stripes and gold and red braiding across the top. Does this image indicate that hats like this were a high fashion item in the fourteenth century, or is this an idealised costume, a shorthand means of denoting an important imperial official? In the case of the personifications, it is perhaps easier to describe this as 'imagined (but appropriate)' dress and to see Theodore's clothes as representing a 'real' costume. However, the basis for these judgements is essentially based on whether the images themselves are perceived as images of 'imaginary' or 'real' people. The *Homilies* manuscript has another miniature depicting the emperor with John Chrysostom and the archangel Michael.[6] The question of whether the dress of the figures in these scenes is 'real' or 'imaginary' is again relevant. Should we see the 'real' figure, the emperor, as wearing 'real' dress and the 'imaginary' figures, Truth, Justice and even Michael, as dressed in 'imaginary' clothing? Is it possible that they wear clothing appropriate for figures in attendance on the emperor and thus reflect clothing appropriate for the emperor's court? Where does this leave the dress of the 'real' but long-dead John Chrysostom?

This is a question of dress codes and what these say about both status and the person depicted. In the case of Theodora, her garments depict a dress code suitable for an empress, an imperial figure, rather than those suitable for a woman. It is her position rather than her sex that is denoted by her garments. The mosaic is not an image of the woman Theodora but of the empress Theodora (James 2001, 26–49). The same can be argued for the images of the personifications, of Theodore Metochites and of the emperor and the archangel; these are all images in which the clothes serve to mark out the status and position of the person. The case for whether they represent their actual garments remains unproven.

To examine this in a little more detail, we turn to the first of two case studies in this chapter, to ask whether the dress of eunuchs marked them out specifically as eunuchs or whether it concerned only their status. Eunuchs were a staple feature of the imperial courts of the later Roman empire and Byzantium. They played important roles in both state and church, and their status as eunuchs was often of significance in the range of offices and positions to which they had access.[7]

A case to explore is that of the donor miniature of the tenth-century Leo Bible.[8] The eunuch donor, Leo the *patrikios praipositos* and *sakellarios*, is shown offering his Bible to the Virgin Mary. Leo, known only from the manuscript (and identified as a eunuch by his beardlessness, rank and office), is depicted wearing a white tunic (*chiton*) with gold bands at the wrist and hem decorated with red, and over this a red cloak (*chlamys*) with golden palmette decoration on the chest and a golden band ornamented with a red shell-like design, and black shoes.

This is one of the very rare cases in which contemporary literary evidence for appropriate dress survives: the *Kleterologion* of Philotheos, written in 899 AD, during the reign of Leo VI.[9] In this text, Philotheos described those individuals who could be invited to the imperial feasts, their exact order of precedence at that moment in time, and the prominent feasts of the year to which various combinations of these people would be invited. Whilst establishing this system, he paid particular attention to the position of eunuchs. In discussing eunuch offices and titles, Philotheos remarked on the dress appropriate to some of the titles when that dress formed the accompanying insignia, or part of the insignia.[10] He noted that the insignia of the *nipsistarios* was a linen *kamision*, a kind of outer garment, on which was attached a *blattion* (purple silken cloth) in the form of a basin; the insignia of the *cubicularius* was a *kamision* decorated with *blattia*, and the robe known as the *paragaudion* (see Harlow, this volume); the insignia of the *primicerius* was a white tunic with gold-embroidered shoulders and decoration; the insignia of the eunuch *protospatharios*, a golden collar decorated with precious stones and pearls, a white tunic threaded with gold, like the *divitesion*, and a scarlet cloak with *tablia* woven with gold.[11] Philotheos also noted that the costume of the eunuch *patrikios* (which Leo was) only differed from that of the eunuch *protospatharios* in the detail of the *loros* or long jewelled scarf.[12]

In this instance, the literary evidence broadly coincides with the visual evidence and gives some weight to a belief that clothing can be accurately depicted. Presumably it was in Leo's interests to have his costume, a vital signifier of his social status, depicted accurately. The same seems likely for Theodore Metochites. However, the dress of Leo's brother Constantine, a bearded (or non-eunuch) *protospatharios*, shown in the other frontispiece of the Leo Bible is remarkably similar to that of his brother (though Constantine is shown with a sword to indicate his title). This implies that it is court dress rather than eunuch dress that is depicted. The impression that dress marks the position rather than the individual, as was the case with Theodora, is reinforced.

The case of two ecclesiastical eunuchs adds weight to this. The ninth-century eunuch patriarch, Ignatios, is depicted in mosaic in Hagia Sophia, within a series of fourteen Church Fathers in the north and south tympana (Mango & Hawkins 1972, 3–41, esp. 9–11, 28–30). Comparison with the other mosaics indicates that his dress of tunic, chasuble and omophorion matches exactly that of the other bishops depicted. His physical appearance, however, is distinctive for he is shown beardless, a typical mark of the eunuch. Similarly, one of the miniatures of the emperor from the *Homilies* of John Chrysostom includes a figure identified, by dress and inscription, as a monk.[13] He has also been identified as a eunuch on the grounds of his physical appearance (lack of a beard). However, there is nothing significantly distinctive in his dress, in itself, or in comparison to images of other monks from the same period, to mark him as such (Dumitrescu 1987, 79). In both of these cases, eunuchs are obviously depicted according to a dress code which stresses position not sex, a code shared with non-eunuchs.

In the Theodora panel, the two beardless male attendants of the empress are conventionally identified as eunuchs.[14] Beardlessness alone at this date was not necessarily an indication of eunuchhood, so can the dress of these figures help in clarifying their physical status? Are they depicted in clothing appropriate to offices held by eunuchs? Again, can we be sure that their dress (long cloak, decorated with purple *tablion*, over white tunic; shoes; cross-bow brooches) has any basis in reality? Unfortunately lack of knowledge about such details makes it impossible to decide. However, it is worth noting that the two men differ in dress from each other: the man closest to Theodora is dressed akin to the men closest to Justinian, while the man holding the curtain lacks elaborate geometric patterns on his tunic and is dressed in a cloak of golden appearance.

All of this leaves us in an ambivalent position. Representations of dress may or may not be accurate; but clothing does serve to denote status in Byzantium. However, that status does not depend on giving clear and unambivalent clues as to the gender of the wearer of the garments. Rather, empresses and eunuchs are given status by being depicted dressed in male robes. This may help us with 'real' people but what about figures such as personifications and angels? To answer that, the ground needs to be moved away from a concern with the accuracy or otherwise of dress, towards a concern with the appropriateness of clothes. It is not possible to claim that the Archangel Michael in the *Homilies* of John Chrysostom was shown dressed as a specific, or indeed as any sort of, court official. Instead, it is necessary to consider some of the ways in which dress denoted status, a role it clearly does fulfil. To do that, dress has to be considered as more than fashion, and some of the other iconographical elements that make up Byzantine costume need to be unpicked.

The idea that the type of garment worn is indicative of status, gender and standing in society is an iconographical commonplace. A toga, a *loros*, a short tunic, a man's robe on a woman, all appear to indicate different things. Similarly what the body is clothed in, or appears to be clothed in – silk, wool, sack – is also a significant pointer. The question of how different textiles are depicted is one which Byzantine art historians and historians of dress have barely begun to explore (cf. Marcar this volume). A further iconographical pointer is the colour of the clothing. This concern forms the basis of our second case study.

What might the colours chosen to depict an individual's garment mean? Why those colours and not others? Again, in answering this, discussion needs to move beyond the response 'because this is the colour that such a garment was' and the problems inherent in that reply. The colour of clothing requires examination within a consideration of the significance and place of colours within Byzantine society, for the colours used in an image must also be the colours appropriate to the individuals.

In the images discussed, the colours used are gold, purple and red for the empress Theodora, gold and blue for the archangel Michael and gold and blue for the imperial official Theodore Metochites. Purple is, on one level, straightforward. It had been the imperial colour since the Roman period, carrying connotations of expense, exclusivity, power, prestige and wealth.[15] Many of the same things can be said about gold. However, noting that the empress was clothed in purple because purple was the imperial colour is only a part of the story. The colour of garments was important to the Byzantines. The *Book of Ceremonies*, a tenth-century account of ceremonies at the Byzantine court probably put together by an emperor, very often describes what garments of what colour are to be worn for which ceremony by the emperor.[16] These vary in colour: white is particularly popular as a colour for imperial garments, which suggests that purple cannot be taken as an automatic choice for imperial clothing. Rather, it is a deliberate choice, but for what reasons?

The twelfth-century author, Nicholas Mesarites, described the mosaic of Christ Pantocrator in the church of the Holy Apostles in Constantinople. He notes how the lines of this image "are not plain, but... please the senses and impress the mind by their varied colours and the brilliance of the gold and the brightness of their hues", and goes on to state that the robes worn by Christ are blue (*kuaneos*) and gold. There is, Mesarites says, a good and Biblical reason for these colours: to reveal by example the ostentation of purple (he uses that common term *porphureios*), scarlet (*kokkinos*) and blue (*hyakinthos*), the latter blue of a different nature from *kuaneos*-blue since it carries overtones of the precious stone called hyacinth.[17] In this instance, purple is seen as an unsuitable colour for Christ because it symbolises ostentation, as, in this instance also do scarlet and hyacinth-blue. In contrast to these stand gold and *kuaneos*-blue. This is a different symbolism for purple.[18]

This shifting significance of colours is, in part, explained by an image employed by the fourth-century church father, Athanasios, and echoed in later Byzantine writers including the eighth-century theologian, John of Damascus. Athanasios said that wool is common and available to all: "however, when it is dipped in the dye of the sea, it is called purple. Once it takes up this name, it becomes something which is fitting to be used exclusively by kings... [the purple] transcends the common character, because of the dignity of him who uses it." John's version is that: "Purple cloth by itself is a simple thing, and so is silk, and a cloak is woven from both. But if a king should put it on, the cloak receives honour from the honour given to him who wears it."[19] What both appear to be saying is that purple is royal because it is worn by kings; the implication is that if not worn by royalty it need not carry the same connotations.

The significance of the colour purple – indeed of any colour – depended on the context of its use (James 1996, 91–110). Purple was not always a symbol of imperial dignity: it was only so if worn by a king. Indeed, this may explain something of the stress placed on keeping purple exclusive to the emperor. If purple was put into a negative context, then it fulfilled a negative function, which was striking because unusual. It did not take on a negative aspect for all time and in all places. In the case of the image of Theodora, to echo John of Damascus and Athanasios, two writers from either side of the date of the Theodora panel, if the purple cloak derives honour from him (or her) who wears it, there is no problem. In contrast, in the image of herself in the Dioscorides Herbal, the sixth-century noblewoman Anicia Juliana is depicted in purple.[20] Here, in contrast to the image of Theodora, Anicia Juliana may have been making a less than accurate claim about her imperial status. In other words, individuals might appropriate colours to sell a line. If the purple of Theodora tells us about her real status as empress, the purple of Anicia Juliana is about her claimed status as empress.

In Byzantium, colour also works in two further dimensions beyond that of hue: brilliance and saturation. In answering the question 'what colour is Theodora's robe?' our immediate impulse is to describe it in terms of its hues: purple and gold. However, Classical Greek and Byzantine colour vocabulary tends to reflect saturation and brilliance rather than hue. Purple (*porphurios*) for example, is used in contexts where 'dark' is a better translation, and 'gushing', 'surging' and 'heaving' are also found as alternative meanings. In addition, Byzantine accounts of art describe colour first in terms of its brilliance and brightness. A sixth-century author describes the church of Hagia Sophia in Istanbul in these terms: "The roof is compacted of gilded tesserae from which a glittering stream of golden rays pours abundantly and strikes men's eyes with irresistible force. It is as if one were gazing at the midday sun in spring when it gilds each mountain top".[21]

In this way, it is conceivable that a Byzantine beholder saw brightness and brilliance in Theodora's robes. Both gold and purple were also colours of brilliance and light, valued because of their light-bearing aspect (James 1996, 91–110). Cloth too can carry light and brilliance. Anna Muthesius has seen how Byzantine silks reflect light and create their pattern through changing the weave. Muthesius notes, in the context of discussing Byzantine silk chasubles surviving in Western Europe, that two faces of tabby weave can often be found contrasted (1995, 203). Weft-faced tabby binding used for the pattern areas reflects more light than the warp-faced tabby binding used on the background areas. This is because the weft-faced area uses silk that is untwisted and thus reflects the maximum amount of light whilst the warp-faced areas have twisted silk threads with a smaller surface and thus less reflection of light. In this context, gold thread was valued not only for its cost but also because it helped to create the sparkling effect so valued by the Byzantines.

A Byzantine viewer might have said Theodora's robe was deep, bright, sparkling and flashing in colour, qualities that were also significant. Gold and blue, Christ's robe in Mesarites, are also described as colours of light. The value of gold as the purest and highest of the metals is underlined by its use as a representation of divine light in haloes and backgrounds, and its possession of the essential qualities of reflectance and brilliance. Blue is a colour frequently used to portray divine light, such as Christ's mandorla in scenes of the Transfiguration. Mesarites' description of Christ in blue and gold thus clothes him in the spiritual holiness of light rather than in ostentatious earthly splendours, costly dyes and precious stones. By taking the iconography of the colour of clothing this far, we then arrive at the question of what it might mean to depict the clothed body not only in purple but also in light.

Here again eunuchs offer an interesting example. In literary texts, court eunuchs of the emperor are often confused or blurred or identified with the angels of God, or, rather, vice versa.[22] As Mango says, "The angels, being sexless and acting as God's attendants, had their closest earthly analogy in the eunuchs of the imperial palace. The chief of the eunuchs was the *praepositus sacri cubiculi*, whose position was, therefore, analogous to that of St. Michael" (1980, 155). One example of this blurring of angels and eunuchs is the famous 'dream of Bardas' from the tenth-century *Life of Ignatios*.[23] Other texts spell out the association more clearly, and relate it to dress. In Pantaleon's late ninth or early tenth-century account of a miracle at the church of Michael at Eusebios, Constantinople, the Archangel Michael is described as being dressed in the robe of a *praipositos*; not just a court official, but a eunuch court official.[24] The important point here is that both angels and eunuchs can be associated with a bright shining quality which can also be reflected in their clothing. Both visually and verbally, the colour of the garments associated with both angels and eunuchs are those which also carry connotations of light and luminosity. White vestments were thought particularly appropriate to angels, as is the case with the mosaic of the angel in the apse of Hagia Sophia, and angels mistaken for eunuchs are often described as being dressed in white robes, such as the angel guardian of Hagia Sophia.[25] In Genesios' version of the dream of Bardas, he describes the *praipositoi* as wearing golden robes.[26] Visual images can also depict angels in imperial dress, thus, as we have seen, in colours associated with light (Maguire 1997, 255–256).

In conclusion, when we look at images of the clothed body, we cannot be sure that this is what X ever wore, but we can be very sure that this was the appropriate way to depict X. As far as clothing the body goes, it is not the depiction of the garment alone, but its style and cut, material, texture, and colour which bear meaning to the nature of the clothed body beneath it, appropriate to that body, nuanced with the same sophistication which underlay every aspect of Byzantine imagery. It is for us to unpick that fabric.

NOTES

1. Since the writing of this paper other relevant work has been published. Unfortunately we have been unable to incorporate this into the paper due to time constraints, but provide the details here: T. Dawson, *The Forms and Evolution of the Dress and Regalia of the Byzantine Court: c. 900 – c. 1400* (PhD thesis, University of New England, 2003); M. G. Parani, *Reconstructing the Reality of Images: Byzantine Material Culture and Religious Iconography (11th – 15th Centuries)* (Leiden and Boston, Brill, 2003); and K. M. Ringrose, *The Perfect Servant: Eunuchs and the Social Construction of Gender in Byzantium* (Chicago, University of Chicago Press, 2003).
2. Stout 1994, 77–100, esp. 83–85; Croom 2000, pl. 1 and 2; Houston 1947, 136–142.
3. The silk is T.104–1949 in the collection of the Victoria and Albert Museum, London. It is worth noting that Justinian and Theodora actually never went to Ravenna, which might add to the sense that the clothing they are depicted in is imagined rather than real.

4 Paris, Coislin 79, fols 2r. Spatharakis 1976, 107–118; Dumitrescu 1987, 32–45; Evans & Wixom (1997, cat.143, 207–209) also outlines the complex history of these miniatures.
5 For the Kariye Camii and its mosaics, Underwood 1967; Ousterhout 2002; for Theodore Metochites, see Ševcenko 1975, 17–92.
6 Coislin 79, fol.2v. Illustrated in Durand *et al.* 1992, cat.271, 361.
7 On late Roman and Byzantine eunuchs: Guilland 1943, 197–238; Hopkins 1978, 172–196; Ringrose 1994, 85–109 and 507–518; Tougher 1997, 168–184.
8 Ms. Vat. Reg. gr. I, fol. 2v. Spatharakis 1976, 7–14; Evans and Wixom 1997, cat.42, 88–90.
9 On middle Byzantine court dress see Piltz 1997, 39–51. See also Ringrose's comments on eunuch dress (1996, 75–93, esp. 78). *Kletorologion*: Oikonomidès 1972, 65–235.
10 Some of the insignia are objects rather than clothes: e.g. the insignia of the *spatharocandidatos* is a golden-headed sword.
11 Edition by Oikonomidès 1972, 125.23, 127.1–4.
12 Philotheos also describes the insignia of the non-eunuch titles, some of which can also be items of costume: Oikonomidès 1972, 88–99.
13 Ms. Coislin 79 fol. 1r; illustrated in Evans & Wixom 1997, 82.
14 As eunuchs: Andreescu-Treadgold & Treadgold 1997, 708–723, esp. 708 and 718, cf. Barber 1990, 21 less certain.
15 For a discussion and bibliography of purple, see James 1996, 121 and Janes 1998.
16 *Book of Ceremonies*: Vogt 1935; Reiske 1832.
17 Mesarites 14.8. See Downey 1957, 859–918, cf. Ziderman 2004, 40–45.
18 For the well-known problem of Greek colour vocabulary, see James 1996, 47–68.
19 Athanasios: *Letter to Eupsychius*, PG 26, col.1245–48; John of Damascus: *First Treatise on the Divine Images*, PG 94, 1264B.
20 Vienna, Nationalbibliothek, cod.med.gr.1, fol.6v. Colour image: Weitzmann 1977, pl.15.
21 Paul the Silentiary, lines 668–72 in Friedländer 1912.
22 Ringrose 1996, 75–93, esp. 86–89; Maguire 1997, 247–258, esp. 255–256; Sidéris 2002, 161–175, esp. 166–168.
23 *PG* 105, 533D–536C. In his dream Bardas sees his own divinely sanctioned death. Bardas says that in his dream he went to Hagia Sophia with the emperor, and that at all the windows archangels were looking in. When they came to the pulpit two chamberlains (thus eunuchs) appeared and dragged away the emperor. Then two more dragged Bardas too. He then saw an old man seated on the patriarchal throne looking like an icon of St Peter, flanked by two *praipositoi* (eunuchs again). Implored by Ignatios, Peter ordered that Bardas be led away and cut to pieces.
24 *Pace* Peers (2001,186). *Narration of the Miracles of the Mighty Archangel Michael*: PG 140.
25 Discussed by Mango (1980, 155) and Peers (2001, 74–75).
26 Genesios 4.21: Lesmüller-Werner & Thurn 1978, 74.93.

Chapter 15

Tunics from Kasr al-Yahud

Orit Shamir

INTRODUCTION

In 1985 a rescue excavation was carried out at Kasr al-Yahud by the anthropologist Joe Zias (1991; 2002). The site is situated along the Jordan River near the Monastery of Saint John the Baptist (believed to be the traditional site of the Baptism of Jesus and the 'washing of the lepers'). A mass grave of around 300 individuals was discovered at the site, 90% of which had been destroyed by road construction. However, thirty-four skeletons were retrieved, probably representing a hospital population of tuberculosis, leprosy and facial disfigurement cases. Such individuals traveled enormous distances, attracted to the site in the hope of washing away their illness. Anthropological evidence indicates that the individuals were probably Egyptian in origin, while structural analysis of the skulls proved that some were Nubian.

The fact that special leper hospitals were established early in the fourth century (by Byzantine authorities and monasteries) attests to the severity of the problem, which had clearly reached epidemic proportions. In the Byzantine period it was customary to build hospitals, in association with monasteries and churches, at places frequented by pilgrims. The monasteries at Mt. Sinai, St. Theodosius, and the Nea Church in Jerusalem, are examples of this Byzantine tradition of combining ecclesiastical institutions with hospitals. Some of these monasteries and their hospitals continued in use during the Islamic period. The custom of travelling vast distances in hope of washing away illness also continued – an impressive feat when one realizes that debilitating diseases would have made long journeys difficult. Additional hospital facilities, specifically for lepers, were established in Jerusalem and Bethlehem during the Crusader period (after 1099 AD).

BALÁNITES AEGYPTIACA (EGYPTIAN BALSAM)

Some of the burial customs at this site, such as placing seeds from the tree *Balánites Aegyptiaca* in the hands of the deceased, conform to Egyptian traditions. The distribution of this tree covers east and west Africa, Arabia, the Nile Valley and Judean Desert: its stones have often been found in ancient tombs at Gizeh, Thebes, and various other sites in Lower and Upper Egypt. The economic value of Egyptian Balsam was known in Egypt since ancient times, its most important product being the oil extracted from its kernel: the fruit pulp was eaten raw or made into cakes, and also went into the preparation of alcoholic drink. Different parts of the Balánites tree were traditionally used to treat a wide range of illnesses. Alongside this evidence was the find of a walnut shell placed on the thorax of one of the deceased. Walnuts theologically symbolized paradise, while their oil was prescribed for various illnesses including leprosy (Zias 2002).

THE TEXTILES

The arid climate of the Judean Desert helped to preserve textiles and a few cords, most from garments. Carbon dating of the textiles placed the date at the eighth to ninth centuries AD (787–877). The excavation lasted only two days, and because of these difficult conditions, no loci or basket numbers were given to the artifacts. All the textiles were catalogued by myself and Dr. Robert Janaway. With the help of a computer, it was possible to match fragments according to material, spin direction, weaving techniques etc.: for example, matching a separate sleeve with the front of a tunic. We were left with two hundred and fifty textiles, which were analyzed and described, but our research is still at an early stage.

Linen textiles

Linen is known in Israel from the Neolithic period (c. 6500 BC) onwards (Schick 1988). It became a major economic factor in many locations in Israel from the middle of the second century AD, most notably Bet She'an (Diocletian Ch. 26). A decline in flax growing set in after the Arab conquest of Israel and Syria at the beginning of the seventh century AD, and by the early Middle Ages its cultivation had ceased almost entirely. Despite this, the use of flax and its products remained popular and widespread in Israel; it was apparently imported from various countries, particularly Egypt (Amar 1998, 114).

One hundred and seventy-two textiles from Kasr al-Yahud are of linen, mostly S-spun in both warp and weft. They are woven in various tabby techniques, and all are undyed cream or beige. Thirty-two textiles are decorated with selfbands (**Figure 15.1**): a number weft threads being used together in one shed. A few are decorated with blue stripes, and one a plait (**Figure 15.2**). Another is decorated with wool bands, and brocading of dark red and black Z-spun threads. It is patched with a rectangular cotton fragment (**Figure 15.3**).

One bleached linen textile is decorated with two bands of foliated tapestry of brown wool and white linen (**Figure 15.4**). There were probably some other colors but the wool threads had disintegrated and only a few wool fibres were preserved. It also has a decoration of four selfbands, and is probably part of a Coptic tunic woven to shape (Baginski & Tidhar 1980, 44): the only one of this type from the site.

Cotton Textiles

These are found in Israel from the Early Christian period, but are very rare (Bellinger

Figure 15.1. Textile, decorated with a selfband (No. 36.8).

1962; Sheffer & Tidhar 1991:22–23). However, a change occurrs after the Arab conquest, relating to the development of trade ties with Asia, especially India, where cotton was more common. Cotton has been found at only two Early Islamic sites in Israel ('En Yahav, and Nahal Omer; Baginski & Shamir 1995). From the eighth century onwards, all the sites in Israel with textiles have yielded cotton textiles, either imported or locally produced (Baginski & Shamir 2001a). By the tenth century cotton was an important agro-industrial product in the economies of Israel and Syria. The S-spun cotton textiles from Kasr al-Yahud could have come from Nubia with the sick individuals.

Seventy-eight cotton textile fragments were found at Kasr al-Yahud. Of these, thirty are S-spun both in the warp and the weft; thirty S-spun in the warp and Z in the weft; and seventeen are Z-spun in both. They are woven in various tabby techniques, and all are undyed cream or beige (except two which are faded blue): some few are decorated with selfbands.

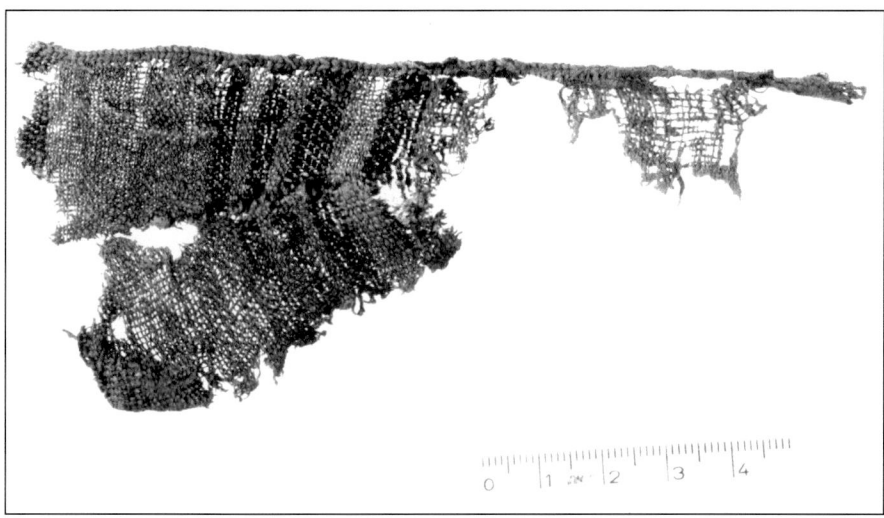

Figure 15.2. Linen textile, decorated with blue strips and a plait (No. 43.1.ii).

Figure 15.3. Linen textile, decorated with wool bands and brocade. It is patched with a rectangle of cotton (No. 43.2).

Figure 15.4. Linen tunic, decorated with tapestry bands (No. 35.2R).

TUNICS

Around fifteen tunics were found at Kasr al-Yahud, none complete. Many other smaller fragments probably belonged to tunics (it seems that the deceased were buried with their clothing). All except one were cut to shape, a later method than weaving to shape. The sleeves, if any, were made from separate pieces. The tunics can be divided into two groups according to their cut: straight tunics cut and sewn to form a cylindrical tube of cloth; and tunics with gores, creating a cone shape. Triangular gores are used in the lower parts of the side seams. Usually each gore is composed of two triangular panels of the same cloth as the ground weave. Tunics with cut construction have a long history in Central Asia, and can be traced back to Halabiyeh at the begining of the seventh century, becoming more common following the Arab expansion. Within two hundred years this form had become predominant (Linscheid 2001, 76; Granger-Taylor 1983).

We will mention two examples:

No. 3R (**Figure 15.5**) is made of linen. The width of the front is fully preserved at ninety-one cm. The side panel consists of two vertical gores of sixty cm in height, sewn in to increase the width by twenty cm on each side. The tunic is finished at the bottom with a two cm hem.

No. AB1A (**Figure 15.6**) is made of one main piece for front and back with a V-shaped neck opening and wool loops for buttons The loops are made of grouped brown

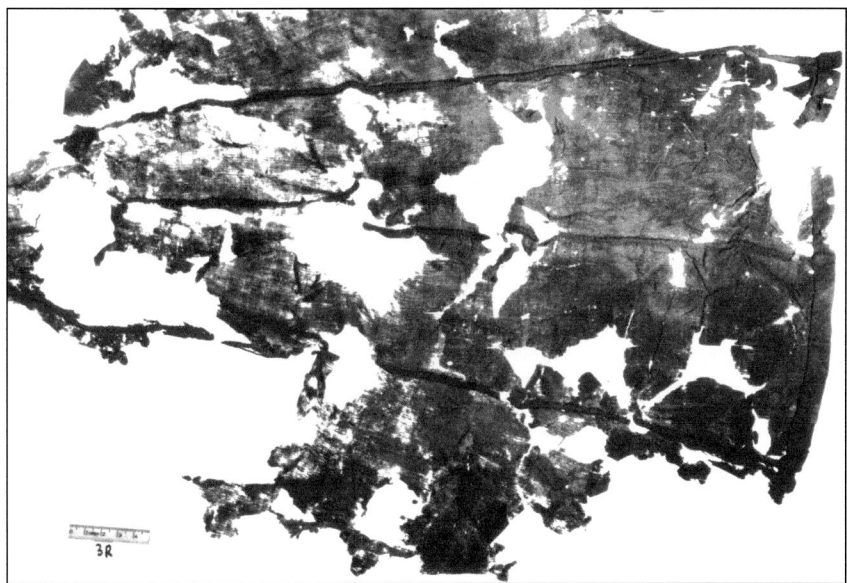

Figure 15.5. Cotton tunic with gores (No. 3R).

threads wrapped by thinner blue threads. The main panel running over the shoulder is made of two layers of cloth stitched one on top of the other: one gore is preserved. It is the largest piece found at the site and measures one hundered and fifty-five by one hundred and ninteen cm over all.

These cotton tunics have Z-spun, S-plied, sewing threads. Most sewing is run and fell seams but there are also hemming, binding and overcasting. The stitches are uniform in size and neat, used mainly for joining textiles together.

CONCLUSION

There is a transition from 'woven to shape' tunics in the Roman and Byzantine periods to 'cut to shape' tunics during the Early Islamic period and onwards, which is also observed in finds of cut and sewn Medieval textiles from Judean Desert caves. The status of the deceased from Kasr al-Yahud can be studied from their clothes – most were undyed and undecorated, of simple materials and weaving technique. On the other hand, few textiles were mended or patched. Apparently some individuals used new clothes for the long jurney from Nubia and Egypt to Israel. This research is not yet finished: we will continue to examine the other uses of textiles at the site, such as head coverings and bandages.

Figure 15.6. Tunic made of cotton with a neck opening (No. AB1).

ACKNOWLEDGEMENTS

The research at Kasr al-Yahud was financed by the Civil Administration in Judea and Samaria and the Israel Antiquities Authority. I thank Dr. Robert Janaway, who preserved the textiles and shared hours with me checking the artifacts, and the organisers of the conference (Dr. Mary Harlow and Dr. Lloyd Llewellyn-Jones) for their invitation and the grant towards my costs.

Photographs: Shlomo Ammy. Courtesy of Staff Officer of Archaeology, Civil Administration in Judea and Samaria.

Balánites Aegyptiaca
http://www.jicakenya.org/SOFEM/treelist/BAegy.htm
http://www.reshafim.org.il/ad/texts/kahun/49.htm
http://www.aun.eun.eg/co munity/cultivation_of_indigenous_medici1.htm

Bibliography

Abrahams, E. (1908) *Greek Dress. A study of the costumes worn in ancient Greece from pre-hellenic times to the hellenistic age.* London, J. Murray.
Aélion, R. (1983) Rois en haillons. In Aélion (ed.), 159–65.
Aélion, R. (ed.) (1983) *Euripide, Héritier d'Eschyle* II. Paris, Belles Lettres.
Alden, M. J. (1998) Divine underwear – in all the better shops. *Omnibus* 36, 32–3.
Aldred, C. (1957) Hairstyles and History. *Boston Museum of Fine Art* 15, 141–147.
Aldrete, G. S. (1999) *Gestures and Acclamations in Ancient Rome*. Baltimore/London, Johns Hopkins University Press.
Aleshire, S. B. (1989) *The Athenian Asklepion*. Amsterdam, Gieben.
Alföldi, A. (1935) Insignien und Tracht der Römischen Kaiser. *Römische Mitteilungen* 50, 1–171.
Alston, R. (1998) Arms and the man. Soldiers, masculinity and power in republican and imperial Rome. In Foxhall & Salmon (eds.) (1998b), 205–223.
Amar, Z. (1998) Written Sources Regarding the Jaziret Fara'un (Coral Island) Textiles. *'Atiqot* 36, 114–119.
Anawalt, P. R. (1981) *Indian Clothing Before Cortés: Mesoamerican costumes from the codices.* Oklahoma, University of Oklahoma Press.
Anderson, J. (1984) *The Historical Topography of the Imperial Fora*. Brussels, Latomus.
Andreescu-Treadgold, I. & Treadgold, W. (1997) Procopius and the imperial panels of S. Vitale. *The Art Bulletin* 79, 708–723.
Annas, A., La Valley, S., Maeder, E. & Jenssen, E. (eds.) (1987) *Hollywood and History. Costume Design in Film.* Los Angeles, Thames & Hudson.
Anstey, E., Manvell, R., Lindgren, E., Rotha, P. & Blumenthal, G. (eds.) (1951) *Shots in the dark: A collection of reviewers' opinions of some of the leading films released between January 1949 and February 1951.* London, Rowman & Littlefield.
Archer, L. J., Fischler, S. & Wyke, M. (eds.) (1994) *Women in Ancient Societies*. London, Routledge.
Arscott, C. & Scott, K. (eds) (2000) *Manifestations of Venus*. Manchester, Manchester University Press.
Arthur, L. B. (1999) Dress and the Social Control of the Body. In Arthur (ed.), 1–7.
Arthur, L. B. (ed.) (1999) *Religion, Dress, and the Body*. Oxford/New York, Berg.
Ash, R. (1989) *Sir Lawrence Alma-Tadema*. London, Thames & Hudson.
Ash, R. (1995) *Lord Leighton*. London, Thames & Hudson.
Ash, R. (1999) *Victorian Masters and Their Art*. London, Phaidon.
Austin, M., Harries, J. & Smith, C. (eds.) (1998) *Modus Operandi. Essays in Honour of Geoffrey Rickman.* London, Institute of Classical Studies.
Babington, B. & Evans, P. W. (1993) *Biblical Epics. Sacred Narrative in the Hollywood Cinema.* Manchester/New York, Manchester University Press.
Baginski, A. & Shamir, O. (1994) Textiles from Jesiret Fara'un (Coral Island). *Archaeology Textiles Newsletter* 18/19, 2–5.

Baginski, A. & Shamir, O. (1995) Early Islamic Textiles, Basketry and Cordage from Nahal Omer, Israel. *'Atiqot* 26, 21–42.

Baginski, A. & Shamir, O. (1997) The Earliest Ikats. *The International Magazine of Antique Carpet and Textile Art* 95, 86–87.

Baginski, A. & Shamir, O. (1998a) Textile Remains in the Umayyad Hoard. In Piccirillo & Alliata (eds.), 565.

Baginski, A. & Shamir, O. (1998b) Textiles, Basketry and Cordage from Jeziret Fara'un (Coral Island). *'Atiqot* 36, 39–122.

Baginski, A. & Shamir, O. (2001a) Textiles and Cordage from 'Avdat – the Saints Cave. *'Atiqot* 42, 243–260.

Baginski, A. & Shamir, O. (2001b) The Textiles, Basketry and Cordage from Qarantal – Cave 38: The First Medieval Assemblage Discovered In Palestine. *Archaeology Textiles Newsletter* 32, 19–20.

Baginski, A. & Tidhar, A. (1980) *Textiles from Egypt 4th–13th Centuries CE*. Jerusalem, Tavinit Press.

Bahrani, Z. (2001) *Women of Babylon. Gender and Representation in Mesopotamia*. London/New York, Routledge.

Bald Romano, I. (1988) Early Greek Cult Images and Cult practices. In Hägg *et al.* (eds.), 127–34.

Balensiefen, L. (1990) *Die Bedeutung des Spiegelbildes als ikonographisches Motiv in der antiken Kunst*. Tübingen, Ernst Wasmuth.

Barber, C. (1990) The imperial panels at San Vitale: a reconsideration. *Byzantine and Modern Greek Studies* 14, 19–42.

Barber, E. J. W. (1991) *Prehistoric Textiles: The Development of Cloth in the Neolithic and Bronze Ages with Special Reference to the Aegean*. Princeton, Princeton University Press.

Barber, E. J. W. (1992) The Peplos of Athena. In Neils (ed.), 103–17.

Barber, E. J. W. (1994) *Women's Work: the first 20,000 years*. New York, Norton.

Barber, E. J. W. (1999) *The Mummies of Ürümchi*. London, Norton.

Barber, E. J. W. (2000) Minoan Fashion: Skin Deep? *Archaeology* 53/6, 6–7.

Barker, A. W. (1923) *A Classification of the Chitons Worn by Greek Women as Shown in Works of Art*. Diss. University of Pennsylvania.

Barnes, S. J. & Melion, W. S. (eds.) (1989) *Cultural Differentiation and Cultural Identity in the Visual Arts*. Washington, National Art Gallery Press.

Barthes, R. [trans. Miller] (1975) *S/Z*. London, Cape.

Barthes, R. [trans. Ward & Howard] (1990) *The Fashion System*. Berkeley, University of California Press.

Bartman, E. (1999) *Portraits of Livia*. Cambridge, Cambridge University Press.

Barton, C. (2002) Being in the eyes. Shame and sight in ancient Rome. In Fredrick (ed.), 216–25

Bartsch, S. (1994) *Actors in the Audience. Theatricality and Doublespeak from Nero to Hadrian*. Cambridge Mass., Harvard University Press.

Beard, M. (1980) The Sexual Status of the Vestal Virgins. *Journal of Roman Studies* 70, 12–47.

Beard, M. (2003) The triumph of the absurd: Roman street theatre. In Edwards & Woolf (eds.), 21–43.

Beard, M., North, J. & Price, S. (1998) *Religions of Rome* Vol. 1. Cambridge, Cambridge University Press.

Beare, W. (1954) The Costume of the Actor in Aristophanic Comedy. *Classical Quarterly* 4, 64–74.

Beaujeu, J. (1955) *La religion romaine a l'apogée de l'empire vol 1. La politique religieuse des Antonins (96–162)*. Paris, Belles Lettres.

Beazley, J. (1960) Some inscriptions on vases: VIII. *American Journal of Archaeology* 64, 219–5.

Becker, W. A. (1866) *Charicles or Illustrations of the Private Life of the Ancient Greeks*. London/New York, Longman.
Bellinger, L. (1962) Textiles. In Colt (ed.), 91–105.
Bender, H. (1994) *De habitu vestis*: clothing in the Aeneid. In Sebesta & Bonfante (eds.), 146–52.
Berczelly, L. (1992) Pandora and the Panathenaia: The Pandora Myth and the Sculptural Decoration of the Parthenon. *Acta Art Hist* 8, 53–86.
Bernabo-Brea, L. (1998) *Le Maschere ellenistiche della tragedia greca*. Naples, Centre Jean Bérard.
Berry, S. (2000) *Screen Style. Fashion and Femininity in 1930s Hollywood*. Minneapolis, University of Minnesota Press.
Beschi, L. (1984) Il Fregio del Partenone: une proposta di lettura. *Accademia Nazionale dei Lincei, Rendiconti della Classe di Scienze morali, storiche e filologiche*, Series 8, Vol. 39, fasc. 5–6 (May–June), 1–23.
Bezantakos, N. P. (1987) *He Archaia Hellenike mitra: hermeneia ton schetikon keimenon apo ton Homero os ton Nonno*. Athens, Ekdoseis Kardamitsa.
Bieber, M. (1928) *Griechische Kleidung*. Berlin, Walter de Gruyter & Co.
Bieber, M. (1931) s.v. Strophium. *Paulys Real-Encyclopädie der Classischen Altertumswissenschaft*, 2nd series, Vol. 4a.7, cols. 378–81.
Bietak, M. (1995) Connections between Egypt and the Minoan World. New results from Tell El-Dab'a/Avaris. In Davies & Schofield (eds.), 19–28.
Bietak, M. (2000) Rich beyond the dreams of Avaris: Tell el-Dab'a and the Aegean world – a guide for the perplexed. A response to Eric H. Cline. *Annual of the British School at Athens* 95, 185–205.
Bietak, M. & Marinatos, N. (1995) The Minoan Wall Paintings from Avaris. *Ägypten und Levante* 5, 49–62.
Bloesch, H., & Mühletaler, B. (1967) Stoffreste aus spätgeometrischen Gräbern südlich des Westtores von Eretria. *Antike Kunst* 10, 130–2.
Boardman, J. (1975) *Athenian Red Figure Vases: the Archaic Period*. London, Thames & Hudson.
Boardman, J. (1985) *Greek Sculpture: the Classical Period*. London, Thames & Hudson.
Boardman, J. (1989) *Athenian Red Figure Vases: the Classical Period*. London, Thames & Hudson.
Boardman, J. (1995) *Greek Sculpture: the Late Classical Period*. London, Thames & Hudson.
Boardman, J. & Arrigoni, C. (1984) s.v. Atalante. *Lexicon Iconographicum Mythologiae Classicae* II, 940–50.
Bobrick, E. (1997) The tyranny of roles: playacting and privilege in Aristophanes' Thesmophoriazusae. In Dobrov (ed.), 177–97.
Boels-Janssen, N. (1993) *La Vie religieuse des Matrones dans la Rome archaïque*. Collection de l'Ecole Française de Rome 176. Rome, Ecole Française de Rome.
Bol, R. (1984) *Das Stauen programm des Herodes-Atticus-Nymphäums* (Olympische Forschungen XV). Berlin, de Gruyter.
Bonfante, L. (1975) *Etruscan Dress*. Baltimore/London, Johns Hopkins University Press.
Bonfante, L. (1989) Nudity as a costume in classical art. *American Journal of Archaeology* 93, 543–70.
Bonnamour, J. & Delavault, H. (eds.) (1979) *Aristophane, les femmes et la cité*. Paris, Fontenay-aux-Roses.
Bonner, C. (1949) *Kestos himas* and the saltire of Aphrodite. *American Journal of Philology* 70, 1–6.
Booth, C. (2001) Possible Tattooing Instruments in the Petrie Museum. *Journal of Egyptian Archaeology* 87, 172–175.
Borbé, T. (ed.) (1983) *Semiotics Unfolding: Proceedings of the Second Congress of the International Association for Semiotic Studies, Vienna, July, 1979*, III (Approaches to Semiotics 68) Berlin/New York/Amsterdam, Walter de Gruyter.

Borchardt, L. (1897) Gebrauch von Henna im alten Reiche. *Zeitschrift fur Agyptische Sprache und Altertumskunde* 35, 168–170.
Botham, M. & Sharrad, L. (1982) *Manual of Wigmaking*. London, Heinemann.
Böttiger, C. A. (1794) *Über den Raub der Cassandra auf einem alten Gefässe von gebrannter Erde*. Weimar, Meyer.
Boulter, C. G. (ed.) (1985) *Greek Art: Archaic into Classical*. Leiden, Brill.
Bowie, A. M. (1993) *Aristophanes: Myth, ritual and cult*. Cambridge, Cambridge University Press.
Brain, R. (1979) *The Decorated Body*. New York, Harper & Row.
Bratton, J., Cook, J. & Gledhill, C. (eds.) (1994) *Melodrama. Stage, Picture, Screen*. London, British Film Institute.
Bremmer, J. & Roodenburg, H. (eds.) (1991) *A Cultural History of Gesture*. Cambridge, Polity Press.
Brenk, E. E. (1977) Aphrodite's girdle: no way to treat a lady. *Classical Bulletin* 54, 17–20.
Brenner, A. (1993) Afterword. In Brenner (ed.), 231–235.
Brenner, A. (ed.) (1993) *A feminist companion to Judges*. Sheffield, Sheffield Academic Press.
Brothwell, D. (1986) *The Bog Man and the Archaeology of People*. London, British Museum Press.
Brovarski, E., Doll, S. K. & Freed, R. E. (1982) *Egypt's Golden Age: the Art of Living in the New Kingdom 1558–1058 BC*. Boston, Boston Museum of Fine Arts.
Brown, C. (1983) *Rubens Samson and Delilah*. London, Thames & Hudson.
Brubaker, L. (forthcoming 2005) Every cliché in the book: the linguistic turn and the text-image discourse in Byzantine manuscripts. In James (ed.).
Brubaker, L. & Smith, J. (eds.) (forthcoming 2005) *Gender and the Early Medieval World*. Cambridge, Cambridge University Press.
Bruhl, A. (1953) *Liber Pater*. Paris, Boccard.
Brulé, P. (1987) *La fille d'Athènes*. Paris, Belles Lettres.
Brulé, P. (1990) Retour à Brauron. Repentirs, avancées, mises au point. *Dialogues d'Histoire Ancienne* 16 (2), 61–90.
Brumfiel, E. M. (1991) Weaving and Cooking: Women's Production in Aztec Mexico. In Gero & Conkey (eds.), 224–251.
Buckley, S. A. & Evershed, R. (2001) The Organic Chemistry of Embalming Agents in Pharaonic and Graeco-Roman Mummies. *Nature* (Vol. 413, Issue 6858), 837–841.
Buitron-Oliver, D. (ed.) (1991) *New Perspectives in Early Greek Art. Proceedings of the Symposium "New Perspectives in Early Greek Art". Sponsored by the Center for Advanced Study in the Visual Arts, 27–28 May, 1988*, (Studies in the History of Art, 32). Hanover/London, University Press of New England.
Burkert, W. (1985) *Greek Religion*. Cambridge Mass., Harvard University Press.
Burkert, W. (1987) Offerings in Perspective: Surrender, Distribution, Exchange. In Linders & Nordquist (eds.), 43–50.
Cairns, D. (ed.) (forthcoming) *Gesture and Non-Verbal Communication in Antiquity*. Swansea, Classical Press of Wales.
Calame, Cl. (1986a) La tragédie: le masque pour mettre en scène l'altérité. In Calame (ed.), 85–100.
Calame, Cl. (1986b) La céramique: représentation et énonciation dans le regard et le masque. In Calame (ed.), 101–117.
Calame, Cl. (ed.) (1986c) *Le récit en Grèce ancienne. Enonciations et représentations de poètes*. Paris, Klincksieck.
Callu, J-P. (forthcoming) L'habit et l'ordre social: le témoinage de l'*Histoire Auguste*. Delivered at *Tissus et vetements dans l'Antiquité tardive*, Lyons, 2003 (*L'Antiquité Tardive* 12).
Cameron A. & Kuhrt, A. (eds.) (1983) *Images of Women in Antiquity*. London, Croom Helm.

Cameron, M. A. S. (1974) *A general study of Minoan frescoes*, Vols. I–II. Unpublished Ph.D. University of Newcastle upon Tyne.
Cannadine, D. & Price, S. (eds.) (1987) *Rituals and Royalty: Power and Ceremonial in Traditional Societies*. Cambridge, Cambridge University Press.
Cantarella, E. (1991) *I supplizi capitali in Grecia e a Roma*. Milan, Rizzoli.
Canterella, R. (1967) Agatone e il prologo delle "*Tesmoforiazuse*". In Koster (ed.), 7–15.
Capart, J. (1907) *L'Art et la Parure Feminine dans l'Ancienne Egypte*. Brussels, Annales de la Societe d'archaeologie de Bruxelles.
Capel, A. K. & Markooe, G. E. (eds.) (1996) *Mistress of the House. Mistress of Heaven: Women in Ancient Egypt*. New York, Hudson Hills Press.
Carandini, A., Ricci, A. & de Vos, M. (1982) *Filosofiana: the Villa of Piazza Armerina*. Palermo, S. F. Flaccovio.
Cardon, D. & Feugère, M. (eds.) (2000) *Archéologie des textiles des origines au Ve siècle*. Montaignac, Éditions Monique Mergoil.
Carington-Smith, J. (1975) Spinning, Weaving and Textile Manufacture in Prehistoric Crete. Unpublished PhD, University of Tasmania (Hobart).
Carington-Smith, J. (1992) Spinning and Weaving Equipment. In McDonald & Wilkie (eds.), 674–711.
Carr, K. (2000) Women's work: spinning and weaving in the Greek home. In Cardon & Feugère (eds.), 163–6
Cary, J. (1974) *Spectacular! The story of epic films*. London, Castle Books.
Casevitz, M. (1993) Remarques sur la langue des inventaires de Tanagra. In Fossey (ed.), 3–10
Castriota, D. (1995) *The Ara Pacis Augustae and the Imagery of Abundance in Later Greek and Early Roman Imperial Art*. Princeton, Princeton University Press.
Chabot, G. (2000) Femme fatale? I THINK NOT! http://www.epinions.com/mvie-review-10F6-168207C0-39648F88-prod5. 1–3. Accessed November 2002.
Chadwick, J. (1988) The Women of Pylos. In Olivier & Palaima (eds.), 43–95.
Chaniotis, A. (1997) Theatricality beyond the theatre: staging public life in the hellenistic world. *Pallas* 47, 219–59.
Chapman, A. C. & Plenderleith (1926) Examination of an Ancient Egyptian (Tut-ankh-Amen) Cosmetic. *Journal of Chemical Society* 329, 2614–2619.
Chausson, F. & Inglebert, H. (eds.) (2003) *Costume et Société dans L'Antiquité et le haut Moyen Age*. Paris, Éditions Picard.
Childs, W. A. P. (1988) The Classic as Realism in Greek Art. *Art Journal* 47, 10–14.
Chiotasso, L., Chiotasso, P., Pedrini, L., Rigoni, G. & Sarnelli, C. (1992) La parrucca di Merit. *Sesto Congresso Internazionale di Egittologia* I, 99–105.
Christ, A. T. (1997) The Masculine Ideal of 'the Race that Wears the Toga.' *Art Journal* 56.2, 24–30.
Christie, I. (1991) Cecil B. DeMille: grand illusions. *Sight and Sound* 1.8, 18–21.
Clarke, J. R. (1998) *Looking at Lovemaking: constructions of sexuality in Roman art 100 BC – AD 250*. Berkeley, University of California Press.
Claussen, D. S. (ed.) (2002) *Sex, Religion, Media*. Lanham, MD, Rowman & Littlefield.
Cleland, L. (2003) *Colour in Greek Clothing: A Methodological Investigation*. Unpublished PhD, University of Edinburgh.
Cleland, L. (2004) After-Paper: Colour in Antiquity. In Cleland & Stears (eds.), 139–145.
Cleland, L. (2004b) A Hierarchy of Women at Andania. In Davies (ed.), forthcoming.
Cleland, L. (forthcoming), *Clothing in the Brauron Inventories: Text, Analysis and Translation*. Leiden, Brill.
Cleland, L. & Stears, K. (eds.) (2004) *Colour in the Ancient Mediterranean World*. Oxford, British Archaeological Reports.

Cline, E. H. & Harris-Cline, D. (eds.) (1998) *The Aegean and the Orient in the Second Millennium. Proceedings of the 50th Anniversary Symposium, Cincinnati, 18–20 April 1997*. Liège, Aegaeum.
Cohen, B. (1997) Divesting the female breast of clothes in classical sculpture. In Koloski-Ostrow & Lyons (eds.), 66–92.
Cohen, B. (ed.) (2000) *Not in the Classical Ideal. Athens and the Construction of the Other in Greek Art*. Leiden, Brill.
Cohen, R. & Cohen-Amin, R. (2004) *Ancient Settlement of the Negev Highlands, Vol. II, The Iron Age and the Persian Period*. Jerusalem. Israel Antiquities Authority.
Coldstream, J. N. (1977) *Geometric Greece*. London, Meuthen.
Cole, S. (1998) Domesticating Artemis. In Williamson & Blundell (eds.), 29–44.
Colt, H. D. (ed.) (1962) *Excavations at Nessana*. London, British School of Archaeology.
Coogan, M. D. (1999) *The Oxford History of the Biblical World*. Oxford, Oxford University Press.
Cooke, W. D. & Shamir, O. (2000) A Textile from Deir Abu Mghar. In Dahari (ed.), 247–8.
Cooper, W. (1971) *Hair: Sex, Society and Symbolism*. London, Aldus.
Corbeill, A. (2002) Political movement: walking and ideology in republican Rome. In Fredrick (ed.), 182–215.
Corbeill, A. (2004) *Nature Embodied. Gesture in Ancient Rome*. Princeton/Oxford, Princeton University Press.
Cornell, T. & Lomas, K. (eds.) (1997) *Gender and Ethnicity in Ancient Italy*. London, Accordia Research Institute.
Cox, J. S. (1977) The Construction of an Ancient Egyptian Wig (c.1400 B.C.) in the British Museum. *Journal of Egyptian Archaeology* 63, 67–71.
Cox, J. S. (1989) *An Illustrated Dictionary of Hairdressing and Wigmaking*. London, Batsford.
Crielaard, J. P. (1995) Homer, history and archaeology: some remarks on the date of the Homeric world. In Crielaard (ed.), 201–88.
Crielaard, J. P. (ed.) (1995) *Homeric Questions. Essays in philology, ancient history and archaeology*. Amsterdam, Gieben.
Croom, A. T. (2000) *Roman Clothing and Fashion*. Stroud, Tempus.
D'Ambra, E. (1996) The Calculus of Venus: Nude Portraits of Roman Matrons. In Kampen (ed.), 219–32.
D'Ambra, E. (1998) *Art and Identity in the Roman World*. London, Everyman Art Library.
Dahari, U. (ed.) (2000) *Monastic Settlements in South Sinai in the Byzantine Period. The Archaeological Remains*. Jerusalem, IAA Reports.
Dakoronia, F. & Gounaraounopolou, L. (1992) Atremiskult auf einem neuen Weihrelief aus Achinos bei Lamia. *Mittelungen des Deutschen Archaeologischen Instituts* 107, 219–227.
Daressy, G. (1907) Les Cercueils des pretres d'Ammon (Deuxieme trouvaille de Deir el-Bahari). *Annales du Service des Antiquites de l'Egypte* 8, 3–36.
David, E. (1984) *Aristophanes and Athenian Society of the Early Fourth Century B.C.* Leiden, Brill.
David, E. (1989) Dress in Spartan society. *The Ancient World* 19/20, 1–14.
Davies, G. (1997) Gender and Body Language in Roman Art. In Cornell & Lomas (eds.), 97–107.
Davies, G. (2002) Clothes as Sign: the case of the large and small Herculaneum women. In Llewellyn-Jones (ed.), 227–242.
Davies, G. (ed.) (fortchoming 2004) *Proceedings of the Inaugural Celtic Classics Conference*. Swansea, Classical Press of Wales.
Davies, N. de G. (1941) *The Tomb of the Vizier Ramose*. New York, Egypt Exploration Society.
Davies, W. V. & Schofield, L. (eds.) (1995) *Egypt, the Aegean and the Levant: Interconnections in the Second Millennium B.C.* London, British Museum Press.
Davis, M. & Weitz, S. (1981) Sex Differences in Body Movements and Positions. In Mayo & Henly (eds.), 81–92.

Davis, R. L. (1993) *The Glamour Factory. Inside Hollywood's big studio system*. Dallas, Southern Methodist University Press.
Dayagi-Mendels, M. (1989) *Perfumes and Cosmetics in the Ancient World*. Jerusalem, Israel Museum.
de Sélincourt, A. [trans.] (1954) *Herodotus The Histories*. London, Harmondsworth.
Delivorrias, A. et al. (1984) s.v. Aphrodite. *Lexicon Iconographicum Mythologiae Classicae* II, 2–151.
DeMille, C. B. (1960) *The Autobiography of Cecil B. DeMille* (ed. Hayne). London, Taylor & Francis.
Derchain, P. (1975) La Perruque et le Cristal. *Studien zur altagyptischen Kultur* 2, 56–74.
Dewald, C. (1981) Women and Culture in Herodotus' *Histories*. In Foley (ed.), 91–125.
Dexheimer D. (2000) Portrait figures on funerary altars of Roman *liberti* in Northern Italy: Romanization or the assimilation of attributes characterising higher social strata? In Pearce et al. (eds.) 78–84.
Di Benedetto, V. (1975) *Euripide: teatro e società*. Turin, Einaudi.
Dillon, M. (2002) *Girls and Women in Classical Greek Religion*. London/New York, Routledge.
Dobrov, G. W. (1995) The poet's voice in the evolution of dramatic dialogism. In Dobrov (ed.), 47–97.
Dobrov, G. W. (ed.) (1995) *Beyond Aristophanes: Transition and diversity in Greek comedy*. Atlanta, Scholars Press.
Dobrov, G. W. (1997) *The City as Comedy: Society and representation in Athenian drama*. Chapel Hill/London, University of North Carolina Press.
Dobrov, G. W. & Urios-Apiarsi, E. (1995) The maculate music: gender, genre, and the Chiron of Pherecrates. In Dobrov (ed.), 139–74.
Donald, M. & Hurcombe, L. (eds.) (1999) *Gender and Material Culture in Historical Perspective*. London, Macmillan.
Doniol-Valcroze, J. (1989) Samson, Cecil and Delilah. *Wide Angle* 11(4), 32, 34–41.
Donohue, A. A. & Fullerton, M. D. (eds.) (2003) *Ancient Art and its Historiography*. Cambridge, Cambridge University Press.
Douglas, M. (1966) *Purity and Danger: an analysis of the concepts of pollution and danger*. London/New York, Routledge.
Doumas, C. (1992) *The Wall-Paintings of Thera*. Athens, Thera Foundation & Petros M. Nomikos.
Downey, G. (1957), Nikolaos Mesarites. Description of the church of the Holy Apostles. *Transactions of the American Philosophical Association* NS 47.6, 859–918.
duBois, P. (1988) *Sowing the Body: Psychoanalysis and Ancient Representations of Women*. Chicago/London, University of Chicago Press.
Duigan, M. (2004) Colour and the Deceptive Gift. In Cleland & Stears (eds.), 78–84.
Dumitrescu, C. L. (1987) Quelques remarques en marge du Coislin 79. *Byzantion* 57, 32–45.
Dunant, C. (1994) Olympian Dreamscapes: The photographic canvas. The wide-screen paintings of Leighton, Poynter and Alma-Tadema. In Bratton et al. (eds.), 21–30.
Durand, J. (ed.) (1992) *Byzance: l'art byzantin dans les collections publiques françaises*. Paris, Musée du Louvre.
Dyck, A. R. (2001) Dressing to kill: attire as a proof and means of characterisation in Cicero's speeches. *Arethusa* 34, 119–30.
Edgerton, W. F. (1951) The Strikes in Ramses III's Twenty-Ninth Year. *Journal of Near Eastern Studies* 10, 137–145.
Edwards, C. (1993) *The Politics of Immorality in Ancient Rome*. Cambridge, Cambridge University Press.
Edwards, C. & Woolf, G. (eds.) (2003) *Rome the Cosmopolis*. Cambridge, Cambridge University Press.
Edwards, D. R. (1994) The social, religious and political aspects of costume in Josephus. In Sebesta & Bonfante (eds.), 153–9.

Egg, M. (1997) L' Homme dans la glace. *Dossiers d' Archaeologie* No. 224/June, 28–35.
Ehrenberg, V. (1951[1961]) *The People of Aristophanes: A Sociology of Old Attic Comedy*. Oxford, Blackwell.
Elley, D. (1984) *The Epic Film. Myth and history*. London/New York, Routledge & Kegan Paul.
Elsner, J. (1995) *Art and the Roman Viewer*. Cambridge, Cambridge University Press.
Ercolani, A. (ed.) (2002) *Spoudaiogeloion: Form und Funktion der Verspottung in der aristophanischen Komödie, Drama 11*. Stuttgart, J. B. Metzler.
Evans, A. J. (1921) *The Palace of Minos at Knossos* Vol. I. London, Macmillan.
Evans, H. C. & Wixom, W. D. (eds.) (1997) *The Glory of Byzantium. Art and Culture of the Middle Byzantine Era A.D. 843–1261*. New York, The Metropolitan Museum of Art.
Evans, M. M. (1893) *Chapters on Greek Dress*. London, Macmillan & Co.
Evely, D. (2000) *Minoan Crafts: Tools and Techniques*. Göteborg, Paul Astroms Forlag.
Ewing, E. (1978) *Dress and Undress: a history of women's underwear*. London, Bibliophile.
Eyre, C. (ed.) (1998) *Proceedings of the Seventh International Congress of Egyptologists*. Leuven, Peeters.
Faraone, C. A. (1990) Aphrodite's KESTOS and apples for Atalanta: aphrodisiacs in early Greek myth and ritual. *Phoenix* 44, 219–43.
Farrell-Beck, J. & Gau, C. (2002) *Uplift: the Bra in America*. Philadelphia, University of Pennsylvania Press.
Ferris, L. (1989) *Acting Women: Images of women in theatre*. New York, University Press.
Fewell, D. N. (1992) Judges. In Newsom & Ringe (eds.), 67–77.
Finkel, A. (1996) *Romantic Stages. Set and costume design in Victorian England*. Jefferson/London, McFarland & Co.
Fisher, N. & van Wees, H. (eds.) (1998) *Archaic Greece: new approaches and new evidence*. London/Swansea, Classical Press of Wales.
Fittschen, K. & Zanker, P. (1983) *Katalog der römischen Porträts in den Capitolinischen Museen und den anderen kommunalen Sammlungen der Stadt Rom*. Vol. III Mainz am Rhein, von Zabern.
Fittschen, K. & Zanker, P. (1985) *Katalog der römischen Porträts in den Capitolinischen Museen und den anderen kommunalen Sammlungen der Stadt Rom*. Vol. I Mainz am Rhein, von Zabern.
Fletcher, J. (1994a) A Tale of Wigs, Hair and Lice. *Egyptian Archaeology* 5, 31–33.
Fletcher, J. (1994b) Cosmetica en lichaamsverzorging. In Vogelsang-Eastwood (ed.) 103–111.
Fletcher, J. (1994c) Pruiken en haarversiering. In Vogelsang-Eastwood (ed.) 127–138.
Fletcher, J. (1995) *Ancient Egyptian Hair: a Study in Style, Form and Function*. Unpublished PhD, Manchester University.
Fletcher, J. (1997) Marks of Distinction: the Tattooed Mummies of Ancient Egypt. *NILE Offerings* I, 28, 30.
Fletcher, J. (1998) *Oils & Perfumes in Ancient Egypt*. London, British Museum Press.
Fletcher, J. (1999) The Wig & Wig Box. In Vogelsang-Eastwood (ed.), 67–68.
Fletcher, J. (2000) Hair. In Nicholson & Shaw (eds.), 495–501.
Fletcher, J. (forthcoming a) *Ancient Egyptian Wigs and Hairstyles*. Austin, University of Texas Press.
Fletcher, J. (forthcoming b) *Ancient Egyptian Cosmetics and Tattoos*. Austin, University of Texas Press.
Fletcher, J. & Montserrat, D. (1998) The Human Hair from the tomb of Tutankhamun: a re-evaluation. In Eyre (ed.), 403–407.
Foley, H. P. (1981) *Reflections of Women in Antiquity*. New York, Gordon and Breach.
Foley, H. P. (1993) The Politics of Tragic Lamentation. In Sommerstein (ed.), 101–143.
Forbes, J. R. (1965) *Studies in Ancient Technology* III. Leiden, Brill.
Fossey, J. M. (ed.) (1993) *Boeotia antiqua III*. Amsterdam, Gieben.

Fountoulakis, A. (2004) Colours of Desire and Death: Colour terms in Bion's *Epitaph on Adonis*. In Cleland & Stears (eds.), 110–16.
Fowler, W. W. (1920) The Toga Praetexta of Roman Children. In Fowler (ed.), 42–52.
Fowler, W. W. (ed.) (1920) *Roman Essays and Interpretations*. Oxford, Clarendon Press.
Foxhall, L. (1998) Cargoes of the heart's desire. The character of trade in the archaic mediterranean world. In Fisher & van Wees (eds.), 295–309.
Foxhall, L. & Salmon, J. (eds.) (1998) *Thinking Men: masculinity and its self-representation in the classical tradition*. London/New York, Routledge.
Foxhall, L. & Salmon, J. (eds.) (1998b) *When Men Were Men. Masculinity, power and identity in classical antiquity*. London, Routledge.
Foxhall, L. & Stears, K. (1999) Redressing the Balance: Dedications of Clothing to Artemis and the Order of Life Stages. In Donald & Hurcombe (eds.), 1–22.
Fredrick, D. (ed.) (2002) *The Roman Gaze. Vision, Power & the Body*. Baltimore, Johns Hopkins University Press.
French, E. B. & Wardle, K. A. (eds.) (1988) *Problems in Greek Prehistory: papers presented at the centenary conference of the British School at Athens, Manchester, April 1986*. Bristol, Bristol Classical Press.
Friedländer, P. (ed.) (1912) *Johannes von Gaza und Paulus Silentarius*. Leipzig-Berlin, B. G. Teubner.
Frontisi-Ducroux, Fr. (1987) 'Prosopon.' Le masque et le visage. *Cahiers du GITA* 3, 83–92.
Frontisi-Ducroux, Fr. (1995) *Du masque au visage. Aspects de l'Identitée en Grèce ancienne*. Paris, Flammarion.
Frontisi-Ducroux, Fr. & Vernant, J-P (1997) *Dans l'Oeil du Miroir*. Paris, Odile Jacob.
Frost, D. (1997) *Billy Graham in conversation*. Sandy Lane West, Chivers Press Ltd.
Gabelmann, H. (1985) Römische Kinder in toga Praetexta, *Jahrbuch des Deutschen Archäologischen Instituts* 100, 497–591.
Gaines, J. & Herzog, C. (1990) *Fabrications. Costume and the female body*. New York/London, Routledge.
Gais, R. M. (1978) Some Problems of River-God Iconography. *American Journal of Archaeology* 82, 335–70.
Gardner, J. (1998) Sexing a Roman: imperfect men in Roman law. In Foxhall & Salmon (eds.) (1998b), 136–52.
Garetto, E. (1955) L'accocianture e la cosmesi della donna egizia nel Nuovo Imperio I. *Aegyptus* 35, 218.
Gauthier-Laurent, M. (1938) Les Scènes de coiffure féminine dans l'ancienne Egypte. *Mélanges Maspero* I. 2, 673–696
Gelzer, T. (2002) Spott auf Personen des öffentlichen Lebens mit den Mitteln der Traditionellen Formen der Alten Komödie. In Ercolani (ed.), 345–74.
Genders, R. (1972) *A History of Scent*. London, Hamilton.
Gentili, B. & Cerri, G. (1988) The Idea of Biography. *London Studies in Classical Philology* 20, 61–85.
George, A. (1999) *The Epic of Gilgamesh. The Babylonian Epic Poem and Other Texts in Akkadian and Sumerian*. London, Penguin Press.
Gerber, D. E. (1978) The female breast in Greek erotic literature. *Arethusa* 11.1.2, 203–12.
Gernet, L. (1968) *Droit et Institutions en Grèce antique*. Paris, Flammarion.
Gero, J. M. & Conkey, M. W. (eds.) (1991) *Engendering Archaeology: Women and Prehistory*. Oxford, Blackwell.
Giesecke, H. E. (1988) Kretische Schurze. *Opuscula Atheniensia* 17, 91–98.
Ginouvès, R. (1962) *Balaneutikè. Recherches sur le bain dans l'antiquité grecque*. Paris, de Boccard.

Gleason, M. (1995) *Making Men. Sophists and Self-Presentation in Ancient Rome*. Princeton, Princeton University Press.
Gnecchi, F. (1912) *I medaglioni romani*. Vol. 3. Milan, V. Hoepli.
Goette, H. R. (1990) *Studien zu rö´mischen Togadarstellungen*. Mainz am Rhein, von Zabern.
Goldhill, S. (1990) Character and action, representation and reading: Greek tragedy and its critics. In Pelling (ed.), 100–27.
Goldman, N. (1994) Reconstructing Roman clothing. In Sebesta & Bonfante (eds.), 213–37.
Gopnik, M. (1983) The Cognitive Aspects of Style Change. In Borbé (ed.), 1319–27.
Gould, J. (1978) Dramatic character and 'human intelligibility' in Greek tragedy. *Proceedings of the Cambridge Philological Society* 24, 43–67.
Gowland, W. (1898) An Ancient Egyptian Toilet Box belonging to W. L. Nash FSA, with an analysis of its contents by W. Gowland FCS, FSA. *Proceedings of Biblical Archaeology* 20, 268–269.
Goyon, J-Cl. & Le Dinahet, M.-Th. (eds.) (1996) *Aspects de l'Artisanat du Textile dans le Monde Mediterraneen*. Paris-Lyons, Presses du Universite Lyons.
Graf, F. (1991) Gestures and Conventions: the Gestures of Roman Actors and Orators. In Bremmer & Roodenburg (eds.), 36–58.
Granger-Taylor, H. (1982) Weaving Clothes to Shape in the Ancient World: The Tunic and Toga of the Arringatore. *Textile History* 13.1, 3–25.
Granger-Taylor H. (1983) The Construction of Tunics. In Rogers (ed.), 11.
Granger-Taylor, H. (1996) s.v. dress. *Oxford Classical Dictionary*, 3rd ed., 497–8.
Greenberg, H. R. (1975) *The movies on your mind*. New York, Saturday Review Press.
Gregory, A. (1994) Powerful images: responses to portraits and the political uses of images in Rome. *Journal of Roman Archaeology* 7, 80–99.
Grene, D. [trans.] (1987) *Herodotus: The History*. Chicago, Chicago University Press.
Gröning, K. (1997) *Decorated Skin: a world survey of body art*. London, Thames & Hudson.
Guarducci, M. (1962) *Epigrafia greca II. Epigrafi di carattere pubblico*. Roma, Istituto Poligrafico e Zecca dello Stato.
Guilland, R. (1943) Les eunuques dans l'empire byzantin. Etude de titulaire et de prosopographie byzantines. *Revue des Etudes Byzantines* 1, 197–238.
Günther, W. (1988) 'Vieux et inutilisable' dans un inventaire de Milet. In Knoepfler & Quellet (eds.), 215–237.
Guthridge, I. (1995) *Great women in history and art*. Middle Park, Vic., Watson-Guptill Publications.
Hägg, R., Marinatos, N. & Nordquist, G. C. (eds.) (1988) *Early Greek Cult Practice*. Stockholm, Astrom.
Hales, S. (2002) How the Venus de Milo Lost Her Arms. In Ogden (ed.), 253–74.
Hall, R. (1986) *Egyptian Textiles*. Buckinghamshire, Shire Archaeology 4.
Hallet, J. P. & Skinner, M. B. (eds.) (1997) *Roman Sexualities*. Princeton, Princeton University Press.
Hamilton, J. A. & Hamilton, J. W. (1989) Dress as a Reflection and Sustainer of Social Reality: A Cross-Cultural Perspective. *Clothing and Textiles Research Journal* 7, 16–22.
Hamilton, R. (1989) Alkman and the Athenian Arkteia. *Hesperia* 58, 449–72.
Harcourt-Smith, S. (1951) The Siegfried of sex: Thoughts inspired by Cecil B. de Mille's 'Samson and Delilah.' *Sight and Sound* 19(10), 410–412, 424.
Harlow, M. (forthcoming 2005) Clothes maketh man: power dressing in the later Roman empire. In Brubaker & Smith (eds.).
Harlow, M. (forthcoming 2005b) Female Dress in the third to sixth centuries: the message in the media? *Antiquité Tardive* 12.

Harpur, Y. (2001) *The Tombs of Nefermaat and Rahotep at Medum: Discovery, Destruction and Reconstruction*. Oxford, Oxford Expedition to Egypt.
Harris, A. C. (1992) From Codpieces to Spoonerisms: Semiolinguistic Approaches to Communication in Culture. *Approaches to a Semiotics of Language Behaviour*, www.csun.edu/~vcspc005/codpie92.html. Accessed August 2004.
Harris, D. (1995) *The Treasures of the Parthenon and Erechtheion*. Oxford, Clarendon Press.
Harris. D. R. (ed.) (1996) *The Origins and Spread of Agriculture and Pastoralism in Eurasia: an Overview*. London, UCL Press.
Harrison, A. R. W. (1968) *The Law of Athens* II. Indianapolis, Hatchett.
Harrison, E. B. (1977) The shoulder-cord of Themis. In Höckmann & Krug (eds.), 155–61.
Harrison, E. B. (1989) Hellenic Identity and Athenian Identity in the Fifth Century B.C. In Barnes & Melion (eds.), 41–61.
Harrison, E. B. (1991) The Dress of the Archaic Korai. In Buitron-Oliver (ed.), 217–239.
Hassan, A. A. & Hassan, F. A. (1981) Source of Galena in Predynastic Egypt at Nagada. *Archaeometry* 23 (1), 77–82.
Havelock, C. M. (1995) *The Aphrodite of Knidos and her successors: a historical review of the female nude in Greek art*. Ann Arbor, University of Michigan Press.
Hawley, R. (1998) The male body as spectacle in Attic drama. In Foxhall & Salmon (eds.) (1998b), 83–99.
Hayes, W. C. (1953–9) *The Scepter of Egypt I–II*. New York, Harper & Bros.
Haynes, J. (1978) The Development of Women's Hairstyles in Dynasty Eighteen. *Journal of the Society for the Study of Egyptian Antiquities* 8.1, 18–24.
Head, E & Castro, P. (1983) *Edith Head's Hollywood*. New York, Penguin USA.
Head, E. & Ardmore, J. K. (1960) *The dress doctor*. Kingswood, Little Brown & Co.
Helbig, W. (1884) *Das homerische Epos aus den Denkmälern erläutert*. Leipzig, B.G. Teubner.
Henderson, J. (1987) Old Women in Attic Old Comedy. *Transactions and Proceedings of the American Philological Association* 117, 105–29.
Henderson, J. (1991) *The Maculate Muse: obscene language in Attic comedy*. 2nd ed. Oxford/New York, Oxford University Press.
Henderson, R. M. (1972) *D.W. Griffith. His life and work*. Oxford, Taylor & Francis.
Henrichs, A. (1982) Changing Dionysiac identities. In Meyer & Sanders (ed.), 137–60.
Herdt, G. (ed.) (1994) *Third Sex, Third Gender: Beyond Sexual Dimorphism in Culture and History*. New York, Zone Books.
Heskel, J. (1994) Cicero as evidence for attitudes to dress in the Late Republic. In Sebesta & Bonfante (eds.), 133–45.
Heuzey, L. (1922) *Historie du costume antique, d'après des études sur le modèle vivant*. Paris, Champion.
Higham, C. (1978) *Cecil B. DeMille. A biography of the most successful film maker of them all*. London, Scribner.
Hildesheim, V. (1984) *Nofret die Schöne: Die Frau im alten Ägypten*. Mainz, von Zabern.
Hirsch, F. (1978) *The Hollywood Epic*. London, Oak Tree Publications.
Höckmann, U. & Krug, A. (eds.) *Festschrift für Frank Brommer*. Mainz, von Zabern.
Hodge, R. & Kress, G. (1988) *Social Semiotics*. Ithaca, Cornell University Press.
Hollander, A. (1993) *Seeing Through Clothes*. Berkley, University of California Press.
Holt, P. (1951) Samson and Delilah. In Anstey *et al.* (eds.), 250–251.
Honigsberg, P. (1940) Sanitary Installations in Ancient Egypt. *Journal of the Egyptian Medical Association* 23, 199–246.
Hopkins, K. (1978) *Conquerors and Slaves*. Cambridge, Cambridge University Press.
Houston, M. G. (1920) *Ancient Egyptian, Mesopotamian and Persian Costume and Decoration*. London, Black.

Houston, M. G. (1931) *Ancient Greek, Roman and Byzantine Costume and Decoration*. London, Black.
Houston, M. G. (1947) *Ancient Greek, Roman and Byzantine Costume and Decoration*. 2nd ed. London, Black.
Hughes, G. (1959) The Cosmetic Arts in Ancient Egypt. *Journal of Society of Cosmetic Chemists* 10 (3), 159–176.
Hurwit, J. M. (1995) Beautiful Evil: Pandora and the Athena Parthenos. *American Journal of Archaeology* 99, 171–86.
Immerwahr, S. (1990) *Aegean Painting in the Bronze Age*. University Park/London, Pennsylvania State University Press.
James, L. (1996) *Light and Colour in Byzantine Art*. Oxford, Clarendon Press.
James, L. (ed.) (1997) *Women, Men and Eunuchs: Gender in Byzantium*. London/New York, Routledge.
James, L. (2001) *Empresses and Power in Early Byzantium*. London, Leicester University Press.
James, L. (ed.) (forthcoming 2005) *Art and Text*. Cambridge, Cambridge University Press.
Janes, D. (1998) *God and Gold in Late Antiquity*. Cambridge, Cambridge University Press.
Johnson, D. M. (ed.) (1964) *Ancient Greek Dress: a new illustrated edition*. Chicago, Argonaut. [= Abrahams, E. B. (1908) *Greek Dress a study of the costumes worn in ancient Greece, from pre-Hellenistic times to the Hellenistic age*. London, John Murray. = Evans, M. M. (1893) *Chapters on Greek Dress*. London/New York, Macmillan.]
Jonckheere, F. (1952) La "mesdemet": cosmetique et medicaments egyptiens. *Histoire de la Medicine* 2/7, 1–12.
Jones, B. (1998) *Minoan Women's Clothes: An Investigation of their Construction from the Depicitons in Aegean Art*. Unpublished Ph.D, Institute of Fine Arts, New York University.
Jones, B. (2000) Revealing Minoan Fashions. *Archaeology* 53/3, 36–41.
Jørgensen, L. B. (1992) *North European Textiles until AD1000*. Denmark, Åarhus University Press.
Jouan, Fr. (1966) *Euripide et les légendes des chants cypriens. Des origines de la guerre de Troie à l'Iliade*. Paris, Belles Lettres.
Just, R. (1989) *Women in Athenian Law and Life*. London/New York, Routledge.
Kahil, L. (1963) Quelques vases du sanctuaire d'Artémis à Brauron. *Antike Kunst* 1, 5–29.
Kahil, L. (1983) Mythological repertoire of Brauron. In Moon (ed.), 231–44.
Kampen, N. B. (ed.) (1996) *Sexuality in Ancient Art*. Cambridge, Cambridge University Press.
Kantor, H. J. (1947) *The Aegean and the Orient in the second Millennium B.C.* (I, Part IV). Indiana, Archaeological Institute of America.
Karageorghis, V. (1998) *Greek Gods and Heroes in Ancient Cyprus*. Athens, Commercial Bank of Greece.
Keimer, L. (1943) Un Bes tatoue. *Annales du Service des Antiquites de l'Egypte* 42, 159–163.
Keimer, L. (1948) Remarques sur la tatouage dans l'Egypte Ancienne. *Memoirs de l'Institut d'Egypte* 53, 1–113.
Kemp, B. J. & Vogelsang-Eastwood, G. (2001) *The Ancient Textile Industry at Amarna*. Oxford, Oxbow.
Kent, R. (1958) *Varro On the Latin Language*. Cambridge Mass., Harvard University Press.
Keuls, E. (1985) *The Reign of the Phallus: sexual politics in Ancient Athens*. New York, Harper & Row [reprinted 1993, Berkeley, University of California Press].
Kilmer, M. F. (1993) *Greek Erotica on Attic Red-Figure Vases*. London, Duckworth.
King, G. A. (1962) Royalty in Rags. *The Classical Bulletin* 1, 61–62.
King, H. (1983) Bound to Bleed: Artemis and Greek Women. In Cameron & Kuhrt (eds.), 109–127.
King, H. (1994) Producing Woman: Hippocratic Gynaecology. In Archer *et al.* (eds.), 102–114.

King, P. J. & Stagger, L. E. (2001) *Life in Biblical Israel*. Louisville/London, Westminster John Knox Press.
Kirk, G. (1990) *The Iliad: A Commentary. Vol. II*. Cambridge, Cambridge University Press.
Kleiner, D. E. E. (1977) *Roman Group Portraiture: The Funerary Reliefs of the Late Republic and the Early Empire*. New York, Garland Press.
Kleiner, D. E. E. (1981) Second Century Mythological Portraiture: Mars and Venus. *Latomus* 40, 512–44.
Kleiner, D. E. E. (1987) *Roman Imperial Funerary Altars with Portraits*. Rome, Brettschneider.
Kleiner, D. E. E. (1992) *Roman Sculpture*. New Haven/London, Yale University Press.
Kleiner, D. E. E. (2002) Now you see them now you don't: the presence and absence of women in Roman art. In Varner (ed.), 45–57.
Kleiner, D. E. E. & Matheson, S. B. (eds.) (1996) *I, Claudia: Women in Ancient Rome*. New Haven, Yale University Art Gallery.
Knoepfler D. & Quellet, N. (eds.) (1988) *Comptes et inventaires dans la cité grecque*. Genèva, Droz.
Kolb, F. (1974) Die *paenula* in der *Historia Augusta*. Historia Augusta Colloquium Bonn 1974, 81–101.
Koloski-Ostrow, A. O. & Lyons, C. L. (eds.), *Naked Truths: Women, Sexuality, and Gender in Classical Art and Archaeology*. London/New York, Routledge.
Konstan, D. & Dillon, M. (1981) The Ideology in Aristophanes' Wealth. *American Journal of Philology* 102, 371–94.
Kontorli-Papadopoulou, L. (1996) *Aegean Frescoes of Religious Character*. Jonsered, Astrom.
Koosed, J. L., & Linafelt, T. (1996) How the west was not one: Delilah deconstructs the western. *Semeia: An Experimental Journal for Biblical Criticism* 74, 167–181.
Kopaka, K. & Platon. L. (1993) *Lino Minoiko* Installations minoennes de traitement des produits liquides. *Bulletin de Correspondance Hellenique* 117, 35–101.
Koster W. J. (1967) *KWMWDOTRAGHMATA: studia Aristophanea viri Aristophanei*. Amsterdam, Hakkert.
Kozloff, A. & Bryan, B. (1992) *Egypt's Dazzling Sun: Amenhotep III and his World*. Cleveland, Indiana University Press.
Kozlovic, A. K. (2002) The whore of Babylon, suggestibility, and the art of sexless sex in Cecil B DeMille's 'Samson and Delilah' (1949). In Claussen (ed.), 21–31.
Kurke, L. (1992) The politics of *habrosyne* in archaic Greece. *Classical Antiquity* 11, 91–120.
La Follette, L. (1994) The Costume of the Roman Bride. In Sebesta & Bonfante (eds.), 58–59.
Labarre, G. & Le Dinahet, M-Th. (1996) Les Metiers du Textile en Asie Mineure de l'Epoque Hellensitique a l'Epoque Imperiale. In Goyon & Le Dinahet (eds.), 49–116.
Lamarr, H. (1966) *Ecstasy and me: My life as a woman*. New York, Penguin USA.
Lambert, R. (1997) *Beloved & God. The Story of Hadrian and Antinous*. London, Phoenix.
Landau, D. (2000) *Gladiator. The making of the Ridley Scott epic*. New York, Newmarket Press.
Lane, E. (1966) *The Manners and Customs of the Modern Egyptians*. Princeton, Princeton University Press.
Lang, M. (1969) *The Palace of Nestor, Vol. II (The Frescoes)*. Princeton, Princeton University Press.
Lansing, A. & Hayes, W. C. (1937) The Egyptian Expedition 1935–1936: The Museum's Excavations at Thebes. *Bulletin of the Metropolitan Museum of Art* 32 (Egyptian Supplements, January), 4–39.
Laskowska-Kusztal, E. (1978) Un Atelier de perruquier à Deir el-Bahari. *Etudes et Travaux* 10, 84–120.
LaValley, S. (1987) Hollywood and Seventh Avenue: the impact of period films in fashion. In Annas *et al.* (eds.), 78–96.
Lavine, W. R. (1981) *In a glamorous fashion. The fabulous years of Hollywood costume design*. London, Scribner Book Co.

Leary, T. J. (1996) *Martial Book XIV: the Apophoreta*. London, Duckworth.
Lee, M. M. (1999) The Myth of the Classical *Peplos*. Unpublished PhD. Bryn Mawr College.
Lee, M. M. (2000) Deciphering Gender in Minoan Dress. In Rautman (ed.), 111–123.
Lee, M. M. (2003) The Ancient Greek *Peplos* and the 'Dorian Question'. In Donohue, & Fullerton (eds.), 118–147.
Lee, M. M. (2004) 'Evil Wealth of Raiment': The Tragic *Peplos*. *The Classical Journal* 99.3, 253–279.
Lesko, L. H. (ed.) (1986) *Egyptological Studies in Honor of Richard A. Parker*. London, University of New England Press.
Lesmüller-Werner, A. & Thurn, H. (eds.) (1978), *Iosephi Genesii regum libri quattuor*. Berlin, de Gruyter.
Lev, Y. (ed) (2002) *Towns and Material Culture in the Medieval Age in Middle East*. Leiden, Brill.
Lewis, S. (2002) *The Athenian Woman: an iconographic handbook*. London/New York, Routledge.
Lichtheim, M. (1973) *Ancient Egyptian Literature, I: The Old and Middle Kingdoms*. Berkeley, University of California Press.
Lichtheim, M. (1976) *Ancient Egyptian Literature, II: The New Kingdom*. Berkeley, University of California Press.
Lilyquist, C. (1979) *Ancient Egyptian Mirrors from the Earliest Times through the Middle Kingdom*. Munich, Muncher Egyptologisches Studien 27.
Linders, T. (1972) *Studies in the Treasure Records at Artemis Brauronia*. Stockholm, Åström.
Linders, T. & Nordquist, G. (eds.) (1987) *Gifts to the Gods*. Upsala, Upsala University Press.
Lindgren, M. (1973) *The People of Pylos*, 3/II. Uppsala, Boreas.
Linscheid, P. (2001) Late Antique to Early Islamic Textiles from Egypt. *Textile History* 32, 75–80.
Liversidge, M. & Edwards, C. (eds.) (1996) *Imagining Rome. British artists and Rome in the nineteenth century*. London, Merrell Holberton.
Llewellyn-Jones, L. (2002) Celluloid Cleopatras or did the Greeks ever get to Egypt? In Ogden (ed.), 275–304.
Llewellyn-Jones, L. (ed.) (2002) *Women's Dress in the Ancient Greek World*. London/Swansea, Duckworth/Classical Press of Wales.
Llewellyn-Jones, L. (2003) *Aphrodite's Tortoise: the veiled women of ancient Greece*. Swansea, Classical Press of Wales.
Llewellyn-Jones (forthcoming 2005) Herakles Re-Dressed. In Rawlings (ed.).
Lonsdale, S. H. (1993) *Dance and Ritual Play in Greek Religion*. Baltimore/London, Johns Hopkins University Press.
Loraux, N. (1990) *Les mères en deuil*. Paris, Editions du Seuil.
Loraux, N. (1999) *La voix endeuillée*. Paris, Gallimard.
Lorimer, H. (1950) *Homer and the Monuments*. London, Macmillan.
Losfeld, G. (1991) *Essai sur le costume grec*. Paris, de Boccard.
Louvre (1993) *Rites et Beaute, objets de toilette egyptien*. Paris, Louvre.
Lucas, A. (1930) Ancient Egyptian Wigs. *Annales du Service des Antiquites de l'Egypte* 30, 190–196.
Lucas, A. (1930b) Cosmetics, Perfumes and Incense. *Journal of Egyptian Archaeology* 16, 41–53.
Lucas, A. (1989) *Ancient Materials and Industries*. London, Histories and Mysteries of Man.
Luppe, W. (1984) Euripides-Hypothesis in den Hygin-Fabeln 'Antiope' und 'Ino'. *Philologus* 128, 41–59.
Luraghi, N. & Alcock, S. (eds.) (2003) *Helots And Their Masters in Laconia and Messenia. Histories, ideologies, structures*. Washington DC, Harvard University Press.
MacDonald Fraser, G. (1988) *The Hollywood history of the world*. Marlborough, St. Martin's Press.
McDonald, W. A. & Wilkie, N. C. (eds.) (1992) *Excavations at Nichoria in Southwestern Greece, Vol. 2: The Bronze Age Occupation*. Minneapolis, University of Minnesota Press.

MacDowell, D. M. (1995) *Aristophanes and Athens: An introduction to the plays*. Oxford, University Press.
Macleod, C. N. (1974) Euripides' Rags. *Zeitschrift furPapyrologie und Epigraphie* 15, 221–222.
MacMullen, R. (1964) Some pictures in Ammianus Marcellinus. *Art Bulletin* 46, 435–55.
Maguire, H. (1997) The heavenly court. In Maguire (ed.), 247–258.
Maguire, H. (ed.) (1997) *Byzantine Court Culture from 829 to 1204*, 247–258. Washington DC, Dumbarton Oaks.
Mango, C. (1980) *Byzantium: The Empire of the New Rome*. London, Weidenfeld & Nicolson.
Mango, C. & Hawkins, E. J. W. (1972) The mosaics of St. Sophia at Istanbul. The church fathers in the north tympanum, *Dumbarton Oaks Papers* 26, 3–41.
Manniche, L. (1987) *Sexual Life in Ancient Egypt*. London, Kegan Paul International.
Manniche, L. (1989) *An Ancient Egyptian Herbal*. Austin, University of Texas Press.
Marcar, A. (2001) *Ancient Aegean Textiles and Dress Design: ca. 2500 to 1200 B.C.E.* Unpublished PhD, University of London.
Marcar, A. (2004) Aegean costume and the dating of the Knossian frescoes. *British School at Athens Studies* 12, 225–238.
Marcar, A. (in press). Fashion changes during the Aegean LBA: their nature and potential significance. In *Proceedings of the 9th International Congress of Cretan Studies, Elounda, Crete*, 1–7 October, 2001.
Marinatos, N. (1984) *Art and Religion in Thera. Reconstructing a Bronze Age Society*. Athens, Mathioulakis.
Marinatos, N. (1993) *Minoan Religion. Ritual Image and Symbol*. S. Carolina, Columbia.
Marinatos, S. (1967) *Kleidung. Haar- und Barttracht. Archaiologia Homerica*, Bd I, kapitel A, B. Göttingen, Vandenhoeck & Ruprecht.
Marinatos, S. (1986) *Kreta, Thera und das Mykenische Hellas*. Munich, Hirmer Verlag.
Marinatos, S. & Hirmer, M. (1960) *Crete and Mycenae*. New York, Abrams.
Massey, A. (2000) *Hollywood beyond the screen. Design and material culture*. Oxford/New York, Berg/New York University Press.
Matheson, S. (1996) The Divine Claudia: Women as Goddesses in Roman Art. In Kleiner & Matheson (eds.), 182–194.
Matthäus, H. (1995) Representations of Keftiu in Egyptian Tombs and the Absolute Chronology of the Aegean Late Bronze Age. *Bulletin of the Institute of Classical Studies* 40, 177–186.
Matz, F. & Biesantz, H. (eds.) (1964) *Die Minoischen und Mykenischen Siegel Des National Museums in Athen, Corpus der minoischen und mykenischen Siegel* I. Berlin, Verlag Gebr, Mann.
Mau, A. (1909) s.v. Fasciae. *Paulys Real-Encyclopädie der Classischen Altertumswissenschaft*. Vol. 6, cols. 2006–9.
Maunder, J. W. (1983) The Appreciation of Lice. *Proceedings of the Royal Institute of Great Britain* 55, 1–31.
Mayer, D. (1994) *Playing out the Empire. Ben-Hur and other Toga Plays and films. A critical anthology*. Oxford, Clarendon Press.
Mayo, C. & Henly, N. M. (eds.) (1981) *Gender and Nonverbal Behaviour*. New York/Heidelberg/Berlin, Springer-Verlag.
McCafferty, S. D. & McCafferty, G. G. (1991) Spinning and Weaving as Female Gender Identity in Post-Classic Mexico. In Schevill *et al.* (eds.), 19–44.
McClure, L. K. (2002) *Sexuality and Gender in the Classical World*. Oxford, Blackwell.
McCracken, G. (1988) *Culture and Consumption*. Bloomington, Indiana University Press.
McHardy, F., Robson, J. E. & Harvey, F. D. (eds.) (forthcoming) *Lost Dramas of Classical Athens: Greek Tragic Fragments*. Exeter, Exeter University Press.
McLeish, K. (1980) *The Theatre of Aristophanes*. London, Thames & Hudson.

Meckler, M. (1993) The Beginning of the *Historia Augusta*. *Historia* 45, 364–75.
Mendoni, L. G. & Mazarakis, A. A. (eds.) (1998) *Kea – Kythnos: History and Archaeology. Proceedings of an International Symposium Kea – Kythnos, 22–25 June 1994*. Athens, Research Centre for Greek and Roman Antiquity/National Hellenic Research Foundation.
Meskell, L. (2002) *Private Life in New Kingdom Egypt*. Princeton/Oxford, Princeton University Press.
Meyer, B. F. & Sanders, E. P. (eds.) (1982) *Jewish & Christian Self-definition* Vol. 3. London, SCM Press.
Meyer, H. (1991) *Antinoos*. Munich, W. Fink.
Michel, C. (1900) *Recueil des Inscriptions Grecques* I. Brussels, H. Lamertin.
Migeotte, L. (1992) *Les souscriptions publiques dans les cités grecques*. Genève-Quebec, École pratique des Hautes Études.
Migeotte, L. (1994) Ressources financières des cités béotiennes. In Fossey (ed.), 16–28.
Millar, M. C. (1997) *Athens and Persia in the 5th Century BC*. Cambridge, Cambridge University Press.
Mills, M. (1984) Greek Clothing Regulations: Sacred and Profane. *Zeitschrift fur Papyrologie und Epigraphie* 55, 255–65.
Mommsen, A. (1899) 'Rhakos' auf attischen Inschriften. *Philologus* 58, 345–47.
Montserrat, D. (ed.) (1998) *Changing Bodies, Changing Meanings. Studies on the Human Body in Antiquity*. London, Routledge.
Moon, W. G. (ed.) (1983) *Ancient Greek Art and Iconography*. Madison, University of Wisconsin Press.
Morgan, L. (1988) *The Miniature Wall Paintings of Thera. A Study in Aegean Culture and Iconography*. Cambridge, Cambridge University Press.
Morgan, L. (1995) The Wall-Paintings of Ayia Irini, Kea. *Bulletin of the Institute of Classical Studies* 40, 243–244.
Morgan, L. (1998) The Wall-Paintings of the North-Bastion at Ayia Irini, Kea. In Mendoni & Mazarakis (eds.), 201–210.
Morris, D. (1969) *The Human Zoo*. London, Cape.
Morris, I. (1996) The strong principle of equality and the archaic origins of Greek democracy. In Ober & Hedrick (eds.), 19–48.
Morris, S. P. (1984) *The Black and Write Style: Athens and Aegina in the Orientalizing Period*. New Haven/London, Yale University Press.
Moulton, C. (1981) *Aristophanic Poetry, Hypomnemata* 68. Göttingen, Vandenhoeck & Ruprecht.
Muecke, F. (1982) A portrait of the artist as a young woman. *Classical Quarterly* 32, 41–55.
Muller, C. (1960) *Die Frauenfrisur im alten Aegypten*. Unpublished PhD, University of Leipzig.
Munn, M. (1982) *The stories behind the scenes of the great film epics*. Watford, Voyageur Press.
Musée de l'Homme (1985) *La Momie de Ramsès II*. Paris, Musée de l'Homme.
Muthesius, A. (1995) *Studies in Byzantine and Islamic Silk Weaving*. London, Pindar Press.
Naguib, S. (1990) Hair in Ancient Egypt. *Acta Orientalia* 51, 7–26.
Neils, J. (ed.) (1992) *The Panathenaic Festival in Ancient Athens*. Hanover, Princeton University Press.
Newiger, H.-J. (ed.) (1975) *Aristophanes und die alte Komödie (Wege der Forschung* 265). Darmstadt, Wissenschaftliche Buchgesellschaft.
Newsom, C. A. & Ringe, S. H. (eds.) (1992) *The woman's Bible commentary*. London, Sheffield Academic Press.
Nicholson, P. & Shaw, I. (eds.) (2000) *Ancient Egyptian Materials and Technology*. Cambridge, Cambridge University Press.
Nock, A. D. (1928) Notes on ruler cult I–IV. *Journal of Hellenic Studies* 48, 21–43.

Noerdlinger, H. S. (1956) *Moses and Egypt. The documentation to the motion picture 'The Ten Commandments.'* Los Angeles, University of Southern California Press.
Ober, J. & Hedrick, C. (eds.) (1996) *Demokratia: a conversation on democracies, ancient and modern*. Princeton, Princeton University Press.
Ogden, D. (ed.) (2002) *The Hellenistic world: New perspectives*. London/Swansea, Duckworth/Classical Press of Wales.
Oikonomidès, N. (1972) *Les listes de préséance byzantines des IXe et Xe siècles*. Paris, Centre National de la Recherche Scientifique.
Olivier, J-P. & Palaima, T. G. (eds.) (1988) *Texts, Tablets and Scribes: Studies in Mycenaean Epigraphy and Economy offered to Emmett L. Bennett, Jr.* (Minos Suppl. 10). Salamanca, Ediciones Universidad de Salamanca.
Olson, K. (2003) Roman underwear revisited. *Classical World* 96, 201–10.
Orlandou, A. K. (ed.) (1966) Crete (Microanaskafai), (in Greek). *Ergon* 1968, 152–156.
Orrison, K. (1999) *Written in stone. Making Cecil B. DeMille's epic 'The Ten Commandments.'* Lanham/New York/Oxford, Vestal Press Ltd.
Orther, D. J. & Aufderheide, A. C. (eds.) (1991) *Human Paleopathology*. Washington, Smithsonian Institute Press.
Osborne, R. (1996) Desiring women on Athenian pottery. In Kampen (ed.), 65–80.
Ousterhout, R. (2002) *The Art of the Kariye Camii*. London, Scala.
Paduano, G. (1967) Il motivo del re mendicante e lo scandalo del Telefo. *Studi Classici e Orientali* 16, 333–335.
Palaiokrassa, L. (1991) *To Hiero tes Artemidos Mounichias*. Athens, Archaiologike Etaireia.
Palmer, R. E. A. (1974) *Roman Religion and Roman Empire: Five Essays*. Philadelphia, University of Pennsylvania.
Panagiotakopulu, E. *et al.* (1997) A lepidopterous cocoon from Thera and evidence for silk in the Aegean Bronze Age. *Antiquity* 71, 420–429.
Parisinou, E. (2002) The 'language' of female hunting outfit in Ancient Greece. [sic.] In Llewellyn-Jones (ed.), 55–72.
Parker, R. (1990 [1983]) *Miasma. Pollution and Purification in Early Greek Religion*. Oxford, Oxford University Press.
Paszthory, E. (1992) *Salben, Schminken und Parfume im Altertum*. Mainz, von Zabern.
Pearce, J. *et al.* (eds.) (2000) *Burial, Society and Context in the Roman World*. Oxford, Oxbow.
Peers, G. (2001) *Subtle Bodies: Representing Angels in Byzantium*. Berkeley/Los Angeles/London, University of California Press.
Pekridou-Gorecki, A. (1989) *Mode im Antiken Griechenland*. Munich, C. H. Beck.
Pelling, C. B. R. (ed.) (1990) *Characterization and Individuality in Greek Literature*. Oxford, Clarendon Press.
Persson, A. W. (1931) *The Royal Tombs at Dendra near Midea*. Lund, C. W. Gleerup.
Pfister, R. (1951) *Textiles de Halabiyhe*. Paris, Geuthner.
Piccirillo, M. & Alliata, E. (eds.) (1998) *Mount Nebo. New Archaeological Excavations 1967–1997*. Jerusalem, Studium Biblicum Franceiscanum.
Pickard-Cambridge, A. (1966) *Dithyramb, Tragedy and Comedy*. Oxford, Clarendon.
Pickard-Cambridge, A. (1988) *The Dramatic Festivals of Athens*. Oxford, Clarendon.
Piltz, E. (1997) Middle Byzantine court costume. In Maguire (ed.), 39–51.
Pinch, G. (1994) *Magic in Ancient Egypt*. London, British Museum Press.
Pirenne-Delforge, V. (1994) *L' Aphrodite Grecque. Contribution à l'étude de ses cultes et de sa personnalité dans le panthéon archaïque et classique* (= Kernos Suppl. 4). Athens/Liège, Centre International d'Étude de la Religion Grecque Antique.
Pochna, M. F. (1995) Dior Invents the Postwar Woman and Women's Fashions. *Historia* 584, 72–77.

Pomeroy, S. B. (1994) *Xenophon. Oeconomicus: A Social and Historical Commentary*. Oxford, Oxford University Press.
Popham, M. et al. (1980) *Lefkandi I. The Iron Age*. Supplement 11. London, British School of Archaeology.
Porter, J. I. (ed.) (1999) *Constructions of the Classical Body*. Ann Arbor, University of Michigan Press.
Posener, G. (1969) "Maquilleuse" en Egyptien. *Revue d'Egyptologie* 21, 150–151.
Posener, G. (1986) La légende de la tresse d'Hathor. In Lesko (ed.), 111–117.
Powell, A. (1992) *Roman Poetry & Propaganda in the Age of Augustus*. Bristol, Bristol Classical Press.
Poyatos, F. (ed.) (1988) *Cross-Cultural Perspectives in Nonverbal Communication*. Toronto, Hogreafe.
Price, S. (1987) From noble funerals to divine cult: the consecration of Roman emperors. In Cannadine & Price (ed.), 56–105.
Pritchett, W. K. (1956) The Attic Stelai II. *Hesperia* 25, 210–54.
Quibell, J. E. (1908) *The Tomb of Yuaa and Thuiu*. Cairo, Musee du Cairo.
Rau, P. (1967) *Paratragödie: Untersuchung einer komischen Form des Aristophanes Zetemata* 45. Munich, Beck.
Rau, P. (1975) Das Tragödienspiel in den "Thesmophoriazusen". In Newiger (ed.), 339–56.
Rautman, A. E. (ed.) (2000) *Reading the Body: Representations and Remains in the Archaeological Record*. Philadelphia, University of Pennsylvania Press.
Rawlings, L. (ed.) (forthcoming 2005) *Herakles-Hercules in the Ancient World*. Swansea, Classical Press of Wales.
Rees, N. (2000) *Cassell's Movie Quotations*. London, Cassell.
Rehak, P. (1996) Aegean Breechcloths, Kilts, and the Keftiu Paintings. *American Journal of Archaeology* 100/1, 35–51.
Rehak, P. (1998) Aegean Natives in the Theban Tomb Paintings: The Keftiu Revisited. In Cline & Harris-Cline (eds.), 39–50.
Rehak, P. (ed.) (1995) *The Role of the Ruler in the Preshistoric Aegean. Proceedings of a Panel Discussion Presented at the Annual Meeting of the Archaeological Institute of America, New Orleans, Louisiana 28 December 1992*. Liège, Aegaeum.
Reinach, Th. (1899) Un temple élevé par les femmes de Tanagra. *Revue des Etudes Grecque* 12, 53–115.
Reiske, J. J. (ed.) (1832) *De Ceremoniis*. Bonn, Weber.
Renfrew, C. (1996) Language families and the spread of farming. In Harris (ed.), 70–92.
Reutter, L. (1914) Analyses des parfums egyptiens. *Annales du Service des Antiquites de l'Egypte* 13, 49–78.
Richardson, E. H. & L. (1966) *Ad Cohibendum Bracchium Toga*: An Archaeological Examination of Cicero, *Pro Caelio* 5.11. *Yale Classical Studies* 19, 251–268.
Richlin, A. (ed.) (1992) *Pornography and Representation in Greece and Rome*. Oxford, Oxford University Press.
Richlin, A. (2002 [1997]) Pliny's brassiere. In McClure (ed.), 225–52.
Richter, G. M. A. (1929) Silk in Greece. *American Journal of Archaeology* 33, 27–33.
Ridgway, B. S. (1970) *The Severe Style in Greek Sculpture*. Princeton, Princeton University Press.
Ridgway, B. S. (1984) The Fashion of the Elgin Kore. *Getty Museum Journal* 12, 29–58.
Ridgway, B. S. (1985) Late Archaic Sculpture. In Boulter, C. G. (ed.), 1–17.
Ridgway, B. S. (1993) *The Archaic Style in Greek Sculpture*. Chicago, Ares.
Riefstahl, E. (1952) An Ancient Egyptian Hairdresser. *Bulletin of the British Museum* 13.4, 7–16.
Riefstahl, E. (1956) Two Hairdressers of the Eleventh Dynasty. *Journal of Near Eastern Studies* 15, 10–17.

Rinaldi, M. (1964–5) Il costumo Romano e i mosaici di Piazza Armerina. *Revista dell'instituto nazionale d'Archaeolgia e Storia dell'Arte* 13–14, 200–268.

Ringrose, K. M. (1994) Living in the shadows: eunuchs and gender in Byzantium. In Herdt (ed.), 85–110, 504–518.

Ringrose, K. M. (1996) Eunuchs as cultural mediators. *Byzantinische Forschungen* 23, 75–93.

Roberts, C. A., Lewis, M. E., & Manchester, K. (eds.) (2002) *The Past and Present of Leprosy – Archaeological, Historical, Palaeopathological and Clinical Approaches. Proceedings of the International Congress on the Evolution and Palaeoepidemiology of the Infectious Diseases 3, University of Bradford, 26th–31st July 1999*. Oxford, British Archaeological Reports.

Robinson, D. (1955) Spectacle. *Sight and Sound* 25, 22–27 & 55–56.

Robson, J. E. (1999) *Humour and Obscenity in Aristophanes*. Unpublished PhD, University of London.

Robson, J. E. (forthcoming) Aristophanes on how to write tragedy: what you wear is what you are. In McHardy *et al.*

Roehrig, C. H. (1996) Woman's work: Some occupations of non royal women as depicted in ancient Egyptian art. In Capel & Markooe (eds.), 13–24.

Rogers, C. (ed.) (1983) *Early Islamic Textiles*. Brighton, Rogers & Podmore.

Rogers, P. W., Jorgensen, L. B. & Rast-Eicher, A. (eds.) (2001) *The Roman Textile Industry and its Influence. A Birthday Tribute to John Peter Wild*. Oxford, Oxbow Books.

Rose, C. B. (1997) *Dynastic Commemoration and Imperial Portraiture in the Julio-Claudian Period*. Cambridge, Cambridge University Press.

Rosental-Heginbottom, R. (2003) *The Nabateans in the Negev*. Haifa, Reuben and Edith Hecht Museum/University of Haifa.

Roy, J. (1998) The masculinity of the hellenistic king. In Foxhall & Salmon (eds.) (1998b), 111–35.

Rubinstein, R. P. (1995) *Dress Codes: Meanings and Messages in American Culture*. Colorado/Oxford, Westview Press.

Ruffle, J. (1967) Four Egyptian Pieces in Birmingham City Museum. *Journal of Egyptian Archaeology* 53, 39–46.

Sagay, E. (1983) *African Hairstyles: Styles of Yesterday and Today*. New Hampshire, Heinemann.

Saïd, S. (1979a) L'Assemblée des femmes: les femmes, l'économie et la politique. *Les Cahiers de Fontenay* 17. Paris, Fontenay aux Roses.

Saïd, S. (1979b) L'Assemblée des femmes, l'économie et la politique. In Bonnamour & Delavault (eds.), 33–69.

Saïd, S. (1987) Travestis et Travestissements dans les comédies d'Aristophane. *Cahiers du GITA*, 3, 217–248.

Sakellariou, A. (1974) Un cratère d'argent avec scène de bataille provenant de la IVème tombe de l'acropole de Mycènes. *Antike Kunst* 17, 3–20.

Samson, J. (1973) Amarna Crowns and Wigs. *Journal of Egyptian Archaeology* 59, 47–59.

Sapouna-Sakellaraki, E. (1971) *Minoan Costume* (in Greek). Athens, Athens Archaeological Society.

Sapouna-Sakellaraki, E. (1995) *Die bronzenen Menschenfiguren auf Kreta und in der Ägäis*. Stuttgart, Prähistorische Bronzefunde Abteilung.

Scanlon, T. F. (2002) *Eros and Greek Athletics*. Oxford/New York, Oxford University Press.

Scheid, J. & Svenbro, J. [trans.Volk] (1996) *The Craft of Zeus: Myths of Weaving and Fabric*. Cambridge Mass., Harvard University Press.

Schevill, M. B., Berlo, J. C. & Dwyer, N. (eds.) (1991) *Textile Traditions of Mesoamerica and the Andes: An Anthology*. Austin, University of Texas Press.

Schiaparelli, E. (1927) *La Tomba Intatta dell Architetto Cha nella necropoli di Tebe*. Turin, R. Museo di antichita.

Schick, T. (1988) Nahal Hemar Cave-Cordage, Basketry, and Fabrics. *'Atiqot* (English series) 18, 31–42.

Schilling, R. (1982) *La religion romaine de Vénus*. Paris, Boccard.

Schoske, S., Grimm, A. & Kreißl, B. (1990) *Schonheit abglanz der Gottlichkeit*. Munich, SSAK.

Sebesta, J. (1994a) Symbolism in the Costume of the Roman Woman. In Sebesta & Bonfante (eds.), 46–53.

Sebesta, J. (1994b) Tunica Ralla, Tunica Spissa: The Colors and Textiles of Roman Costume. In Sebesta & Bonfante (eds.), 65–76.

Sebesta, J. & Bonfante, L. (eds.) (1994) *The World of Roman Costume*. Madison, University of Wisconsin Press.

Segal, Ch. (1993) *Euripides and the Poetics of Sorrow. Art, Gender and Commemoration in Alcestis, Hippolytus and Hecuba*. Durham NC, Duke University Press.

Seltman, C. (1956) *Women in Antiquity*. London, Thames & Hudson.

Serpico, M. & White, R. (1996) A Report on the analysis of the contents of a cache of jars from the tomb of Djer. In Spencer (ed.), 128–139.

Serpico, M. & White, R. (2000) Oil, Fat & Wax. In Nicholson & Shaw (eds.), 390–429.

Server, L. (1987) *Screenwriter: Words become pictures*. Pittstown, NJ, Sterling Pub Co. Inc.

Serwint, N. (1993) The female athletic costume at the Heraia and prenuptial initiation rites. *American Journal of Archaeology* 97, 403–22.

Ševčenko, I. (1975) Theodore Metochites, the Chora and the intellectual trends of his time. In Underwood (ed.), 17–92.

Shamir, O. (1995) Textiles from Nahal Shahak, Israel. *'Atiqot* 26, 43–48.

Shamir, O. (1999) Textiles, Basketry, and Cordage from 'En Rahel. *'Atiqot* 38, 91–124.

Shamir, O. (2001) Byzantine and Early Islamic Textiles Excavated in Israel. *Textile History* 32, 93–105.

Shamir, O. (2002) Textile Production in Eretz-Israel. *Michmanim* 16, 19–32.

Shamir, O. (2003) Textiles, Basketry and Cordage from Nabatean Sites along the Spice Route between Petra and Gaza. In Rosental-Heginbottom (ed.), 35–38.

Shamir, O. (2004a) Coloured Textiles found along the Spice Route joining Petra and Gaza – Examples from the First Century CE till the Eighth Century CE. In Cleland & Stears (eds.), 49–52.

Shamir, O. (2004b) Loomweights of the Persian Period from Horbat Rogem, Horbat Mesura and Horbat Ha-Ro'a. In Cohen & Cohen-Amin (eds.), 18–28.

Shamir, O. & Baginski, A. (2002a) Medieval Mediterranean Textiles, Basketry and Cordage Newly excavated in Israel. In Lev (ed),135–158.

Shamir, O. & Baginski, A. (2002b) The Later Textiles, Basketry and Cordage from Caves in the Northern Judean Desert ("Operation Scroll"). *'Atiqot* 41, 241–256.

Sheffer, A. & Tidhar, A. (1991) The Textiles from the 'En-Boqeq Excavation in Israel. *Textile History* 22, 3–46.

Sidéris, G. (2002) "Eunuchs of light". Power, imperial ceremonial and positive representations of eunuchs in Byzantium (4th – 12th centuries). In Tougher (ed.) 161–175.

Sieber, R. & Herreman, F. (eds.) (2001) *Hair in African Art & Culture*. London, Prestel.

Silk, M. S. (2000) *Aristophanes and the Definition of Comedy*. Oxford, Oxford University Press.

Slater, N. W. (1997) Waiting in the Wings: Aristophanes' *Ecclesiazusae*. *Arion* 5.1, 97–129.

Slater, N. W. (2002) *Spectator Politics: Metatheatre and performance in Aristophanes*. Philadelphia, University of Pennsylvania Press.

Smith, C. (1999) Delilah: A suitable case for (feminist) treatment? In Brenner (ed.), 93–116.

Smith, G. E. (1912) *The Royal Mummies*. Cairo, Musee du Cairo.

Smith, R. R. R. (1988) *Hellenistic Royal Portraits*. Oxford, Clarendon Press.

Smith, R. R. R. (1998) Cultural choice and political identity in honorific portrait statues in the Greek East in the second century AD. *Journal of Roman Studies* 88, 56 93.
Solomon, J. (2001) *The Ancient World in the Cinema*. (2nd edition) New Haven/London, Yale University Press.
Sommerstein, A. H. (1980) *The Comedies of Aristophanes, Volume 1: Acharnians*. Warminster, Aris & Phillips.
Sommerstein, A. H. (1990) *The Comedies of Aristophanes, Volume 7: Lysistrata*. Warminster, Aris and Phillips.
Sommerstein, A. H. (1994) *The Comedies of Aristophanes, Volume 8: Thesmophoriazusae*. Warminster, Aris and Phillips.
Sommerstein, A. H. (1998) *The Comedies of Aristophanes, Volume 10: Ecclesiazusae*. Warminster, Aris and Phillips.
Sommerstein, A. H. (ed.) (1993) *Tragedy, Comedy and the Polis. Papers from the Greek Drama Conference*. Bari, Levante.
Sousa e Silva, M. de F. (1987) *Critica do teatro na comédia antiga*. Lisbon, Coimbra.
Spatharakis, I. (1976) *The Portrait in Byzantine Illuminated Manuscripts*. Leiden, Brill.
Speidel, M. A. (1990) *Die Frisure des ägyptischen alten Reiches. Ein historisch-prosopographische Untersuchung zu Amt und Titel (jr-sn)*. Konstanz, Hartung-Gorre.
Spencer, D. (2002) *The Roman Alexander. Reading a Cultural Myth*. Exeter, Exeter University Press.
Spencer, J. (ed.) (1996) *Aspects of Early Egypt*. London, British Museum Press.
Spindler, K. (1993) *The Man in the Ice*. London, British Museum Press.
Squire, G. (1972) *Dress and Society*. London, Viking Press.
Stevenson Smith, W. (1984) *The Art and Architecture of Ancient Egypt*. London, Harmondsworth.
Stewart, A. (1997) *Art, Desire and the Body in Ancient Greece*. Cambridge, Cambridge University Press.
Stohn, G. (1993) Zur Agathonszene in den "Thesmophoriazusen" des Aristophanes. *Hermes* 121, 196–205.
Stone, L. M. (1980) *Costume in Aristophanic Comedy*. Salem (New York), Arno Press.
Stone, S. (1994) The Toga: From National to Ceremonial Costume. In Sebesta & Bonfante (eds.), 13–45.
Storm, P. (1987) *Functions of Dress: Tool of Culture and the Individual*. New Jersey, Prentice Hall.
Stout, A. M. (1994) Jewellery as a symbol of status in the Roman empire. In Sebesta & Bonfante (eds.), 77–100.
Strack, P. L. (1937) *Untersuchungen zur römischen Reichsprägung des Zweiten Jahrhundert*. Vol. 3. Stuttgart, Kohlhammer.
Strathern, A. & Strathern, M. (1971) *Self-Decoration in Mount Hagen*. London, Backworth.
Stratiki, K. (2004) *Melas* in Greek Cultural Practices. In Cleland & Stears (eds.), 106–9.
Studniczka, F. (1886) *Beiträge zur Geschichte der altgriechischen Tracht*. Vienna, O. Gerold's Sohn.
Sutherland, A. (1975) *Gypsies: The Hidden Americans*. New York, Free Press.
Sutton, R. F. (1992) Pornography and persuasion on Attic pottery. In Richlin (ed.), 3–35.
Syme, R. (1968) *Ammianus and the Historia Augusta*. Oxford, Clarendon Press.
Syme, R. (1971) *Emperors and Biography: Studies in the Historia Augusta*. Oxford, Clarendon Press.
Symons, D. J. (1987) *Costume of Ancient Greece*. London, Batsford Ltd.
Taaffe, L. K. (1993) *Aristophanes and Women*. London/New York, Routledge.
Taillardat, J. (1965) *Les Images d'Aristophane. Etudes de langue et de style*. Paris, Belles Lettres.
Tanitch, R. (2000) *Blockbusters. 70 Years of best-selling movies*. London, Batsford.
Tanner, J. (2000) Portraits, power and patronage in the late Roman republic. *Journal of Roman Studies* 90, 18–60.

Taplin, O. (1995 [1978]) *Greek Tragedy in Action*. Oxford, Oxford University Press.
Tashiro, C. S. (1998) *Pretty Pictures. Production design and the history film*. Austin, University of Texas Press.
Televantou, C. (1982) Women's Dress from Prehistoric Thera (in Greek). *Archaiologike Ephemeris*, 113–135.
Thomas, A. (1981) *Gurob*. London, Uphill.
Thompson, D. B. (1944) The Golden Nikai Reconsidered. *Hesperia* 13, 173–209.
Thompson, W. (1982) Weaving: A Man's Work. *Classical World* 75, 217–22.
Tölle-Kastenbein, R. (1980) *Frühklassische Peplosfiguren Originale*. Mainz, von Zabern.
Torelli, M. (1984) *Lavinio e Roma: Riti iniziatici e matrimonio tra archeolgia e storia*. Rome, Quasar.
Tougher, S. (1997) Byzantine eunuchs: an overview, with special reference to their creation and origin. In James (ed.), 168–184.
Tougher, S. (ed.) (2002) *Eunuchs in Antiquity and Beyond*. London, Classical Press of Wales/ Duckworth.
Tsetskhladze, G. R., Prag, A. J. N. W. & Snodgrass, A. M. (eds.) (2000) *PERIPLOUS. Papers on classical art and archaeology presented to Sir John Boardman*. London, Thames & Hudson.
Tzachili, I. (1997) *Weaving and weavers in the prehistoric Aegean, 2000–1000BC* (in Greek). Herakleion, Ekdoseis Kritis.
Tzachili, I. (2000) Etin aparxi tis istorias *Kathimerini*, 30th Jan 2000, 4–7.
Underwood, P. A. (1967) *The Kariye Djami*, vols 1–3. London, Routledge & Kegan Paul.
Underwood, P. A. (ed.) (1975) *The Kariye Djami*, vol. 4. London, Routledge & Kegan Paul.
Ungar, T. *et al.* (2002) Revealing the powdering methods of black makeup in Ancient Egypt by fitting microstructure based Fourier coefficients to the whole x-ray diffraction profiles of galena. *Journal of Applied Physics* 91 (4), 2455–2465.
Ussher, R. G. (1969) The staging of the *Ecclesiazusae*. *Hermes* 97, 22–37.
van Wees, H. (1995) Princes at dinner: social event and social structure in Homer. In Crielaard (ed.), 147–82.
van Wees, H. (1998a) A brief history of tears: gender differentiation in archaic Greece. In Foxhall & Salmon (eds.) (1998b), 10–53.
van Wees, H. (1998b) Greeks bearing arms: the state, the leisure class, and the display of weapons in archaic Greece. In Fisher & van Wees (eds.), 333–78.
van Wees, H. (2002) Homer and early Greece. *Colby Quarterly* 38.1, 94–117 (corrected reprint from I. de Jong [ed. 1999] *Homer: Critical Assessments. Vol. II*, London, 1– 32).
van Wees, H. (2003) Conquerors and serfs: wars of conquest and forced labour in archaic Greece. In Luraghi & Alcock (eds.), 33–80.
van Wees, H. (forthcoming) Clothes, class and gender in Homer. In Cairns (ed.).
Vandier d'Abbadie, J. (1972) *Les objets de toilettes egyptien au Musee du Louvre*. Paris, Louvre.
Varner, E. (2000) Tyranny and the transformation of the Roman visual landscape. In Varner (ed.), 9–26.
Varner, E. (ed.) (2000) *From Caligula to Constantine. Tyranny and Transformation in Roman Portraiture*. Atlanta, Michael C Carlos Museum.
Varone, A. [trans. Fant] (2000) *Eroticism in Pompeii*. Rome, L'Erma di Bretschneider.
Ventris, M. & Chadwick, J. (1973) *Documents in Mycenaean Greek*. 2nd ed. Cambridge, Cambridge University Press.
Vermeule, C. (1977) *Greek Sculpture and Roman Taste*. Ann Arbor, University of Michigan Press.
Versnel, H. S. (1970) *Triumphus: an inquiry into the origin, development and meaning of the Roman triumph*. Leiden, Brill.
Vicary, G. Q. (1988) The Signs of Clothing. In Poyatos (ed.), 291–314.
Vidal, G. (1992) *Screening History*. London, Harvard University Press.

Villing, A. (2000) *Kestos, zoster* and Athena's crossband aegis. Anatomy of a classical attribute. In Tsetskhladze *et al.* (eds.), 361–70.

Vogelsang-Eastwood G. (1999) *Tutankhamun's Wardrobe: garments from the tomb of Tutankhamun*. Rotterdam, van Doorn & Co.

Vogelsang-Eastwood, G. (ed.) (1993) *Pharaonic Egyptian Clothing*. Leiden, Brill.

Vogelsang-Eastwood, G. (ed.) (1994) *De Kleren van de Farao*. Leiden, Brill.

Vogt, A. (1935) *Le Livre des cérémonies*, 2 Vols. Paris, Belles Lettres.

von Möllendorff, P. (2002) *Aristophanes*. Hildesheim, Olms.

Vout, C. (1996) The Myth of the Toga: Understanding the History of Roman Dress. *Greece and Rome* 43, 204–20.

Wachsmann, S. (1987). *Aegeans in the Theban Tombs*. Leuven, Orientalia Lovaniensia Analecta 20.

Wagner-Hasel, B. (2002) The graces and colour weaving. In Llewellyn-Jones (ed.), 17–32.

Wallace-Hadrill, A. (1982) Civilis Princeps: Between Citizen and King. *Journal of Roman Studies* 72, 32–48.

Wallace-Hadrill, A. (1998) To be Roman, go Greek: thoughts on Hellenistic art at Rome. In Austin *et al.* (eds.), 79–92.

Walter, P. *et al.* (1999) Making Make-up in Ancient Egypt. *Nature* 397, 483–484.

Walters, H. (1931) Corpus Vasorum Antiquorum: Great Britain, fasc. 8: *The British Museum*. Oxford, Oxford University Press.

Walton, J. M. & Arnott, P. D. (1996) *Menander and the Making of Comedy*. Westport/London, Praeger.

Wardle, D. (1988) Does Reconstruction Help? A Mycenaean Dress and the Dendra Suit of Armour. In French & Wardle (eds.), 469–476.

Webster, T. B. L. (1955) The Costume of the Actors in Aristophanic Comedy. *Classical Quarterly* 5, 94–95.

Webster, T. B. L. (1974) *An Introduction to Menander*. Manchester, Manchester University Press.

Weitzmann, K. (1977) *Late Antique and Early Christian Book Illumination*. London, George Braziller.

West, M. (1995) The date of the *Iliad*. *Museum Helveticum* 52, 203–19.

Wex, M. (1979) *Let's Take Back Our Space. "Female" and "Male" Body Language as a Result of Patriarchal Structures*. Munich, Frauenliteraturverlag Hermine Fees.

Wiedemann, T. (1989) *Adults and Children in the Roman Empire*. New Haven/London, Yale University Press.

Wild, J. P. (2000) Textile production and trade in Roman literature and written sources. In Cardon & Feugère (eds.), 209–14.

Wiles, D. (1991) *The Masks of Menander: Sign and meaning in Greek and Roman performance*. Cambridge, Cambridge University Press.

Wilfong, T. (1997) *Women and Gender in Ancient Egypt from Prehistory to Late Antiquity*. Ann Arbor, The Museum.

Wilkinson, J. G. (1988) *A Popular Account of the Ancient Egyptians*. New York, Crescent.

Willett, C. & Cunnington, P. (1992 [1951]) *The History of Underclothes*. New York, Dover Publications.

Williams, C. (1999) *Roman Homosexuality: Ideologies of Masculinity in Classical Antiquity*. New York/Oxford, Oxford University Press.

Williamson, M. & Blundell, S. (eds.) (1998) *The Sacred and the Feminine*. London, Routledge.

Wilson, L. (1924) *The Roman Toga*. Baltimore, Johns Hopkins Press.

Wilson, L. (1938) *The Clothing of the Ancient Romans*. Baltimore, Johns Hopkins Press.

Winkler, J. J. (1990) *The Constraints of Desire: The Anthropology of Sex and Gender in Ancient Greece*. New York, Routledge.

Winlock, H. E. (1916) Ancient Egyptian Kerchiefs. *Bulletin of the Metropolitan Museum of Art* 16, 238–242.

Winlock, H. E. (1923) The Egyptian Expedition 1922–1923: The Museum's Excavations at Thebes. *Bulletin of the Metropolitan Museum of Art* 18, 11–39.

Winlock, H. E. (1932) *The Tomb of Queen Meryet-Amun at Thebes*. New York, Metropolitan Museum Press.

Winlock, H. E. (1945) *The Slain Soldiers of Neb-hepet-Re' Mentu-hotep*. New York, Metropolitan Museum Press.

Winlock, H. E. (1948) *The Treasure of Three Egyptian Princesses*. New York, Metropolitan Museum Press.

Wood, C. (1983) *Olympian Dreamers. Victorian classical painters 1860–1914*. London, Constable.

Wood, S. (1995) Diva Drusilla Panthea and the Sisters of Caligula. *American Journal of Archaeology* 99, 457–82.

Wrede, H. (1971) Das Mausoleum der Claudia Semne und die Bürgerliche plastik der Kaiserzeit. *Römische Mitteilungen* 78, 125–66.

Wrede, H. (1981) *Consecratio in Formam Deorum*. Mainz am Rhein, von Zabern.

Wright, W. C. [trans.] (1913–23) *The works of the Emperor Julian*, 3 Vols. Cambridge Mass., Harvard University Press.

Wurtzel, E. (1998) *Bitch: In praise of difficult women*. New York, Doubleday Books.

Wyke, M. (1992) Augustan Cleopatras: Female power and poetic authority. In Powell (ed.), 98–140.

Wyke, M. (1997) *Projecting the Past. Ancient Rome, cinema and history*. London/New York, Routledge.

Wyke, M. (2002) *The Roman Mistress*. Oxford, Oxford University Press.

Xenaki-Sakellariou, A. & Chatziliou, C. (1989) *"Peinture en Métal" à l'époque mycénienne*. Athens, Ekdotike Athenon.

Zanker, P. (1988) *The Power of Images in the Age of Augustus*. Ann Arbor, University of Michigan Press.

Zanker, P. (1995) *The Mask of Socrates*. Berkeley, University of California Press.

Zeitlin, F. I. (1981) Travesties of gender and genre in Aristophanes' *Thesmophoriazousae* [sic]. In Foley (ed.), 169–218.

Zevi, F. & Andreae, B. (1982) Gli scavi sottomarini di Baia. *La Parola del Passato* 37, 114–56.

Zias J. (1991) Leprosy and tuberculosis in the Byzantine Monasteries of the Judaean Desert. In Orther & Aufderhide (eds.),197–199.

Zias, J. (2002) New Evidence for the History of Leprosy in the Ancient Near East: An Overview. In Roberts *et al*. (eds.), 259–268.

Zimmermann, B. (1992) *Dithyrambos: Geschichte einer Gattung*. Göttingen, Vanderhoeck & Ruprecht.

Zivie, A. P. (1988) Portrait de femme: une tête en bois stuqué récemment découverte à Saqqarah. *Revue d'Egyptologie* 39, 179–195.

Zoffili, E. (1992) *Kleidung und Schmuck im Alten Ägypten*. Berlin, Propylaen Verlag.